Reteaching and Practice Workbook

Grade 6

Scott Foresman-Addison Wesley

enVisionMATH®
Common Core

PEARSON

Glenview, Illinois • Boston, Massachusetts • Chandler, Arizona • Upper Saddle River, New Jersey

ISBN-13: 978-0-328-81078-9
ISBN-10: 0-328-81078-9

6 18

Contents

Name ____________________

Reteaching **1-1**

Exponents

base ⟶ 5^4 ⟵ exponent

The number 5 is the **base**. The base is the factor that is being multiplied.

The number 4 is the **exponent.** The exponent tells how many times the base is used as a factor.

$$5^4 = 5 \times 5 \times 5 \times 5 = 625$$

The base (5) is used as a factor the exponent (4) number of times.

To write a product in exponential form: **$4 \times 4 \times 4 \times 4 \times 4 \times 4 \times 4$**

First write the base: **4**

Count the number of times the base is used as a factor. This is the exponent. **4^7**

To evaluate an exponential number: **6^3**

Write the base as a factor the number of times shown by the exponent.

$6^3 = 6 \times 6 \times 6 = 216$

To write the expanded form of a number using exponents:

Write the number in expanded form.

52,965 = $(5 \times 10{,}000) + (2 \times 1{,}000) + (9 \times 100) + (6 \times 10) + (5 \times 1)$

Write the place values as powers of 10.

52,965 = $(5 \times 10^4) + (2 \times 10^3) + (9 \times 10^2) + (6 \times 10^1) + (5 \times 10^0)$

Tip: Any number raised to the first power equals that number. **$8^1 = 8$**

Write each power as a product and evaluate the expression.

1. 9^4 ____________________ **2.** 4^5 ____________________

Write each product in exponential form.

3. $3 \times 3 \times 3 \times 3 \times 3$ ________ **4.** $7 \times 7 \times 7 \times 7 \times 7 \times 7 \times 7 \times 7$ ________

Write the number in expanded form using exponents.

5. 74,271 = ________ + ________ + ________ + ________ + ________

6. Number Sense Explain the difference between 4^6 and 6^4.

____

____

____

Name ______________________

Practice **1-1**

Exponents

Write each expression in exponential form.

1. $5 \times 5 \times 5 \times 5 \times 5 \times 5$ ______ **2.** $2 \times 2 \times 2 \times 2 \times 2 \times 2 \times 2$ ______

3. $3 \times 3 \times 3$ ______ **4.** 9 ______

Write each number in expanded form using exponents.

5. 53,806 ______

6. 527,519 ______

Evaluate.

7. 6^2 ______ **8.** 5^3 ______ **9.** 3^6 ______ **10.** 2^8 ______

11. Reasoning Zach texted 8 different friends each day for three days about a new game. Then Zach texted 8 friends about a new movie. The next day each of Zach's friends texted 8 friends about the movie, and the third day each of those friends texted 8 friends about the movie. Did more people get a text about the game or the movie? Explain.

______

______

______

12. Writing to Explain In 2014, the estimated population of the world was 7,261,087,766 people. When this number is written in expanded form using exponents, one power of 10 would not be represented. Which power of 10? Why?

______

______

13. Number Sense Which is **NOT** equal to 1?

A 10^0

B 4^1

C 1×10^0

D 1^4

Name ______________________

Reteaching
1-2

Properties of Operations

Commutative Properties You can add or multiply numbers in any order and the sum or product will be the same. **Examples:** $10 + 5 + 3 = 5 + 3 + 10 = 18$ $7 \times 5 = 5 \times 7 = 35$	**Associative Properties** You can group numbers differently. It will not affect the sum or product. **Examples:** $2 + (7 + 6) = (2 + 7) + 6 = 15$ $(4 \times 5) \times 8 = 4 \times (5 \times 8) = 160$
Identity Properties You can add zero to a number or multiply it by 1 and not change the value of the number. **Examples:** $17 + 0 = 17$ $45 \times 1 = 45$	**Multiplication Property of Zero** If you multiply a number by zero, the product will always be zero. **Example:** $12 \times 0 = 0$

Find each missing number. Tell what property or properties are shown.

1. $9 \times 5 = 5 \times$ ______

____

2. ______ $\times 89 = 89$

____

3. $(3 + 4) + 19 = 3 + ($______ $+ 19)$

____

4. $128 +$ ______ $= 128$

____

5. ______ $+ 18 = 18 + 12$

____

6. Reasoning What is the product of any number, *x*, multiplied by 1? Explain how you know.

____

____

Name________________________________

Properties of Operations

Find each missing number. Tell what property or properties are shown.

1. $(32 + \_\_\_\_) + 2 + 7 = 32 + (14 + 2) + 7$

____

2. $8 + 6 + 12 = \_\_\_\_ + 12 + 6$

____

3. $(8 \times \_\_\_\_) \times 7 = 8 \times (9 \times 7)$

____

4. $\_\_\_\_ + 0 = 34$

____

5. $12 \times 3 = 3 \times \_\_\_\_$

____

6. $1 \times \_\_\_\_ = 288$

____

7. **Reasoning** Write a number sentence that shows why the associative property does not work with subtraction.

____

8. Which property is shown in $(23 \times 5) \times 13 \times 7 = 23 \times (5 \times 13) \times 7$?

   A Commutative Property of Multiplication
   B Identity Property of Multiplication
   C Associative Property of Multiplication
   D Associative Property of Addition

9. **Writing to Explain** Explain why you do not have to do any computing to solve $15 \times 0 \times (13 + 7)$.

____

____

Name ______________________

Reteaching
1-3

Order of Operations

Order of operations is a set of rules that mathematicians use when computing numbers. Here is how order of operations is used to solve the following problem: $7 + (5 \times 4) \times 3$.

Order of Operations

First, compute all numbers inside parentheses.	$7 + (5 \times 4) \times 3$ $7 + 20 \times 3$
Next, evaluate terms with exponents. If there are no exponents, go to the next step.	$7 + 20 \times 3$
Then, multiply and divide the numbers from left to right.	$7 + 60$
Finally, add and subtract the numbers from left to right.	67

How to use parentheses to make each sentence true:	$6 + 2 \times 9 = 72$
Using order of operations, $6 + 2 \times 9 = 24$, not 72.	
Place parentheses around 6 + 2 so that this operation is done first:	$(6 + 2) \times 9 = 72$ $8 \times 9 = 72$

Evaluate each expression.

1. $8 + 7 \times 5 =$ ________

2. $18 - 3 \times 2 =$ ________

3. $3 \times 7 + 3 \times 5 =$ ________

4. $40 \div (2 \times 4) =$ ________

5. $6 \times 3 - 6 \times 2 =$ ________

6. $9 + 2^3 =$ ________

7. $7 + 12 \times 3 - 2 =$ ________

8. $4 \times (5 + 5) \div 20 + 6 =$ ________

9. $4^2 - (3 \times 5) =$ ________

10. $(3 \times 2) + 3^2 =$ ________

11. Reasoning Which operation should be performed *last* in this problem: $3^2 + 7 \times 4$? Why?

____

Use parentheses to make each sentence true.

12. $0 \times 6 + 9 = 9$ ________________

13. $3^2 + 2 \times 2 = 13$ ________________

Name ______________________

Practice **1-3**

Order of Operations

Evaluate each expression.

1. $3 + 4 \times 7$ ______

2. $88 - 6 \times 6$ ______

3. $8 \times 2 + 7 \times 3$ ______

4. $(5 + 9) + 3 \times 8$ ______

5. $(6 + 3^2) + 5$ ______

6. $9^2 - (7 \times 5) + 3$ ______

7. $48 \div 2 + 6$ ______

8. $26 \div (5 + 8) + 1$ ______

9. $18 + 3 \times (6 \div 2)$ ______

10. Reasoning What operation would you perform *last* in this problem: $(2 \times 3) + (7 \times 2)$? ______

Use parentheses to make each number sentence true.

11. $10 + 5 \times 4^2 \div 2^3 = 20$

12. $124 - 6 \times 0 + 15 = 34$

13. $10^2 - 10 + 3 = 93$

14. $7 + 5 \times 3 \div 3 = 12$

15. Mr. Miller's sixth-grade class went on a field trip to hear the symphony perform. Their seats were grouped in the following ways: 2 groups of 3 seats; 3 groups of 4 seats, 4 groups of 2 seats, and 1 seat (for Mr. Miller). Write a number sentence to calculate how many students went on the field trip.

____

____

16. Evaluate the expression $(4^2 - 4) + 6 \div 2$.

A 4 **B** 9 **C** 12 **D** 15

17. Writing to Explain Suppose you had to evaluate $9^2 + 5 \times 4$. Tell the order in which you would compute these numbers.

____

____

Name ______________________________

The Distributive Property

You can use the distributive property to multiply mentally.

Example A. Evaluate 7×53. 7×53

Break 53 apart into 50 + 3. $7 \times (50 + 3)$

Then distribute the 7 to each part. $(7 \times 50) + (7 \times 3)$

Multiply. $350 + 21$

Add the products. 371

Example B. Evaluate $5(42) - 5(2)$. Remember $5(42)$ means 5×42.

Use the distributive property in reverse. $5(42) - 5(2)$

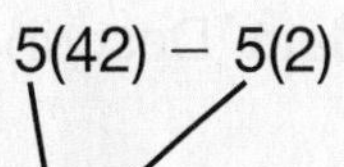

Join 42 and 2 using the minus sign. $5\,(42 - 2)$

Subtract. 5×40

Multiply the difference by 5. 200

Find each missing number.

1. $8 \times (30 + 2) = (8 \times$ ______$) + (8 \times 2)$

2. $(6 \times$ ______$) - (6 \times 7) = 6 \times (37 - 7)$

3. $8(28) = 8\,(20) + 8\,($______$)$

4. $3(22) + 3(4) = 3($______$) + 3(6)$

Use the distributive property and mental math to evaluate.

5. $6(24)$ ______

6. $4(13) - 4(3)$ ______

7. $7(24 + 6)$ ______

8. $2(72)$ ______

9. $9(12) + 9(3)$ ______

10. $5(24 - 3)$ ______

11. Number Sense What are two other ways to write $9(46)$?

____

Name ___________________________

The Distributive Property

Find each missing number.

1. $8 \times (30 + 2) = (8 \times$ ______$) + (8 \times 2)$ **2.** $8(94) = 8($______$) + 8(4)$

3. $5(45 + 5) = 5($______$)$ **4.** $9(42) - 9(4) = 9(30) + 9($______$)$

Use the distributive property and mental math to evaluate.

5. $3(58 - 8)$ ______ **6.** $7(31 + 19)$ ______

7. $9(72)$ ______ **8.** $4(26) - 4(16)$ ______

9. $8(41) + 8(5)$ ______ **10.** $5(22 - 5)$ ______

11. Writing to Explain Describe the mental math steps you would use to find 7(42).

____

____

12. Number Sense Use mental math to evaluate the expression $6(31) + 6(4) - 6(15)$.

____

13. Geometry Write an expression for the area of this rectangle. Evaluate your expression to find the area.

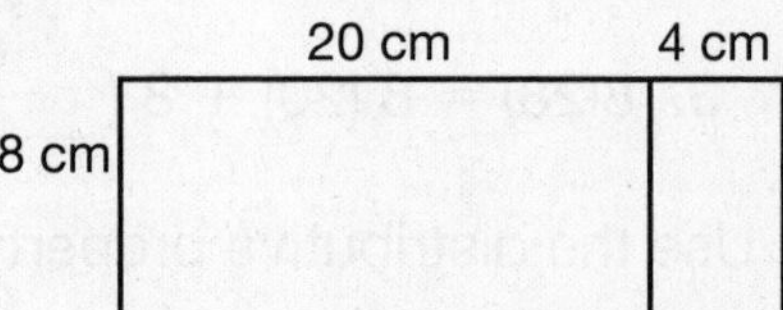

____

14. Algebra Which expression is equal to $12m + 12n$?

A $12mn$

B $12m + n$

C $12m - 12n$

D $12(m + n)$

Name ____________________

Evaluating Numerical Expressions

Brackets and parentheses are both used to show groupings.
Brackets are used to avoid double parentheses: [(instead of ((.

Evaluate expressions according to the order of operations.

1. Evaluate inside parentheses, then evaluate inside brackets.	$2.3^2 + [\mathbf{(9 \times 0.4)} + \mathbf{(3 \times 0.8)}] \times 1.2$ $2.3^2 + \mathbf{[3.6 + 2.4]} \times 1.2$ $2.3^2 + 6 \times 1.2$
2. Evaluate exponents.	$\mathbf{2.3^2} + 6 \times 1.2$ $5.29 + 6 \times 1.2$
3. Multiply and divide from left to right.	$5.29 + \mathbf{6 \times 1.2}$ $5.29 + 7.2$
4. Add and subtract from left to right.	$\mathbf{5.29 + 7.2}$ 12.49

Evaluate each expression.

1. $(7.8 \div 2) \times 12$ ____________

2. $5.6 + (3 \times 9.6 - 4.8)$ ____________

3. $[(4.2 \times 3.4) - 9.28]$ ____________

4. $[4 \times (9.6 \div 3)] + 8.4$ ____________

5. $5 \times [(6 \times 2.3) + 0.9]$ ____________

6. $2^4 \div [(3.2 \times 0.8) + 1.44]$ ____________

7. Reasoning Is it possible to have an expression that uses brackets without using any parentheses? Give your reasons.

____

8. Estimation How could you estimate to get an approximate answer for this expression: $12.3 \times [(2 \times 1.7) + 6] - 2^3$?

____

Name ______________________

Practice
1-5

Evaluating Numerical Expressions

1. $6^2 - (3.1 \times 5 + 2.3)$

2. $[(8 - 3.7) \times 6] + 1.5$

3. $9^2 - [(4.2 \times 3.4) - 9.28]$

4. $3.2^2 - [(12.6 - 2^2) \times 0.6]$

5. $[(0.3 \times 8) + (1.5 \times 3)] + 6^2$

6. $40 \div [9.6 - (8 \times 0.2)]$

7. $3^3 + 4.2 \times 8 \div 0.2$

8. $8.8 + [(0.4 \times 7) + (3.1 \times 2)]$

9. $7^2 - [(6^2 - 22.4) + (8 \div 0.5)] + 3.8$

10. $9 + [(4.2 - 3.3) + (6.4 \div 0.8)] \times 3$

11. $41 - 3^2 + (8 \times 2.3) - 15 + (2.1 \times 4)$

12. $13 + 26 - [(2.8 \times 5) \div 7]$

13. $16 + 23 - [(5 + 2) \times 1.9] - 13 + 6.8$

14. Jessica bought a new computer for \$800. She put \$120 down and got a student discount of \$50. Her mother gave her $\frac{1}{2}$ of the balance for her birthday. Which of these expressions could be used to find the amount Jessica still owes on the computer?

A $800 - 120 + 50 \div 2$

B $[800 - (120 - 50) \div 2]$

C $800 - (120 - 50) \div 2$

D $[800 - (120 + 50)] \div 2$

15. Number Sense A printing error in a math book removed the brackets and parentheses from the original expression of $(7 \times 3.4) - [(2.8 \times 5) - (4.3 \times 2)] + 4^2$. Give the order of operations a student solving this problem would have used to evaluate the expression with the printing error, and find the value of the incorrect expression and the correct expression.

Name ______________________________

Reteaching
1-6

Using Variables to Write Expressions

A variable represents a quantity that can change. To use a variable to write an algebraic expression for a situation, you need to decide which operation is appropriate for the situation. To help you, some words and phrases are listed below.

Word phrase	Variable	Operation	Algebraic Expression
ten **more than** a number *b*	*b*	Addition	$b + 10$
the **sum** of 8 and a number *c*	*c*		$8 + c$
five **less than** a number *d*	*d*	Subtraction	$d - 5$
15 **decreased by** a number *e*	*e*		$15 - e$
the **product** of 8 and a number *f*	*f*	Multiplication	$8f$
19 **times** a number *g*	*g*		$19g$
the quotient of a number *h* **divided by** 2	*h*	Division	$h \div 2$
a number *i* **divided into** 50	*i*		$50 \div i$

Write each algebraic expression.

1. a number *j* **divided by** 5

Identify the operation. __________ Write the expression. __________

2. the **sum** of 2 and a number *k* __________

3. 6 **times** a number *m* __________

4. a number *n* **divided into** 9 __________

5. 4 **less than** a number *p* __________

6. *q* fewer limes than 10 __________

7. *r* tickets at $7 each __________

8. A field goal scores 3 points. Write an algebraic expression to represent the number of points the Raiders will score from field goals.

Identify the operation __________ Write the expression. __________

9. **Writing to Explain** Write an algebraic expression to represent the situation below. Explain how the expression relates to the situation.

Some children share 5 apples equally among themselves.

____

____

Name ____________________

Practice
1-6

Using Variables to Write Expressions

Write each algebraic expression.

1. 6 more than a number *c* ______

2. twice a number *b* ______

3. 25 less than a number *d* ______

4. the product of 7 and a number *e* ______

5. 50 divided by a number *f* ______

6. the sum of a number *g* and 2 ______

7. 8 more stripes than a number *h* ______

8. 12 fewer hats than four times a number *i* ______

9. Alexander has $10. He buys a snack. Which expression shows how much money Alexander has left?

A $s + 10$

B $10 - s$

C $10s$

D $s \div 10$

10. A diner has booths and counter seating. Each booth can seat 4 people. Another 15 people can sit at the counter. Which expression shows how many customers can be seated in the diner?

A $15b - 4$

B $15b + 4$

C $4b - 15$

D $4b + 15$

11. Reasonableness Linnia bought some flats of flowers. Each flat holds 9 flowers. Linnia has planted 10 flowers. Is $9x + 10$ a reasonable way to represent the number of flowers that Linnia has left to plant? Explain your answer.

______

______

______

Name ____________________

Reteaching **1-7**

Parts of an Expression

There are special words you can use to describe expressions and the parts of expressions.

Terms are the parts of an expression separated by a plus or a minus sign.

$3k - 9w + 14$ has three terms: $3k$, $9w$, 14.

$h + 9$ is a **sum**.

$h - 9$ is a **difference.**

A **coefficient** is a number that is multiplied by a variable.

In the term $3k$, 3 is the coefficient of k.

$9h$ is a **product**. The **factors** are 9 and h.

$\frac{h}{9}$ is a **quotient**.

Tell how many terms are in each expression.

1. $4s + 4t$ ____________ **2.** $ab + cd - ef$ ____________

Identify the coefficient of the variable. Then identify the factors.

3. $28p$ ____________

4. $4q$ ____________

Describe each expression using **two** of these words: sum, difference, product, or quotient.

5. $vw - 12$ ____________

6. $\frac{34}{a} + 5$ ____________

7. $6(15 + 3)$ ____________

8. $\frac{13y}{10}$ ____________

9. Writing to Explain Oscar says the expression $t \div u$ has two terms. Vincent says it has one term. Who is right? Explain.

____

____

____

____

Name ____________________

Practice **1-7**

Parts of an Expression

Describe each expression.

1. $n - 4$ ____________________

____

2. $25(b + 4)$ ____________________

____

Tell how many terms are in each expression.

3. $\frac{22x}{3y}$ ____________________ **4.** $\frac{a}{b} + \frac{c}{d}$ ____________________

Identify the coefficient of the variable. Then identify the factors.

5. $37n$ ____________________ **6.** $8.5w$ ____________________

Use the table for **7** and **8**. Inez is buying office supplies for her company. She buys *b* boxes of black ink cartridges and *c* boxes of colored ink cartridges.

Item	Number in box	Cost per box
Black ink cartridges	8	$130
Colored ink cartridges	6	$115

7. Write an expression for the total number of ink cartridges Inez buys.

____

8. Write an expression for the total cost of the cartridges Inez buys.

____

9. Writing to Explain Compare the expressions you wrote in **7** and **8.** How are they alike? How are they different? Use terminology from this lesson in your explanation.

____

____

____

____

10. Which expression shows the sum of two products?

A $2jk$ **B** $(4 + d)(7 + e)$ **C** $5a + bc$ **D** $2 + \frac{u}{4}$

Name ______________________________

Evaluating Algebraic Expressions

Reteaching **1-8**

To evaluate an expression, follow these steps:

1. Substitute or replace the variable with the value given in the problem.
2. Perform the operation or operations.
3. If there is more than one operation, use the order of operations.

Evaluate $4 + 2n$ for 3.

Replace *n* with 3.	$4 + 2(3)$
Multiply first.	$4 + 6$
Then add.	10

The value of the expression is 10.

Evaluate $g^2 - 3(3) + g \div 2; g = 4$.

Replace *g* with 4.	$4^2 - 3(3) + 4 \div 2$
Evaluate terms with exponents.	$16 - 3(3) + 4 \div 2$
Then multiply and divide.	$16 - 9 + 2$
Then subtract and add.	9

The value of the expression is 9.

Apply the substitutions and evaluate.

1. $12n; n = 3$ ______________

2. $2t - 4; t = 6$ ______________

3. $r + 48 \div r; r = 8$ ______________

For **4–7,** evaluate each expression for 3, 6, and 8.

4. $7x$ _____, _____, _____

5. $6x + 4$ _____, _____, _____

6. $14 + x \div 2$ _____, _____, _____

7. $x + 2x$ _____, _____, _____

8. Katie rented a bicycle at the beach for \$3 an hour plus a \$5 fee. Write an expression that shows how much it will cost Katie to rent the bicycle. Then solve the expression for 4 hours.

____

9. Writing to Explain Timothy is solving the problem $50 + 108x \div 4$. What order of operations should he follow?

____

Name ____________________

Practice
1-8

Evaluating Algebraic Expressions

Apply the substitutions and evaluate.

1. $7x - 4; x = 9$ **2.** $3d + (5 - d); d = 4$ **3.** $8 + 2g - g \div 2; g = 6$

For **7–10,** evaluate each expression for 2, 6, and 8.

4. $5x$ ______, ______, ______ **5.** $x + 12$ ______, ______, ______

6. $96 \div x$ ______, ______, ______ **7.** $x^2 - x$ ______, ______, ______

8. Evaluate the expression for the values of *h*.

h	6	18	24	42	54
$(h - 6) + h \div 6$					

9. The table shows how much Tia charges for pet sitting. Write an expression to show how much Tia will earn for sitting two dogs for a day and two cats per hour. Then solve for sitting two dogs for the day and one cat for 6 hours.

Number of Pets	Per Day	Per Hour
One dog	$20	$7
Two dogs	$25	$9
One or two cats	$15	$6

10. Writing to Explain Tia wrote $20 + 7x$ to find how much she earned for one pet sitting job and $15x$ for another job. Explain the difference between the expressions.

11. Evaluate the expression $6 + 8f$ for $f = 4$.

A 8

B 18

C 38

D 56

Name ____________________

Reteaching
1-9

Using Expressions to Describe Patterns

You can write an expression to describe the pattern in an input/output table.

Look at the first input and output values in the table.

INPUT	OUTPUT
11	5
12	6
13	7
15	★
20	★

Ask Yourself: What do I need to do to the input 11 to get the output 5?

You might need to add, subtract, multiply, divide, or perform more than one operation.

In this table, you can subtract 6 from 11 to get 5.

Check the input and output values for 12 and 13.

$12 - 6 = 6$

$13 - 6 = 7$

The pattern is true for all of the values in the table. So, the pattern is subtract 6.

You can write the expression $x - 6$ to describe the pattern.

Substitute input values for the variable x to get the output values.

Find the output values for 15 and 20.

The input/output table shows how much Jake pays for toys. Use the input/output table for **1–4**.

INPUT	OUTPUT
6	18
7	21
8	24
9	27

1. If Jake buys 12 toys, what is the cost? ____________

2. If Jake pays $45, how many toys did he buy? ____________

3. Write an expression to describe the output pattern if the input is the variable t. ____________

4. What inputs and outputs should be added to the table for 20 toys? ____________

5. **Writing to Explain** Jessie says that the expression 2x describes the input/output table. Explain why Jessie's expression is correct or incorrect.

INPUT	2	3	4	5
OUTPUT	4	5	6	7

____

____

Name ____________________

Practice **1-9**

Using Expressions to Describe Patterns

Use this table for **1–4.**

Total Cups in Boxes	18	36	54	66	72	84
Total Number of Boxes	3	6	9	□	□	□

1. How many boxes are needed for 66, 72, and 84 cups? ____________

2. How many cups will be in 20 boxes? ____________

3. Write an algebraic expression that explains the relationship between the input (total cups in boxes) and output values (total number of boxes) if the variable *c* is the input. ____________

4. Writing to Explain Jason thinks he needs 25 boxes to pack 144 cups. Is Jason correct? Explain.

____

____

5. Make a Table Lily is using seashells to make necklaces. Each necklace has 7 shells. Make an input/output table that shows the number of shells used for 10, 15, 20, and 25 necklaces. Write an algebraic expression that explains the relationship between the input and output values.

Use this table for **6** and **7.**

Large White Butterfly Wing Beats					
Number of seconds	1	2	3	4	5
Number of beats	12	24	36	48	60

6. Critical Thinking What algebraic expression shows the number of wing beats for a chosen number of seconds?

A $60 + x$ **B** $x \div 12$ **C** $12 \div x$ **D** $12x$

7. How many times will a large white butterfly beat its wings in 12 seconds?

A 144 **B** 120 **C** 84 **D** 72

Name ______________________________

Reteaching
1-10

Simplifying Algebraic Expressions

Algebraic expressions are simplified by combining **like terms**.
Like terms are terms that look alike such as 4y and 2y, or 5 and 3.

The algebraic expression $2x + 5x + 4$ can be simplified by combining like terms.

The like terms for this expression are $2x$ and $5x$.

$2x + 5x = 7x$ The coefficients are added and an x is placed with the sum. Notice that the variable x does not change when combining the like terms $2x$ and $5x$.

Solution: $2x + 5x + 4 = 7x + 4$

For **1–6**, simplify each algebraic expression.

1. $4x - x$

2. $2y + 6y$

3. $3x + 2 + x$

4. $7y + 3 - 6y$

5. $6x + 5 - 3x$

6. $4y - 3 + 3y$

For **7** and **8**, use the picture shown to the right.

7. Find a simplified expression for the perimeter of the square.

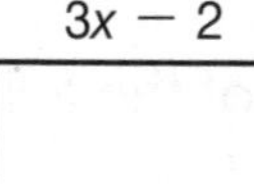

8. Find the perimeter if $x = 3$.

9. Bill says that the algebraic expression $6y + 3 - y$ has been simplified. Is Bill correct? Explain.

____

____

____

Name ____________________

Practice
1-10

Simplifying Algebraic Expressions

For **1–3**, identify the like terms.

1. $3x + 2 - x$ **2.** $y + 3y - 2$ **3.** $6x + 2 - 3x + 4x$

For **4–9**, simplify each algebraic expression.

4. $6x - 3x$ **5.** $4y + 3y$ **6.** $5x + 1 + 3x$

7. $3y - 1 - y$ **8.** $4 + 8x - 2 - 5x$ **9.** $7y - 6 + 4 - 2y$

For **10–15**, determine if the expressions are simplified. If they are not simplified, then simplify them.

10. $6x - x$ **11.** $3y + 4 - 2$ **12.** $8y - 1$

13. $2x + 3 + 5x$ **14.** $9x + 2$ **15.** $4 - 3y$

16. Which of the following algebraic expressions is simplified?

A $9y + 2 - 1$

B $5y + 3 - 7y$

C $4y + 6y$

D $8y + 3$

Name ______________________________

Reteaching 1-11

Writing Equivalent Expressions

You can use the properties of operations to write equivalent expressions. Two algebraic expressions are equivalent if they have the same value when any number is substituted for the variable.

How can you use the properties of operations to write an equivalent expression for the expression below?

$2(5x + 7)$

Use the Distributive Property to expand the expression. Then use Associative Property of Multiplication to regroup the first term and multiply 2×5.

$$\begin{aligned} 2(5x + 7) &= 2(5x) + 2(7) \\ &= (2 \times 5)x + 14 \\ &= 10x + 14 \end{aligned}$$

How can you use the Distributive Property in reverse order to write an equivalent expression for the expression below?

$9x + 3$

Look for a common factor of both terms that is greater than 1. In this expression, the common factor is 3.

$$\begin{aligned} 9x + 3 &= 3(3x) + 3(1) \\ &= 3(3x + 1) \end{aligned}$$

Use the Distributive Property to write an equivalent expression by filling in the missing numbers.

1. $4(x - 2) =$ ____$x -$ ____

2. $15x - 5 = 5($____$x -$ ____$)$

3. $3(6x + 1) =$ ____$x +$ ____

4. $21x + 6 = 3($____$x +$ ____$)$

Find the missing number(s) so that the expressions are equivalent.

5. $2(4x + 6)$ and ____$x + 12$

6. $16x - 14$ and ____$(8x -$ ____$)$

7. $3(8x - 5)$ and ____$x - 15$

8. $10x + 25$ and $5($____$x +$ ____$)$

Use the Distributive Property to write an equivalent expression.

9. $3(2x - 1)$

10. $10x - 5$

11. $7(3x + 4)$

12. $22x - 8$

13. Reasoning Jun writes the expression $5(x + 2)$. Then he uses the Distributive Property to write the equivalent expression $5x + 10$. How can he substitute a value for the variable to check to see if expressions are equivalent?

____

____

Name ________________________________

Practice

1-11

Writing Equivalent Expressions

Use the Distributive Property to write an equivalent expression by filling in the missing numbers.

1. $10(x + 3) =$ ____$x +$ ____

2. $7(8x + 2) =$ ____$x +$ ____

3. $6(7x - 8) =$ ____$x -$ ____

4. $24x - 3 = 3($____$x -$ ____$)$

5. $20x + 4 = 4($____$x +$ ____$)$

6. $9x + 27 = 9($____$x +$ ____$)$

Find the missing number(s) so that the expressions are equivalent.

7. $8(2x - 3)$ and ____$x - 24$

8. $5(3x - 9)$ and ____$x -$ ____

9. $6(2x + 9)$ and ____$x +$ ____

10. $22x - 11$ and ____$(2x -$ ____$)$

11. $18x +$ ____ and ____$(3x + 1)$

12. $36x +$ ____ and ____$(12x + 7)$

Use the Distributive Property to write an equivalent expression.

13. $3(6x - 7)$

14. $4(9x - 2)$

15. $6(8x + 1)$

16. $35x + 30$

17. $70x - 10$

18. $18x - 36$

19. **Geometry** The formula for the perimeter of a rectangle is $2l + 2w$, where l is the length and w is the width. How can you use the Distributive Property to write an equivalent expression for $2l + 2w$? Explain.

____

____

____

20. **Writing to Explain** Eliot uses the Distributive Property to write an equivalent expression for $7(3x + 4)$. He writes $21x + 4$. Emma notices that Eliot made a mistake. How could Emma explain to Eliot where he went wrong? What is the correct equivalent expression?

____

____

____

____

Name ____________________

Reteaching
1-12

Equivalent Expressions

Two expressions are equivalent if they have the same value when the variable is replaced with any number. For example, the following expressions are equivalent:

$2 + 1 + 2x$ $\quad 3 + 2x \quad$ $3 + x + x$

Are the expressions $4(x + 2)$ and $2x + 5 + 2x + 3$ equivalent to $4x + 8$?

You can apply the Distributive Property: $4(x + 2) = 4x + 8$

The expressions $4(x + 2)$ and $4x + 8$ are equivalent.

You can apply the Commutative Property of Addition and combine like terms.

$$2x + 5 + 2x + 3 = 2x + 2x + 5 + 3 = 4x + 8$$

The expressions $2x + 5 + 2x + 3$ and $4x + 8$ are equivalent.

Identify the expressions that are equivalent to expression given.

1. $2(x - 5)$
- **A** $2x - 8 - 2$
- **B** $2x - 8 + 2$
- **C** $2x - 5$
- **D** $2x - 10$

2. $3(x - 3)$
- **A** $3x - 6$
- **B** $3x - 8 - 1$
- **C** $x + 2x - 3$
- **D** $x - 3 + x - 3 + x - 3$

3. $8x + 10$
- **A** $2(4x + 10)$
- **B** $4x + 4x + 10$
- **C** $2(4x + 5)$
- **D** $10x + 8 + 2 - 2x$

4. $7x + 6$
- **A** $6x + x + 6$
- **B** $6(x + 1) + x$
- **C** $4x + 2 + 3x + 4$
- **D** $7x + 8 - 2$

Determine if the expressions are equivalent. Substitute 3 for y to check.

5. $5(y + 4)$ and $2 + 5y + 18$

6. $2y - 6$ and $6y - 6 - 3y$

7. Number Sense Show that $4x - 7$ is equivalent to $4(x - 1) - 3$ when $x = 3$.

____

____

Name ______________________________

Practice
1-12

Equivalent Expressions

Identify the expressions that are equivalent to expression given.

1. $4(x - 4)$

A $4x - 18 - 2$

B $2x - 16 + 2x$

C $16 + 4x$

D $8x - 16 - 4x$

2. $12x - 3$

A $9x - 6 + 3x + 3$

B $12(x - 1)$

C $14x - 6 - 2x - 3$

D $4(3x - 1)$

3. $5x + 7$

A $4x - 7 + 14 + x$

B $5(x + 1) + 2$

C $x - 3 + 4x + 10 + x$

D $5(x + 2) - 3$

4. $10(x + 2)$

A $20 + 2x + 8x - 10$

B $10x + 2$

C $x + 10 + 9x + 2$

D $15 + 20x + 5 - 10x$

5. $2(4x - 7)$

A $2 + 8x - 16$

B $5x - 14 + 3x$

C $2x + 2x - 4 + 4x - 10$

D $8(x - 1) - 6$

6. $12x + 10 - 5x$

A $10x + 2 - 3x + 8$

B $17x + 12 - 2$

C $3 + 7x + 7$

D $2 + 7x + 5$

Determine if the expressions are equivalent. Substitute 4 for y to check.

7. $4y + 10 - y$ and $2(y + 5)$

8. $3y - 12$ and $7y - 6 - 4y - 6$

9. $2(5y + 3)$ and $2 + 10y + 4$

10. $4y - 1 - y$ and $5 + 5y - 6$

11. Writing to Explain Are the algebraic expressions $4(2x + 3)$ and $8x + 12$ equivalent? Explain.

____

____

Name ____________________

Problem Solving: Make an Organized List

You can make an organized list in a table using the information given in a problem. A table organizes the information and helps you solve the problem.

Angie has \$30 to spend at a carnival. Tickets for rides cost \$1.25 each. Write an expression to show how much Angie has left after buying x tickets at the carnival. Make a table to show how much Angie has left after buying $x = 3$ tickets, $x = 8$ tickets, and $x = 15$ tickets.

Write an Expression

x = number of tickets

Spending Money		Price of Tickets		Number of Tickets
↓		↓		↓
30	−	1.25	×	x

The expression $30 - 1.25x$ represents the situation.

Make a Table

Use x as a label for one column.
Use $30 - 1.25x$ for the other column.

Enter the values for x: 3, 8, and 15.

Solve the expression for each x-value and enter it into the table.

x	$30 - 1.25x$
3	26.25
8	20
15	11.25

So, Angie has \$26.25 left after she buys 3 tickets, \$20 left after she buys 8 tickets, and \$11.25 left after she buys \$15 tickets.

1. Arturo works at a horse ranch. He makes \$50 each week for cleaning out stalls and \$12 for each horse that he grooms. Write an expression that describes Arturo's weekly earnings after grooming x horses.

____

2. Using your answer for Exercise 1, complete the table to find how much Arturo earns in a week if he grooms 5 horses, 9 horses, and 12 horses.

x	
5	
9	
12	

3. Gina sells bracelets at a fair for \$6 each. Complete the table to show how much she earns for $x = 12$ bracelets, $x = 35$ bracelets, and $x = 56$ bracelets.

x	$6x$
12	
35	
56	

Name ______________________

Practice 1-13

Problem Solving: Make an Organized List

1. Selena earns $8.75 per hour working at her job. It costs $3.50 to ride the bus to and from work. Write an expression that describes how much Selena has each day after *x* hours of work and paying her bus fare.

____

2. Complete the table to find how much Selena earns each day if she works 3 hours, 5 hours, or 8 hours.

x	
3	
5	
8	

3. A health food store sells protein powder online. A 10-lb carton of protein powder costs $27.25. It costs $4.95 to ship the powder whether you buy 1 or more cartons. Write an expression to show the cost including shipping of *x* cartons of protein powder.

____

4. Complete the table to find how much it costs to have 2, 5, and 9 cartons of protein powder shipped.

x	
2	
5	
9	

5. **Critical Thinking** Lee earns 3 points for every dollar he spends at the pet store. Which value completes this table?

x	3*x*
27	?

A 9 **B** 24 **C** 30 **D** 81

6. **Writing to Explain** A wildlife park charges $18 for each admission ticket *x*. Explain the labels you would use to make a table to find the cost of 4 tickets, 9 tickets, and 12 tickets.

____

____

Name ______________________________

Reteaching **2-1**

Understanding Equations

A solution to an equation is a value that makes the equation true. An equation is true if both sides are equal.

To find out if a given value is a solution to an equation, substitute the value for the variable. If both sides of the equation are equal, the value is a solution to the equation. Use this method to solve the following problem.

Kate is going to babysit for 5 hours. She needs to make exactly $20.00 to buy a concert ticket. How much does Kate need to make each hour in order to buy the concert ticket?

The equation for this situation is $5x = \$20.00$, where x is the amount she makes per hour.

Possible Babysitting Rates
$3.00 per hour
$4.00 per hour
$5.00 per hour
$6.00 per hour

To find the solution to $5x = \$20.00$, substitute the different rates for x.

Try $x = \$3.00$:	$5 \times \$3.00 = \$15.00$	Not a solution
Try $x = \$4.00$:	$5 \times \$4.00 = \$20.00$	Solution
Try $x = \$5.00$:	$5 \times \$5.00 = \$25.00$	Not a solution
Try $x = \$6.00$:	$5 \times \$6.00 = \$30.00$	Not a solution

Since the solution is $4.00, Kate needs to make $4.00 per hour in order to earn enough money to buy the concert ticket.

Substitute the different values of the variable to find the solution to each equation.

1. $5 + x = 22$ $x = 7, 12, 17, 20$

2. $n - 9 = 33$ $n = 14, 24, 32, 42$

3. $27 \div p = 9$ $p = 3, 4, 6, 7$

4. $81 = 9y$ $y = 2, 5, 8, 9$

Tell if each equation is true or false for $k = 4$.

5. $32 \div k = 8$

6. $k = 31 - 27$

7. $43.6 - k = 38.6$

Tell which value of the variable is the solution to the equation.

8. $23.7 = 41.1 - t$ $t = 17.4, 18.4, 27.4, 64.8$

9. $d + 19.6 = 34.5$ $d = 13.1, 13.9, 14.9, 22.9$

10. Reasoning Ada is putting autographed baseballs in a display case. The display case can hold 28 baseballs, and there are already 17 baseballs in the case. Ada thinks that she can display 9 more baseballs and the display case will be full. How can you use the equation $17 + b = 28$ to check if she is right?

____

____

Name ______________________

Practice **2-1**

Understanding Equations

Substitute the different values of the variable to find the solution to each equation.

1. $27 - c = 18$ $c = 9, 11, 35, 45$

2. $q - 19 = 12$ $q = 7, 21, 29, 31$

3. $8 \times s = 96$ $s = 9, 12, 13, 14$

4. $56 = 7f$ $f = 6, 7, 8, 9$

Tell if each equation is true or false for $w = 2.1$.

5. $28.4 - w = 25.3$

6. $w = 39.2 - 37.1$

Tell which value of the variable is the solution to the equation.

7. $t + \$13.38 = \$19.00$ $t = \$5.62, \$5.72, \$6.62, \$7.72$

8. $19.7 = 41.1 - g$ $g = 21.4, 22.4, 30.4, 31.4$

9. $7.7 + r = 8.5$ $r = 0.2, 0.6, 0.8, 1.2$

10. Writing to Explain Lou set up 6 tables for a party. 42 people are coming to the party. Lou is planning to seat 7 people at each table. Use the equation $42 \div p = 6$ to explain whether Lou's plan will work.

____

____

____

11. Reasoning 117 students and teachers participated in a fundraiser. 96 students participated. Did 11, 19, 21, or 29 teachers participate? Use the equation $t + 96 = 117$ to justify your answer.

____

____

____

12. Geometry Jerry built a table with a square top. The perimeter of the tabletop is 18 feet. He knows that each side of the table is either 3, $3\frac{1}{2}$, 4, or $4\frac{1}{2}$ feet long. Use the equation $18 = 4s$ to help him find which is the length of each side of the tabletop.

____

____

____

Name ____________________

Reteaching **2-2**

Properties of Equality

To keep an equation balanced, you must do the same thing to each side.

Balanced Equation

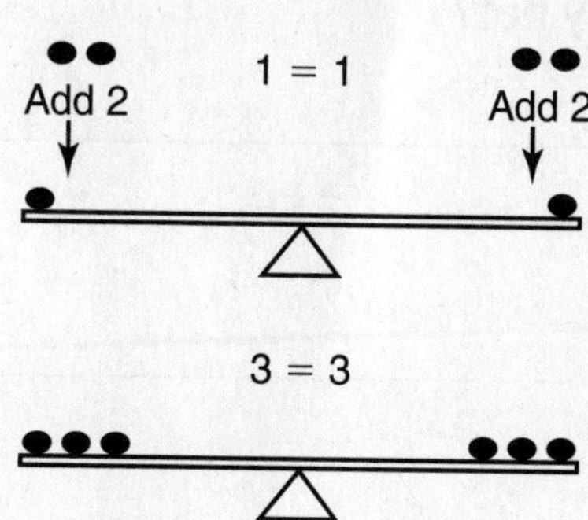

The scale is balanced because both sides **have the same value.** We added the same amount to each side of the equation.

Unbalanced Equation

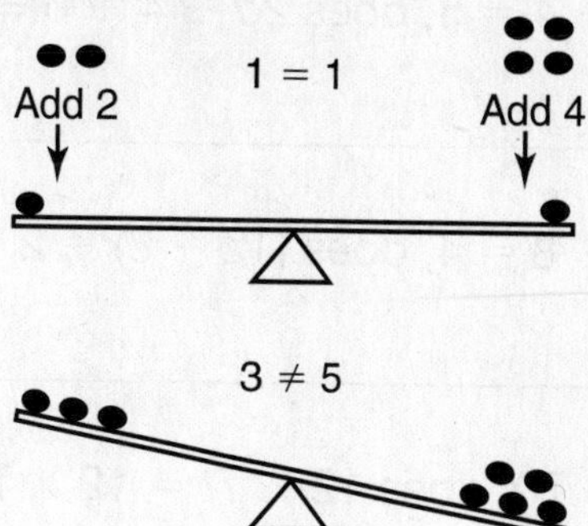

The equation is not balanced. 3 does not equal 5. We did not add the same amount to both sides of the equation.

Use the Properties of Equality to balance equations.

Add the same number to each side.	$3c = 12$, so $3c + 5 = 12 + 5$
Subtract the same number from each side.	$3c = 12$, so $3c - 3 = 12 - 3$
Multiply each side by the same number.	$3c = 12$, so $3c \times 2 = 12 \times 2$
Divide each side by the same number.	$3c = 12$, so $3c \div 4 = 12 \div 4$

Evaluate the equations.

1. If $16 + 5 = 21$, does $16 + 5 - 4 = 21 - 4$? Why or why not?

____

2. If $3p = 27$, does $3p \times 2 = 27 \times 3$? Why or why not?

____

3. If $4s - 6 = 18$, does $(4s - 6) \div 2 = 18 \div 2$? Why or why not?

____

4. **Reasoning** A pan balance shows $x + 2 = 10$. If you add 5 units to one side, can you balance the scale by adding x units to the other side? Explain.

____

Name ___________________________

Practice

2-2

Properties of Equality

1. If $16 + 4 = 20$, does $16 + 4 - 4 = 20 - 4$? Why or why not?

2. If $2d \div 4 = 5$, does $2d \div 4 + 6 = 5 + 4$? Why or why not?

3. If $12 - 8 = 4$, does $(12 - 8) \div 2 = 4 \times 2$? Explain.

4. If $7t = 70$, does $12 \times 7t = 12 \times 70$? Explain.

5. **Critical Thinking** Emil and Jade have equal amounts of play money in two piles. Emil has $1 and a quarter in his pile. Jade has 5 quarters in her pile. If Emil gives Jade $1 and Jade gives Emil 4 quarters, will the two piles still be equal in value? Explain.

6. Which equation shows the Multiplication Property of Equality if $n + 4 = 11$?

   A $(n + 4) \times 2 = 11$

   B $(n + 4) \times 2 = 11 \div 2$

   C $(n + 4) \times 2 = 11 \times 4$

   D $(n + 4) \times 2 = 11 \times 2$

7. **Writing to Explain** Bobbie wrote $y + 6 = 15$. Then she wrote $(y + 6) \div 3 = 15$. Explain why the second equation is not balanced and how to balance it.

Name ____________________

Reteaching **2-3**

Solving Addition and Subtraction Equations

You can use inverse relationships and the properties of equality to get the variable alone to solve an equation. Remember that you need to do the same thing to both sides of the equation to keep the equation equal.

Solve the equation $5 + c = 15$.

To get c alone, undo adding 5 by subtracting 5 from both sides.

$$5 + c = 15$$
$$5 + c - \mathbf{5} = 15 - \mathbf{5}$$
$$c = 10$$

Check your solution by substituting 10 for c in the equation.

$$5 + c = 15$$
$$5 + 10 = 15$$
$$15 = 15 \quad \text{It checks.}$$

Solve the equation $x - 20 = 16$.

To get x alone, undo subtracting 20 by adding 20 to both sides.

$$x - 20 = 16$$
$$x - 20 + \mathbf{20} = 16 + \mathbf{20}$$
$$x = 36$$

Check your solution by substituting 36 for x in the equation.

$$x - 20 = 16$$
$$36 - 20 = 16$$
$$16 = 16 \quad \text{It checks.}$$

Explain how to get the variable alone in each equation.

1. $x + 13 = 25$

$x + 13 - \mathbf{13} = 25 - \mathbf{13}$

____

2. $n - 30 = 10$

$n - 30 + \mathbf{30} = 10 + \underline{\mathbf{?}}$

____

Solve each equation and check your answer. Show your work.

3. $g - 100 = 150$

$g - 100 +$ ________ $= 150 +$ ________

$g =$ ____________________

4. $y + 56 = 63$

____

5. The Olympic triathlon is about 51 km. A contestant has completed two of the three legs of the race and has traveled 42 km. Solve $42 + d = 51$ to find the distance of the third leg.

____

Name ______________________________

Practice
2-3

Solving Addition and Subtraction Equations

Explain how to get the variable alone in each equation.

1. $n + 10 = 100$
$n + 10 - 10 = 100 - 10$

____

2. $x - 75 = 49$
$x - 75 + \_\_ = 49 + \_\_$

____

Solve each equation and check your answer.

3. $g - 8 = 25$ __________

4. $25 + y = 42$ __________

5. $r + 82 = 97$ __________

6. $30 = m - 18$ __________

7. $150 = e + 42$ __________

8. $a - 51 = 12$ __________

9. Jo loaned Al \$15. She had \$15 left. Solve the equation $15 = s - 15$ to find how much money Jo had before she made the loan.

A \$0

B \$15

C \$30

D \$60

10. Critical Thinking If $n + 10 = 40$, then what is the value of the expression $n - 25$?

A 5

B 25

C 30

D 50

11. Writing to Explain Explain how to solve the equation $35 + p = 92$. Then solve.

____

Name ______________________________

Problem Solving: Draw a Picture and Write an Equation

Tico spent \$37.51 at the computer store. Now he has \$29.86 left. How much did Tico have before he went to the computer store?

What do you know?	Tico has \$29.86 now. He spent \$37.51.
What do you need to find out?	How much Tico had before.
1. Assign a variable.	b = how much Tico had before
2. Draw a picture.	b \$29.86 | \$37.51
3. Write and solve an equation.	\$29.86 + \$37.51 = b \$67.37 = b
4. Answer the question.	Tico had \$67.37 before he went to the store.

Draw a picture and write an equation to solve each problem.

1. Gina's book has 349 fewer pages than Terri's. If Gina's book has 597 pages, how many pages does Terri's book have?

2. Peter played a video game. Before dinner, he had collected 24,729 gold coins. At the end of the game he had collected 97,304 gold coins. How many coins did he collect after dinner?

3. SaveMart can store 840 cases of canned food in the big warehouse. This is 394 cases more than the number that can be displayed on the shelves. How many cases can be displayed?

Name ____________________

Practice
2-4

Problem Solving: Draw a Picture and Write an Equation

Draw a picture and write an equation to solve each problem.

1. Mike has already driven 176 laps. The race is 250 laps long. How many more laps does he have to drive to finish the race?

____

2. Antonio found 133 golf balls in the water. He picked up a total of 527 lost golf balls. How many golf balls did he find in the weeds and bushes?

____

3. A lumber company plants 840 trees. If the company cuts down 560 trees, how many more trees did it plant than it cut down?

____

4. Writing to Explain What operation would you use to solve this problem? Why?

Erik wants to buy a new stereo for \$359. He has \$288 saved already. How much more will he have to save to buy the stereo?

____

____

5. Reasonableness Write an estimate that will show if 77 is a reasonable solution to the equation $14 + m = 91$.

____

6. Juan brought 87 pounds of recyclables to the recycling center. He brought 54 pounds of glass, and the rest was plastic. Which equation could be used to find *p*, the number of pounds of plastic Juan recycled?

A $87 + p = 54$

B $54 + p = 87$

C $p - 54 = 87$

D $p + 87 = 54$

Name ___

Reteaching 2-5

Solving Multiplication and Division Equations

To solve an equation, make the two sides of the equation equal with the variable alone on one side. You can use inverse operations and properties of equality.

Remember: **Inverse operations** "undo" each other. **Properties of Equality** say that you can multiply or divide both sides of an equation by the same number and the two sides of the equation remain equal.

Use division to "undo" multiplication.

With numbers:
$3 \times 6 = 18$
$3 \times 6 \div \mathbf{6} = 18 \div \mathbf{6}$
$3 = 3$

In algebra:
$m \times 9 = 54$
$m \times 9 \div \mathbf{9} = 54 \div \mathbf{9}$
$m = 6$

Use multiplication to "undo" division.

With numbers:
$24 \div 2 = 12$
$24 \div 2 \times \mathbf{2} = 12 \times \mathbf{2}$
$24 = 24$

In algebra:
$p \div 8 = 7$
$p \div 8 \times \mathbf{8} = 7 \times \mathbf{8}$
$p = 56$

For **1** through **3**, name the inverse operation you will use to get the variable alone on one side of the equation. In **2** and **3**, also fill in the blanks.

1. $5p = 50$
$5p \div 5 = 50 \div 5$
___

2. $n \div 16 = 4$
$n \div 16 \times 16 = 4 \times$ ___
___

3. $15 = r \times 3$
$15 \div$ ___ $= r \times 3 \div$ ___
___

For **4** through **6** solve the equation.

4. $w \div 5 = 8$
___

5. $20y = 100$
___

6. $3 = s \div 10$
___

7. Writing to Explain Jason solved the equation $r \div 14 = 19$. He got 266. Is his answer correct? Explain how you know.

___

___

Name ____________________

Practice
2-5

Solving Multiplication and Division Equations

For **1** through **3**, explain how to get the variable alone in each equation.

1. $r \times 7 = 42$
$r \times 7 \div 7 = 42 \div 7$

2. $m \div 6 = 12$
$m \div 6 \times \_ = 12 \times \_$

3. $44 = 2k$

For **4** through **9**, solve the equation. Check your answer.

4. $9n = 72$

5. $y \times 5 = 60$

6. $v \div 13 = 2$

7. $w \div 7 = 15$

8. $216 = 36p$

9. $17 = t \div 3$

10. Writing to Explain Tell how you would get the variable *m* alone on one side of the equation $15m = 45$.

11. Write a Problem Write a problem that can be solved with the equation $r \div 6 = 14$.

12. Number Sense Which equation can you use to solve this problem?

There are 12 muffins in a package. Will bought 84 muffins. How many packages did he buy?

A $12 \times p = 84$

B $84 \times 12 = p$

C $12 \div p = 84$

D $84 = 12 + p$

Name ______________________________

Reteaching **2-6**

Solving Equations with Fractions

You can solve equations with fractions and mixed numbers the same way that you solve equations with whole numbers: using inverse relationships and properties of equality to isolate the variable.

Solve the following problem. Remember to find a common denominator before you add or subtract fractions or mixed numbers.

Jason worked at a car wash for 5 hours. For $3\frac{1}{3}$ hours, he vacuumed the interiors of cars. For the other part of his shift, he collected money from customers. For how many hours did Jason collect money? Use the equation $3\frac{1}{3} + h = 5$ to solve the problem.

$3\frac{1}{3} + h = 5$

$3\frac{1}{3} + h - 3\frac{1}{3} = 5 - 3\frac{1}{3}$ ⟵ Subtract $3\frac{1}{3}$ from both sides of the equation.

$h = 4\frac{3}{3} - 3\frac{1}{3}$ ⟵ Find a common denominator.

$h = 1\frac{2}{3}$

Jason collected money from customers for $1\frac{2}{3}$ hours.

Here is another example. Solve the equation $\frac{5}{9}z = \frac{1}{4}$ by getting the variable alone on one side of the equation.

$\frac{5}{9}z = \frac{1}{4}$

$\frac{5}{9}z \times \frac{9}{5} = \frac{1}{4} \times \frac{9}{5}$ ⟵ Multiply both sides by $\frac{9}{5}$, the reciprocal of $\frac{5}{9}$.

$z = \frac{9}{20}$

Solve each equation.

1. $s + \frac{1}{4} = 12\frac{1}{2}$

2. $2\frac{2}{3} + y = 4\frac{1}{4}$

3. $a - 4\frac{3}{8} = 2\frac{1}{2}$

4. $\frac{2}{7}q = 3\frac{3}{5}$

5. $14\frac{1}{6} - d = 12\frac{3}{4}$

6. $f \times \frac{2}{7} = 5\frac{1}{2}$

Solve.

7. Reasonableness 6 people are seated along a counter that is $11\frac{1}{4}$ feet long. Use the equation $\frac{1}{6} \times 11\frac{1}{4} = p$ to find the amount of counter space for one person. Tell one way you can check the reasonableness of your answer.

____

____

____

Name ______________________

Practice
2-6

Solving Equations with Fractions

Solve each equation.

1. $b - 1\frac{1}{3} = 4\frac{4}{9}$

2. $3\frac{2}{9} - k = \frac{1}{5}$

3. $g \times \frac{2}{3} = 6\frac{1}{9}$

4. $t + 1\frac{3}{8} = 2\frac{1}{4}$

5. $3\frac{1}{6} + x = 7\frac{5}{12}$

6. $\frac{2}{9} \times y = 4\frac{5}{6}$

7. $p \times \frac{4}{9} = 4\frac{5}{12}$

8. $m + \frac{3}{5} = 8\frac{1}{2}$

9. $a \times \frac{5}{8} = 100$

10. $5\frac{2}{5} - v = 1\frac{1}{3}$

11. Geometry To find the area of a rectangle, multiply the length and width. Write an equation to find the area of rectangle $3\frac{3}{5}$ feet long and $2\frac{1}{6}$ feet wide. Then find the area in square feet.

____

12. Reasoning Is the solution of $w \times \frac{11}{12} = 19$ greater than or less than 19? How can you tell without solving the equation?

____

____

____

13. Algebra Jill cut a $3\frac{1}{2}$-foot chain into 2 pieces in order to hang 2 birdfeeders. The longer piece of chain was $1\frac{5}{6}$ feet long. Tell how to write and solve an equation to find the length of the shorter piece.

____

____

14. Writing to Explain Antonio is staying in Seattle for the entire month of July. He has been in Seattle for a week and $3\frac{2}{3}$ days. How many more days will he be in Seattle? Explain how you found your answer.

____

____

____

Name ______________________________

Reteaching
2-7

Writing Inequalities

You can write an inequality to show a relationship in a real-world situation. For example, you could write an inequality to show that there were more than 50 people at a picnic. Or you could write an inequality to show that you can spend up to $15.00 at a store. An inequality is a mathematical sentence that contains an inequality symbol.

Inequality Symbols

Symbol	Meaning
$<$	is less than
$\leq$	is less than or equal to
$>$	is greater than
$\geq$	is greater than or equal to
$\neq$	is not equal to

How can you write an inequality to show that there were more than 50 people at a picnic? Here are some numbers of people that might have been at the picnic:

52, 67, 102, 115

There were more than 50 people at the picnic, so every possible number will be greater than 50. Use the variable p to represent the number of people at the picnic. Use the greater than symbol (>) to write the inequality.

$$p > 50$$

How can you write an inequality to show that there were 50 or more people at a picnic? If there were 50 or more, 50 must be included as a possible answer. For this situation, use the greater than or equal to symbol (≥) to write the inequality.

$$p \geq 50$$

Write an inequality for each situation.

1. A number, x, is less than 4.

2. A price, p, is at least $10.00.

3. The time limit, t, is 55 minutes.

4. An age, a, is not 16.

5. A height, h, is greater than 2 meters.

6. Amy knitted more than 7 scarves, s.

7. The temperature, t, was not 53°.

8. There can be up to 20 dogs, d, at a dog park.

9. Writing to Explain The Tornadoes baseball team has not won a game this year. Write an inequality to show the number of games that another team would have to win to have a better record than the Tornadoes. Explain your answer.

____

____

Name ______________________

Practice
2-7

Writing Inequalities

Write an inequality for each situation.

1. A bucket, *b*, holds up to 3 gallons.

2. Chloe's age, *a*, is under 8.

3. The test score, *s*, is not 92.

4. The temperature, *t*, is over 80°.

5. The width, *w*, is at least 10 feet.

Solve each problem.

6. The stadium had seating for 40,000 fans, and it was not full. Write an inequality to show the number of fans at the game.

7. The museum gave a discount to seniors over the age of 65. Write an inequality to represent the age of the seniors who receive a discount.

8. Students may not work in groups of 3. Write an inequality to represent the number of students that may be in a group.

9. Campfires must be at least 30 feet from the nearest tent. Write an inequality to show distance from a campfire to the nearest tent.

10. Jordan had less than 55 minutes to finish his work. Then he got a phone call that lasted 16 minutes. Write an inequality to show how much time he has left to work.

11. Caroline practices piano as much as 2 hours a day Monday through Thursday, and she practices up to 3 hours on Sunday. Write an inequality to show the number of hours that she practices in one week.

12. Writing to Explain How do you know when to use the less than symbol and when to use the less than or equal to symbol when writing an inequality for a situation?

____

____

13. Write a Problem Write a real-world situation that can be represented by $x \leq 5$.

____

Name ______________________________

Solving Inequalities

An equation shows when expressions are equal. Equations use equal signs (=). An inequality is a statement that uses the greater-than symbol (>), the less-than symbol (<), the greater-than-or-equal-to symbol (≥), or the less-than-or-equal-to symbol (≤).

Variables can be used with inequalities. A variable in an inequality stands for all numbers that make the inequality true.

For example, in the inequality $x < 3$, the x stands for all numbers less than 3. So x can be 0, 1, or 2.

The inequality $13 \leq y + 5$ can have solutions $y = 8$, 9, and 10, since $8 + 5 = 13$, $9 + 5 = 14$, and $10 + 5 = 15$.

To graph $x < 3$, first draw an open circle on the number line above 3. Shade a line from the open circle to the left through the arrow. This represents all numbers that are less than 3.

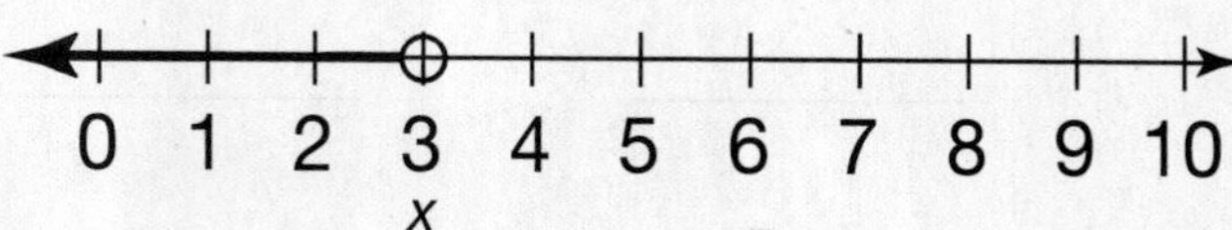

To graph x is greater than or equal to 5, first draw a closed circle on the number line at 5. Then shade a line from the closed circle to the right through the arrow.

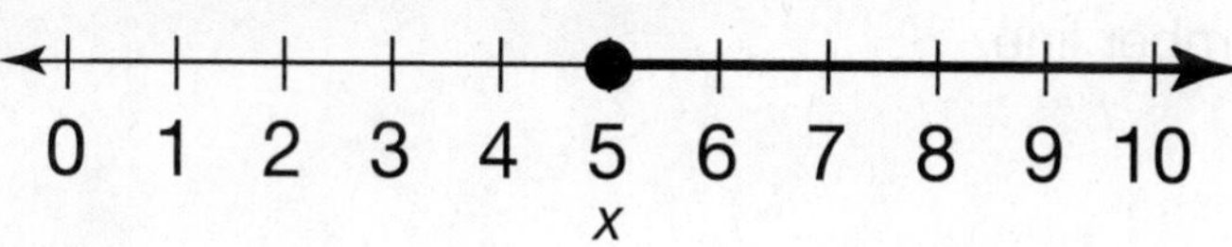

1. Is 0 a solution of $x > 2$? ______________________

2. Is 5 a solution of $y \leq 10$? ______________________

3. Name 3 solutions for $z > 5$. ______________________

4. Name 3 solutions for $x \geq 4$. ______________________

5. Graph the inequality $x < 7$ on the number line below.

0 1 2 3 4 5 6 7 8 9 10

6. Graph the inequality $x \geq 4$ on the number line below.

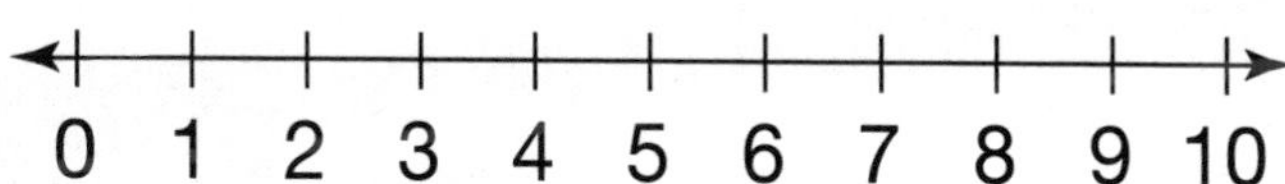

Name ______________________

Practice
2-8

Solving Inequalities

Give 3 values that solve the inequality for Exercises **1** through **16**.

1. $x > 0$ ________

2. $y > 5$ ________

3. $z \leq 10$ ________

4. $z < 3$ ________

5. $x > 4$ ________

6. $x < 4$ ________

7. $x > 170$ ________

8. $x > 1$ ________

9. $x < 9$ ________

10. $x < 6$ ________

11. $y > 2$ ________

12. $y \geq 100$ ________

13. $z < 8$ ________

14. $x \geq 77$ ________

15. $u > 10.9$ ________

16. $u \leq 13.99$ ________

17. Draw the inequality $x < 7$ on a number line.

18. Draw the inequality $x \geq 7$ on a number line.

19. Which is NOT a solution to $x > 18$?

A 18 **B** 18.000001 **C** 19 **D** 30

20. Writing to Explain Is 0 a solution to $x > 0$? Why or why not?

____

____

Name ____________________

Reteaching
2-9

Problem Solving: Draw a Picture and Write an Equation

Zoo keepers divided some land into 4 sections for the monkeys at the zoo. Each section has 23 monkeys. How many monkeys are at the zoo?

Read and Understand

Choose a variable for the unknown. The unknown is the total number of monkeys at the zoo.

Let m = the total number of monkeys.

Draw a picture to show that the total number of monkeys is divided into 4 equal sections of 23 monkeys.

m

23	23	23	23

Plan and Solve
Write an equation using the variable and the picture.

$m \div 4 = 23$ ← Use division.

Solve the equation.

$$m \div 4 = 23$$
$$m \div 4 \times 4 = 23 \times 4$$
$$m = 92$$

There are 92 monkeys at the zoo.

Write an equation for **1**. Solve each problem.

1. Juan has 6 times as many basketball cards as Nick. If Juan has 192 basketball cards, how many does Nick have?

192

x	x	x	x	x	x

____

2. Several sixth grade classes are going on a field trip to a planetarium. The teachers divided the classes into 19 groups. There are 7 students in each group. How many students are going to the planetarium? Use the equation $c \div 19 = 7$.

____

3. Each bus for a field trip can carry 27 students. If 216 students are going on the field trip, how many buses are needed? Use the equation $27n = 216$.

____

Name ___________________________

Practice
2-9

Problem Solving: Draw a Picture and Write an Equation

Draw a picture and write an equation to solve each problem.

1. Mr. Conover bought 6 boxes of pastels for his art class. He paid \$4.50 for each box. What was the total cost of the boxes?

____

2. A company charters boats for whale watching. The company chartered 13 boats. There were a total of 325 passengers on the boats. What was the average number of passengers per boat?

____

3. A store sells 5-gallon bottles of water for \$8. The store made \$288 on Monday selling the water. How many bottles were sold?

____

4. A sign at a recycling center states that 118 pounds of recycled newspapers saves one tree. How many pounds of newspapers will save 3 trees?

____

5. **Algebra** Students mailed invitations to a play to 414 parents. Each student mailed 18 invitations. If s equals the number of students who mailed invitations, which equation best shows the number of invitations that were mailed?

A $s + 18 = 414$

B $s \div 18 = 414$

C $18 \div s = 414$

D $18s = 414$

Name ______________________________

Reteaching
3-1

Dependent and Independent Variables

A **dependent** variable changes in response to another variable, an **independent variable**.

An independent causes the change in a dependent variable. It is called *independent* because another variable does not cause it to change.

For example, the capacity (*c*) of this soup can, can depend in part on the diameter (*d*) of the top of the can. So, the diameter (*d*) is an independent variable that causes the dependent variable, the capacity (*c*) of the can, to change.

Underline the independent variable and circle the dependent variable in each situation.

1. The number of hours (*h*) studying and the score (*s*) on a test

2. The length (*l*) of a pencil and the number of times (*t*) it has been sharpened

3. The length of a book in pages (*p*) and the number of words (*w*) in a story

4. The number of students (*s*) ahead of you in the lunch line and the time (*t*) it takes you to get lunch

5. The amount of time (*t*) to finish a race and the number of laps (*l*) around a track

6. Tickets (*t*) sold for a race and the amount of money (*m*) collected

7. The height (*h*) of a fence and the amount of wood (*w*) to make the fence

8. The height (*h*) of a fence and the time (*t*) it takes to climb the fence

9. Writing to Explain Write your own situation where speed (*s*) is an independent variable.

____

____

Name ____________________

Practice
3-1

Dependent and Independent Variables

Underline the independent variable and circle the dependent variable in each situation.

1. The number of days (d) working and the amount of money (m) you make

2. The pounds (p) of sand in a sandbox and the diameter (d) of a sandbox

3. The thickness of a book in inches (i) and the weight (w) of the book

4. The number of windows (w) in a building and the hours (h) it takes to clean them

5. The hours (h) it takes to clean windows and the number of people (p) cleaning

6. Tickets (t) sold for a play and the amount of money (m) collected

7. The number of gallons (g) a gas tank holds and the cost (c) to fill it

8. The number of laps (l) you swim and the time (t) you spend swimming

9. Which of the following could be an independent variable that affects how long a candle will burn?

A color of the candle

B diameter of the candle

C day the candle was made

D state the candle was made in

10. **Reason** Sue says time (t) can only be an independent variable. Do you agree? Explain.

____

____

____

11. Write your own situation that has an independent and dependent variable. Underline the independent variable and circle the dependent variable in the situation.

____

____

____

Name ______________________________

Patterns and Equations

Write a rule and an equation for the pattern in the table.

x	1	4	7	8	9
y	3	12	21	24	27

Think: How can I get to the value of y if I start at the value of x?
Think: 3 is 1×3 12 is 4×3
State a theory: It seems that $3 \times x$ is equal to y.
Test the other pairs: $7 \times 3 = 21$ ✔ $8 \times 3 = 24$ ✔ $9 \times 3 = 27$ ✔
Write a rule: The value of y is the value of x times 3.
Write an equation: $y = x \times 3$, or $y = 3x$

Write a rule and an equation for the pattern in each table.

1.

x	3	6	11	13	15
y	5	8	13	15	17

____

____

2.

x	2	5	6	8	9
y	6	15	18	24	27

____

____

3.

x	4	12	20	36	40
y	1	3	5	9	10

____

____

4.

x	5	7	9	10	12
y	0	2	4	5	7

____

____

5. Write a Problem Complete the table to show a pattern. Then write a rule and an equation for the pattern.

____

____

x					
y					

6. Writing to Explain Explain how you would find the pattern in this table, and how you would write a rule and an equation for the pattern.

x	4	5	7	10	12
y	0	1	3	6	8

____

Name ____________________

Practice
3-2

Patterns and Equations

Write a rule and an equation to fit the pattern in each table in **1** through **6**.

1.

x	0	1	2	3	4
y	5	6	7	8	9

2.

x	12	18	21	24	36
y	4	6	7	8	12

3.

x	11	14	18	21	25
y	3	6	10	13	17

4.

x	0	1	2	4	6
y	0	4	8	16	24

5.

x	3	9	13	22	27
y	10	16	20	29	34

6.

x	0	1	2	3	4
y	0	3	6	9	12

7. The Gadget Factory sells winkydiddles in different quantities, as shown by the table. How much would ten winkydiddles cost?

Number of Winkydiddles	7	12	26	31
Cost	$24.50	$42.00	$91.00	$108.50

8. Which equation best describes the pattern in the table?

x	4	9	12	16	19
y	2	4.5	6	8	9.5

A $y = 2x$ **B** $y = x - 1$ **C** $y = \frac{x}{2}$ **D** $y = x + 1$

9. Writing to Explain All the values of *x* in a table are greater than the corresponding values of *y*. If *x* is a positive integer, what operation(s) and circumstance(s) could explain this pattern?

Name ____________________

More Patterns and Equations

The entry fee to a carnival is \$3. Each ride ticket is \$2. The cost of going to the carnival equals the entry fee plus two times the number of tickets purchased, $c = 3 + 2t$.

You can substitute numbers into the equation to make a table showing the cost compared to the number of tickets purchased.

$c = 3 + 2t.$

Tickets *t*	**3 + 2*t***	**Cost** *c*
0	3 + 2(0)	\$3
2	3 + 2(2)	\$7
4	3 + 2(4)	\$11
6	3 + 2(6)	\$15

In **1** through **4**, use the equation to complete each table.

1. $y = 3x + 7$

x	0	1	2	3
y				

2. $y = 4x - 4$

x	2	4	6	8
y				

3. $y = 2x + 7$

x	1	3	5	7
y				

4. $y = \frac{1}{4}x + 5$

x	0	4	8	12
y				

5. Reasoning For the equation $y = 1x - 25$, will the value of *y* increase or decrease as *x* increases?

____

6. Algebra Write an equation in words and in symbols to represent this situation:
Grace has \$100. She is buying charms for her bracelet that cost \$5 each. Write an equation showing the relationship between the number of charms (*c*) she buys and the amount of money she has left (*l*).

____

____

7. Number Sense How many charms can Grace buy before she runs out of money?

____

Name ______________________

Practice
3-3

More Patterns and Equations

In **1** through **4,** use the equation given to complete each table.

1. $y = 2x + 4$

x	0	1	2	3
y				

2. $y = 4x - 3$

x	5	6	7	8
y				

3. $y = 100 - 4x$

x	2	4	6	8
y				

4. $y = \frac{1}{3}x + 1$

x	0	3	6	9
y				

5. Writing to Explain Complete the table and write an equation for the pattern. Tell how you do it.

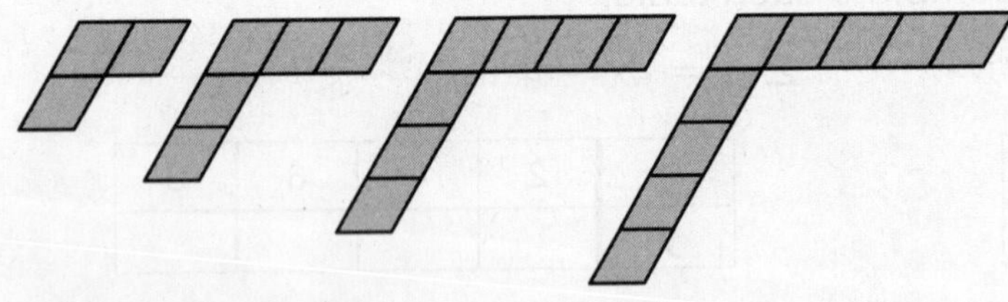

Pattern Number, p	1	2	3	4
Number of Blocks, b	3			

____

____

6. Algebra How many blocks are needed to make the 10th figure in the pattern above?

A 11 **B** 20 **C** 21 **D** 22

7. Reasoning Justin used 35 blocks to make a figure for the pattern above. What was the pattern number for the figure? ______________________

8. Write a Problem Write a problem that can be represented by this equation and table.

$y = 20x + 5$

x	1	2	3	4
y	25	45	65	85

____

Name ____________________

Problem Solving: Use Reasoning

You can use counters, tables, ordered pairs, and graphs to act out a problem and show your reasoning.

Jenna is creating a display of photographs at her school for shark-awareness week. She has 24 photographs that she can display on 4 walls and 4 bulletin boards. She wants to put the same number of photographs on each wall and the same number of photographs on each bulletin board. How many different ways can Jenna display the photographs on the walls and bulletin boards?

Make a Table
Use walls and bulletin boards as the labels in the table.

Use counters to find the possible ways.

Walls	0	1	2	3	4	5	6
Bulletin Boards	6	5	4	3	2	1	0

Write Ordered Pairs
(walls, bulletin boards)

(0, 6), (1, 5), (2, 4), (3, 3), (4, 2), (5, 1), (6, 0)

Make a Graph
You can use the table or ordered pairs to graph the different ways.

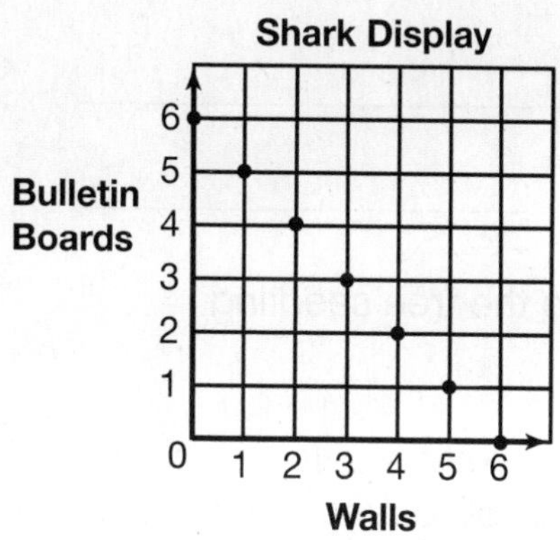

So, Jenna can display the shark photographs in 7 different ways on the walls and bulletin boards.

1. Cory is arranging 12 baseball caps on 2 shelves. He wants at least 2 caps on each shelf and the number of caps on each shelf to be even. How many possible ways can he arrange the caps on 2 shelves? Show your answer as ordered pairs.

____

2. Graph the solution for the above problem.

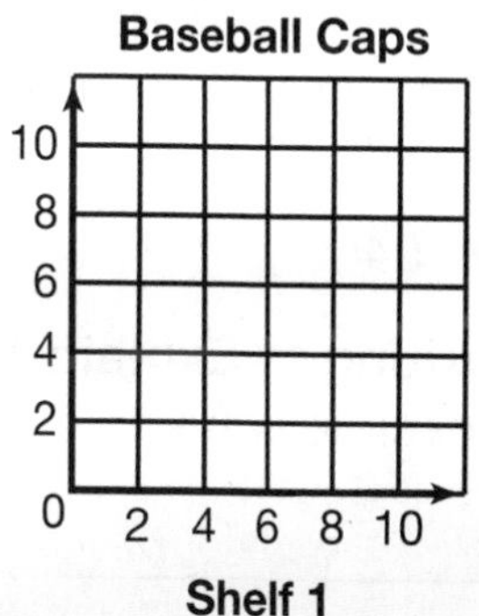

Name ___________________________

Practice
3-4

Problem Solving: Use Reasoning

1. A ranch owner has 18 bales of hay to distribute in 3 cow pastures and 3 horse pastures. He wants each cow pasture to have the same number of bales of hay and each horse pasture to have the same number of bales of hay. He wants at least 1 bale of hay in each pasture. How many different ways can hay be distributed among the pastures? Make a table to show your reasoning.

____

2. A nursery has 10 tree seedlings to give out at 2 workshops. It wants to give out a minimum of 2 seedlings at each workshop. How many different ways can the nursery give out seedlings? Show your answer as ordered pairs.

____

____

3. Graph the solution to the tree seedling problem above.

4. A reading club at a bookstore gives a certificate for one free book after the reader earns 150 points. Each book a person reads is worth 3 points. Sonja has 96 points. What is the least number of books she needs to read to get the certificate?

A 18

B 23

C 23

D 54

5. **Writing to Explain** Explain how you know you found all of the possible ways to distribute the bales of hay in Problem 1.

____

____

____

Name ______________________________

Estimating Sums and Differences

Estimate: 7.382 + 4.97

1. Round each number to the nearest whole number.

   7.382 + 4.97
   ↓ ↓
   7 + 5

2. Add to estimate:

   7 + 5 = 12
   7.382 + 4.97 ≈ 12

≈ is used to show that this is an estimate.

Estimate: 12.57 – 6.806

1. Round each number to the nearest whole number.

   12.57 – 6.806
   ↓ ↓
   13 – 7

2. Subtract to estimate.

   13 – 7 = 6
   12.57 – 6.806 ≈ 6

You can also round the numbers to any decimal place. Estimate the sum. Round to the nearest tenth.

3.947 + 11.286
↓ ↓
3.9 + 11.3 = 15.2, so 3.947 + 11.286 ≈ 15.2

Round each number to the nearest whole number to estimate the answer.

1. 4.38 + 9.179 ______ **2.** 62.873 – 12.7 ______ **3.** 52.83 + 97.288 ______

4. 131.049 – 82.604 ______ **5.** 79.14 + 32.546 ______ **6.** 48.468 + 63.029 ______

7. 112.658 – 81.903 ______ **8.** 586.735 – 204.63 ______ **9.** 107.139 + 90.621 ______

Round each number to the nearest tenth to estimate the answer.

10. 17.058 – 8.623 ______ **11.** 38.8314 + 15.62 ______ **12.** 26.429 – 6.703 ______

13. 238.562 – 104.387 ______ **14.** 400.628 + 291.037 ______ **15.** 76.451 – 68.399 ______

16. Geometry The area of the Davis's living room is 18.087 square yards, and their bedroom has an area of 15.78 square yards. Round to the nearest tenth and estimate the amount of carpet they need to buy.

____

17. Explain It Angela has a \$5-bill, two \$10-bills, and a \$20-bill. She wants to buy a DVD for \$17.89, a pin for \$5.12, and shoes for \$12.99. Estimate the sum to the nearest dollar. Tell which bills she should hand to the cashier.

____

____

Name ________________________________

Practice
4-1

Estimating Sums and Differences

Fill in the blanks to complete the estimate.

1. 4.36 − 2.971 =
____ − 3 = ____

2. 9.384 + 7.713 =
9 + ____ = ____

3. 8.81 + 2.78 =
8.8 + ____ = ____

Round each number to the nearest whole number to estimate the answer.

4. 15.63 − 8.497 ____

5. 3.504 + 7.118 ____

6. 13.09 − 10.902 ____

7. 14.52 + 11.118 ____

8. 9.573 − 4.817 ____

9. 22.174 + 18.561 ____

10. 37.624 − 14.826 ____

11. 15.938 + 7.627 ____

12. 19.394 − 6.943 ____

Round each number to the nearest tenth to estimate the answer.

13. 7.349 + 8.192 ____

14. 14.087 − 5.418 ____

15. 8.991 + 3.475 ____

16. 25.183 − 13.984 ____

17. 11.004 + 5.391 ____

18. 31.038 − 12.861 ____

19. Geometry Estimate the perimeter of the figure to the nearest whole number. ________

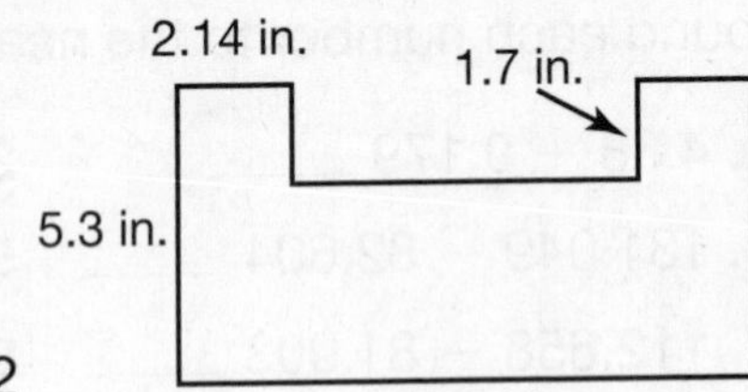

20. Four runners ran the relay. Bill ran his lap in 22.738 seconds, Tory ran in 21.874 seconds, Grace ran in 20.32 seconds, and Jessica ran in 19.047 seconds. Estimate the team's total time to the nearest tenth of a second.

____

On Sale Today

Mustard . . . $1.58
Ice cream . . . $3.27
Popcorn $2.19

21. LuWanda bought a jar of mustard, a half-gallon of ice cream, and two boxes of popcorn. She gave the clerk a $20 bill. Estimate how many dollars she received in change.

A $4 **B** $9 **C** $11 **D** $14

22. Writing to Explain The digit 5 is usually rounded up, but it can also be rounded down. How would you round the numbers in the equation 9.5 + 4.7 + 3.2 + 7.5 = x to the nearest whole number without getting an overestimate or an underestimate?

____

____

____

Name ______________________________

Evaluating Addition and Subtraction Expressions

Find 1.093 + 41.6.

Estimate: Round 1.093 to 1 and 41.6 to 42.
1 + 42 = 43

Write the numbers, lining up the decimal points. Annex zeros so all numbers have the same number of decimal places.

$$\begin{array}{r} 1.093 \\ +41.600 \\ \hline 42.693 \end{array}$$ ← Annex 2 zeros.

Add the numbers. Regroup if necessary. Write the decimal point in your answer.

42.693 is close to 43, so the answer is reasonable.

Find 18.5 − *g* when *g* = 7.82.

Estimate: Round 7.82 to 8.
18.5 − 8 = 10.5

Write the numbers, lining up the decimal points. Annex zeros so all numbers have the same number of decimal places.

$$\begin{array}{r} 18.50 \\ -\ 7.82 \\ \hline 10.68 \end{array}$$ ← Annex a zero. (regrouping: 7 4 10)

Subtract. Regroup if necessary. Write the decimal point in your answer.

10.68 is close to 10.5, so the answer is reasonable.

Use substitution to evaluate each expression.

1. 45.6 + 26.3 ______________

2. $n - 5.14$; $n = 14.25$ ______________

3. 17.2 + 6.08 ______________

4. $24.84 - h$; $h = 22.7$ ______________

5. 13.64 − 8.3 ______________

6. $r + 15.9$; $r = 0.214$ ______________

7. $3.652 - a$; $a = 1.41$ ______________

8. 18.06 + 9.798 ______________

9. $t - 6.38$; $t = 8.006$ ______________

10. Reasonableness Jaime wrote 4.4 − 0.33 = 1.1. Is his answer reasonable? Why or why not?

____

____

Name ______________________

Practice
4-2

Evaluating Addition and Subtraction Expressions

Evaluate each expression.

1. 10.21 − 4.6

____

2. $b + 1.85$; $b = 0.03$

____

3. $5.011 + x$; $x = 1.23$

____

4. $22.9 - k$; $k = 0.61$

____

5. $m - 1.26$; $m = 9.834$

____

6. 24 + 7.45

____

7. Complete the sequence of numbers. 4.25, 5, 5.75, ________, ________

8. **Number Sense** How does the cost for 1 tube of glue compare to the cost for 1 roll of tape?

____

9. What is the difference in cost between 2 packs of markers and 4 sheets of poster board?

____

Craft Supplies	
Poster board	$1.29/sheet
Markers	$4.50/pack
Tape	$1.99/roll
Glue	$2.39/tube
Construction paper	$3.79/pack

10. In a long jump competition, Khaila jumped 3.9 meters. Alicia jumped 3.08 meters. How much farther did Khaila jump?

A 0.01 meter

B 0.82 meter

C 0.98 meter

D 1.01 meters

11. **Writing to Explain** Trey wrote 9.009 − 0.01 = 9.008. Is his answer correct? Why or why not?

____

____

Name ____________________

Reteaching
4-3

Solving Addition and Subtraction Equations

You can solve equations by getting the variable alone. You can use inverse relationships and the properties of equality to get the variable alone. Remember that you need to do the same thing to both sides of the equation to keep the equation equal.

Solve the equation $5.2 + c = 13.6$.

To get *c* alone, undo adding 5.2 by subtracting 5.2 from both sides.

$$5.2 + c = 13.6$$
$$5.2 + c - \mathbf{5.2} = 13.6 - \mathbf{5.2}$$
$$c = 8.4$$

Check your solution by substituting 8.4 for *c* in the equation.

$$5.2 + c = 13.6$$
$$5.2 + 8.4 = 13.6$$
$$13.6 = 13.6 \quad \text{It checks.}$$

Solve the equation $x - 2.4 = 16.1$.

To get *x* alone, undo subtracting 2.4 by adding 2.4 to both sides.

$$x - 2.4 = 16.1$$
$$x - 2.4 + \mathbf{2.4} = 16.1 + \mathbf{2.4}$$
$$x = 18.5$$

Check your solution by substituting 18.5 for *x* in the equation.

$$x - 2.4 = 16.1$$
$$18.5 - 2.4 = 16.1$$
$$16.1 = 16.1 \quad \text{It checks.}$$

Explain how to get the variable alone in each equation.

1. $x + 11.4 = 25$

$x + 11.4 - \mathbf{11.4} = 25 - \mathbf{11.4}$

____

2. $n - 19.1 = 12.4$

$n - 19.1 + \mathbf{19.1} = 12.4 + \mathbf{19.1}$

____

Solve each equation and check your answer. Show your work.

3. $g - 21.3 = 48.4$

$g - 21.3 +$ ______ $= 48.4 +$ ______

$g =$ ____________________

4. $y + 7.7 = 21$

____

5. The Olympic triathlon is 51.5 km. A contestant has completed two of the three legs of the race and has traveled 41.5 km. Solve $41.5 + d = 51.5$ to find the distance of the third leg.

____

Name ______________________

Practice
4-3

Solving Addition and Subtraction Equations

Explain how to get the variable alone in each equation.

1. $n + 1.1 = 22.3$

$n + 1.1 - 1.1 = 22.3 - 1.1$

____

2. $x - 6.7 = 28.8$

$x - 6.7 +$ ______ $= 28.8 +$ ______

____

3. $g - 3.2 = 20$

____

4. $31.7 + y = 54.4$

____

5. $r + 16.9 = 88.2$

____

6. $3.9 = m - 22.1$

____

7. $100 = e + 91.8$

____

8. $a - 31 = 12.6$

____

9. Tom drove 11.8 miles in the morning. He drove more in the afternoon. He drove 32.4 miles in all. Which equation could you use to find how far Tom drove in the afternoon?

A $11.8 + 32.4 = m$

B $11.8 + m = 32.4$

C $11.8 - m = 32.4$

D $m - 32.4 = 11.8$

10. Critical Thinking If $n + 10 = 45.5$, then what is the value of the expression $n - 25$?

A 10.5

B 25

C 25.5

D 45.5

11. Writing to Explain Explain how to solve the equation $4.8 + p = 12.2$. Then solve.

____

Name ____________________

Reteaching **4-4**

Estimating Products

You can use rounding or compatible numbers to estimate products.

Rounding:

Round each factor to the nearest whole number and multiply.

$$\begin{array}{r} 4.287 \longrightarrow 4 \\ \times\, 2.804 \longrightarrow \times\, 3 \\ 12 \end{array}$$

so, $4.287 \times 2.804 \approx 12$

Compatible Numbers:

Find compatible numbers and multiply.

16.173×3.45

$\downarrow \qquad \downarrow$

$15 \times 3 = 45$ so $16.173 \times 3.45 \approx 45$

Use rounding to estimate each product.

1. 3.73×8.16 ______

2. 35.518×9.722 ______

3. 7.349×5.62 ______

4. 4.178×12.513 ______

5. 8.498×5.602 ______

6. 24.534×7.96 ______

7. 41.01×4.88 ______

8. 15.812×9.47 ______

9. 2.81×17.638 ______

Use compatible numbers to estimate each product.

10. 55.93×8.34 ______

11. 61.438×8.72 ______

12. 122.899×5.36 ______

13. 16.954×3.5 ______

14. 17.158×8.99 ______

15. 38.753×8.461 ______

16. 73.724×20.1 ______

17. 79.48×8.512 ______

18. 43.518×18.043 ______

19. Writing to Explain Elena used rounding to estimate $7.864 \times 3.29 \approx 24$. Peter used rounding to estimate $7.864 \times 3.29 \approx 32$. Which student is correct? What mistake was made?

____

____

Name ______________________

Estimating Products

Estimate each answer using rounding.

1. 3.48 × 9.673 ______ **2.** 5.702 × 4.26 ______ **3.** 9.734 × 6.8 ______

4. 8.37 × 2.501 ______ **5.** 7.936 × 2.491 ______ **6.** 5.092 × 3.774 ______

7. 12.123 × 4.802 ______ **8.** 6.98 × 8.502 ______ **9.** 1.948 × 3.728 ______

Estimate each answer using compatible numbers.

10. 19.18 × 3.7 ______ **11.** 14.9 × 8.432 ______ **12.** 31.047 × 5.492 ______

13. 16.07 × 4.989 ______ **14.** 48.614 × 9.01 ______ **15.** 61.503 × 8.041 ______

16. 7.196 × 10.93 ______ **17.** 103.82 × 25.9 ______ **18.** 81.431 × 6.73 ______

19. Number Sense An airliner is 9.34 feet wide. The airline wants to install 5 seats in each row. The seats are each 1.46 feet wide. Rounded to the nearest tenth, about how much space would be left for the aisle? ______

20. Geometry Estimate the area of the rectangle. ______

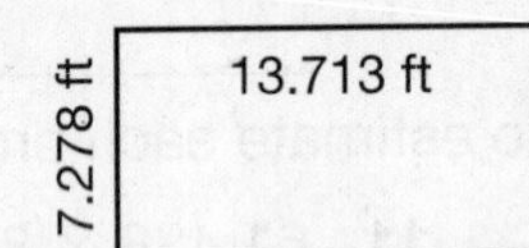

21. Writing to Explain The library has a bookshelf 46.725 inches wide for their new encyclopedia. When the encyclopedia arrived, the librarian found that each of the 24 volumes was 1.65 inches wide. Estimate if the 24 books will fit on the shelf. How does your rounding affect the answer?

____

____

____

22. Algebra Dominick wants to buy 2 CDs for $14.95 each, 3 DVDs for $19.99 each, and a video game for $36.79. Which equation could you use to estimate how much money he needs?

A $15 + 20 + 26 = x$

B $2(14) + 3(20) + 36 = x$

C $2(15) + 3(20) + 37 = x$

D $2(15) + 3(19) + 36 = x$

Name ______________________________

Reteaching 4-5

Multiplying Decimals

Use the same strategy to multiply a decimal by a whole number or to multiply a decimal by a decimal.

Multiply 0.72 × 23.

Ignore the decimal points. Multiply as you would with two whole numbers.

Count the number of decimal places in both factors. Use that number of decimal places to write the answer.

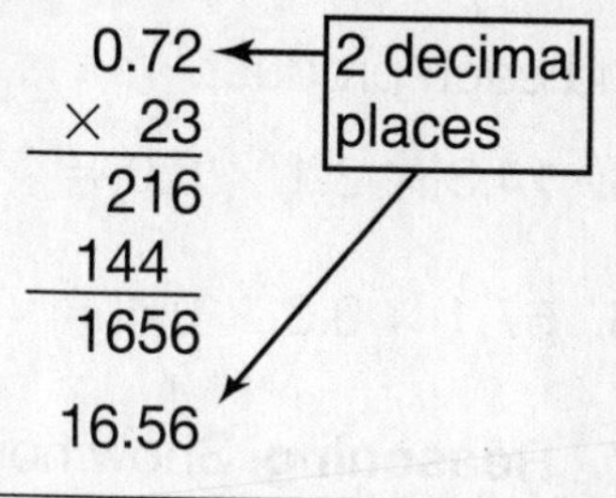

Multiply 0.45 × 0.8.

Ignore the decimal points. Multiply as you would with two whole numbers.

Count the number of decimal places in both factors. Use that number of decimal places to write the answer.

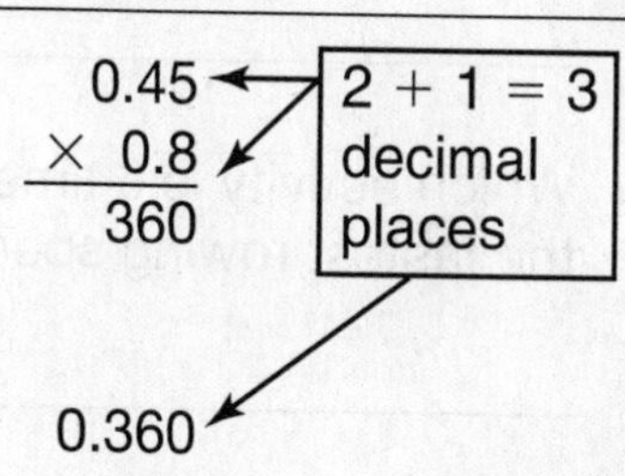

Place the decimal point in each product.

1. 1.2 × 3.6 = 432 ____________

2. 5.5 × 3.77 = 20735 ____________

3. 4.4 × 2.333 = 102652 ____________

Find the product.

4. 7 × 0.5 ________

5. 12 × 0.08 ________

6. 24 × 0.17 ________

7. 0.4 × 0.17 ________

8. 1.9 × 0.46 ________

9. 3.42 × 5.15 ________

10. Writing to Explain If you multiply two decimals less than 1, can you predict whether the product will be less than or greater than either of the factors? Explain.

____

____

11. Number Sense Two factors are multiplied and their product is 34.44. One factor is a whole number. How many decimal places are in the other factor?

____

Name ____________________

Multiplying Decimals

Place the decimal point in each product.

1. $3 \times 6.892 = 20676$ ________ **2.** $0.3 \times 4.57 = 1371$ ________

Find each product.

3. $14.3 \times 2.1 \times 8.9 =$ ________ **4.** $0.45 \times 0.01 =$ ________

5. $67.1 \times 0.3 \times 0.4 =$ ________ **6.** $582.1 \times 4.2 =$ ________

7. Reasoning Show how to find the product of 16.2×4 using addition.

____

8. Which activity is 6 times as fast as the fastest rowing speed?

____

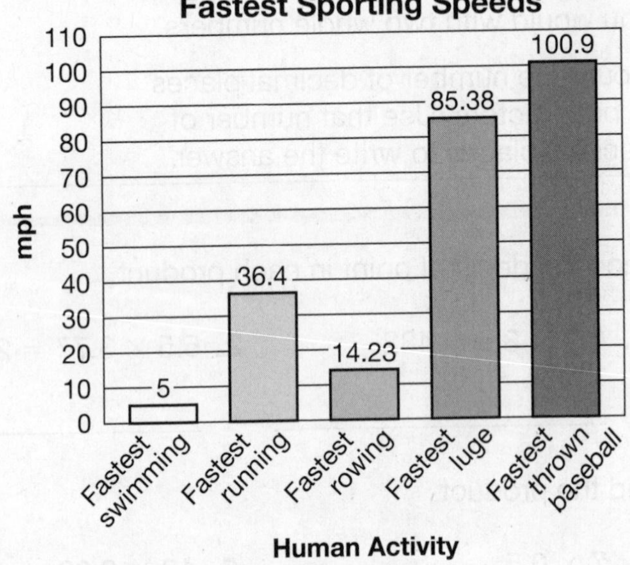

9. The fastest speed a table tennis ball has been hit is 21.12 times as fast as the speed for the fastest swimmer. What is the speed for the table tennis ball?

____

10. How fast would 1.5 times the fastest rowing speed be?

____

11. Which is the product of 110.1×2.5?

A 770.7 **B** 275.25 **C** 77.07 **D** 27.525

12. Writing to Explain Explain why multiplying 37.4×0.01 gives a product that is less than 37.4.

____

____

____

Name ______________________________

Problem Solving: Make a Table and Look for a Pattern

Mario plans to walk $\frac{3}{4}$ mile today. Tomorrow he will walk $\frac{1}{2}$ mile more, then $\frac{1}{2}$ mile more every day after that. How long will it take before Mario walks 3 miles in one day?

Make a table showing each day and the distance he walks every day.

Day	1	2	3	4	5	6
Distance (mi)	$\frac{3}{4}$	$1\frac{1}{4}$	$1\frac{3}{4}$	$2\frac{1}{4}$	$2\frac{3}{4}$	$3\frac{1}{4}$

Start with the first day's distance.

Add $\frac{1}{2}$ mile for every day

$3\frac{1}{4} > 3$

Mario will walk at least 3 miles on Day 6.

Make tables to solve. Write each answer in a complete sentence.

1. The phone company charges 10¢ to connect a call for one minute and 8¢ per minute after that. How long could you talk on the phone for $1?

____

2. A plumber charges $30 for a house call and $20 per $\frac{1}{2}$ hour of work. How much will the plumber charge for $4\frac{1}{2}$ hours of work at Mrs. DiMarco's house?

____

3. **Geometry** The angles of a triangle have a sum of 180°. The angles of a rectangle have a sum of 360°. The angles of a pentagon have a sum of 540°. Continue this pattern to find the sum of the angles of an octagon.

____

4. **Writing to Explain** Write a problem based on the information in the table. Extend the table if necessary.

Day	1	2	3	4	5
Pages Read	23	58	93	128	☐

____

Name ______________________________

Practice

4-6

Problem Solving: Make a Table and Look for a Pattern

Make tables to help solve. Write each answer in a complete sentence.

1. A train has 3 engines, 52 boxcars, and 1 caboose. At every stop, it picks up 8 more boxcars. How many total cars (engines, cars, and cabooses) will the train have after 5 stops?

____

2. Eileen likes to keep scrapbooks. She already has 4 scrapbooks filled with 40 pages each. If she fills 5 pages every month, how many months will it take her to fill up 2 more 40-page scrapbooks?

____

3. Phil's Garage charges $50 for towing and $40 per hour to fix a car. Cliff's Cars charges $60 for towing and $38 per hour to fix a car. After how many hours of working on a car will the cost of towing and fixing a car be the same at the two repair shops?

____

4. Dominic got a new video game. The first time he played the game he scored 80 points. After that, each time he played he increased his score by 60 points. How many times will he have to play before he scores 500 points?

____

5. A scientist is studying certain germs. She places 3 germs in a special solution that will help the germs grow. The number of germs doubles every hour. How many germs will there be after 8 hours?

A 24 **B** 384 **C** 768 **D** 786

6. **Writing to Explain** Ed saved $50 one week. For the next 6 weeks, he saved $25 more than he saved the week before. How much did he save in all? One student solved this problem using the expression $50 + 6($25) = $200. What error was made? What is the correct answer?

____

____

____

Name ______________________

Reteaching **5-1**

Estimating Quotients: 2-Digit Divisors

You can use compatible numbers to estimate a quotient.

Find 1,759 ÷ 32.

Step 1: Find compatible numbers for 1,759 and 32.

32 rounds to 30.

Think: 18 can be divided evenly by 3.

1,800 is close to 1,759 and 30 is close to 32.

1,800 and 30 are compatible numbers.

Step 2: Divide. Use patterns to help you, if possible.

Think: 1,800 ÷ 30 is the same as 180 tens ÷ 3 tens.

18 ÷ 3 = 6
18 tens ÷ 3 tens = 6 tens
So, 1,800 ÷ 30 = 60.

Step 3: Check for reasonableness.

60 × 30 = 1,800

So, a good estimate of 1,759 ÷ 32 is 60.

Estimate each quotient using compatible numbers.

1. 2,983 ÷ 25 ______________

2. 5,391 ÷ 77 ______________

3. 2,403 ÷ 12 ______________

4. 2,765 ÷ 42 ______________

5. 1,347 ÷ 54 ______________

6. 5,564 ÷ 91 ______________

At Elmer Elementary School, fifth-grade students are saving money for a summer trip to Washington, D.C.

Student	Amount Saved
Percy	$1,256
Emily	$800
George	$2,024
James	$401
Bertha	$1,599

7. The money Percy has saved is how many times as great as the money James has saved?

____

____

Name ____________________

Estimating Quotients: 2-Digit Divisors

In **1** through **4**, estimate the quotients using compatible numbers.

1. 5,682 ÷ 81 ________ **2.** 4,506 ÷ 93 ________

3. 1,423 ÷ 69 ________ **4.** 8,631 ÷ 10 ________

5. If you use $99.00 ÷ 11 to estimate $98.69 ÷ 11, is $9.00 greater than or less than the exact answer? Explain.

____

____

6. Suppose there are 26 students in a class. A teacher has 1,022 and passes them out to the class. Estimate the number of pencils each student will receive.

7. At a department store, a package of 12 handkerchiefs costs $58.99. Estimate how much each handkerchief costs. ________

8. Which is the closest estimate for 2,130 ÷ 33?

A 7 **B** 17 **C** 70 **D** 700

9. Explain how to estimate 4,983 ÷ 12.

____

____

Name ______________________________

Reteaching **5-2**

Dividing Whole Numbers: 2-Digit Divisors

Find 8,365 ÷ 34.

Step 1: Round the divisor to the nearest ten. Look at the first digit in the divisor and the first digit in the dividend. What basic division fact is the best estimate of the quotient of these two numbers?

34)8,365 ⟶ 30)8,365

8 ÷ 3 = 2 R2

Step 2: Use this fact to begin the quotient. Write it over the hundreds place.

```
     2
34)8,365
  −68↓
   156
```

Multiply, 2 × 34 = 68.
Subtract and bring down the next digit in the dividend.

Step 3: What basic division fact is the best estimate of the next division? Use this fact and write it over the tens place.

```
     24
34)8,365
  −68
   156
  −136↓
    205
```

Multiply, 4 × 34 = 136. Subtract and bring down the next digit in the dividend.

Step 4: What basic division fact is the best estimate of the next division? Use this fact and write it over the ones place.

```
     246 R1
34)8,365
  −68
   156
  −136
    205
   −204
      1
```

Multiply, 6 × 34 = 204.
Subtract. Compare the remainder with the divisor.
If the remainder is less than the divisor, write it in the quotient.

Check.
246 × 34 = 8,364
8,364 + 1 = 8,365

Complete.

1. 39)4,372   112 R☐

2. 24)6,315   ☐☐☐ R3

3. 26)9,289   ☐☐☐ R☐

Divide. Check by multiplying.

4. 13)1,722

5. 44)6,668

6. April has 905 baseball cards. She wants to organize them on pages that hold 18 cards each. She has 50 pages. Does April have enough pages to organize all her cards?

____

Name ____________________

Practice
5-2

Dividing Whole Numbers: 2-Digit Divisors

In **1** through **6**, find each quotient.

1. $14\overline{)4{,}139}$ ____________ **2.** $29\overline{)6{,}304}$ ____________

3. $35\overline{)7{,}168}$ ____________ **4.** $19\overline{)4{,}001}$ ____________

5. $45\overline{)3{,}942}$ ____________ **6.** $26\overline{)5{,}073}$ ____________

7. The school student council sponsored a Switch Week where students were able to switch classes every 20 minutes. The students are in school for 7 hours each day, Monday through Friday. If a student switched as often as possible, how many times in all did that student switch classes? (Hint: There are 60 minutes in 1 hour.)

____

8. 456 students participated in Switch Week. The students raised money for charity so that the principal would approve of the week. If the total amount of money raised was $8,208, and each student brought in the same amount of money, how much did each student raise?

____

9. The total dinner bill at a buffet came out to $1,240 for 62 people. About how much was the buffet cost per person?

A $15.00 **B** $20.00 **C** $22.00 **D** $25.00

10. If you have a two-digit divisor and a four-digit dividend, does the quotient always have the same number of digits?

____

____

Name ______________________________

Reteaching
5-3

More Dividing Whole Numbers

Find 8,037 ÷ 77.

You can use estimation to check that a quotient is reasonable.

Step 1: Estimate. Round the divisor and the dividend.

8,037 ÷ 77 ⟶

8,000 ÷ 80 = 100

The quotient should be close to 100.

Step 2: Now, find the quotient.

8,037 ÷ 77

```
    104 R29
77)8,037
  -77↓
    33
    -0↓
    337
   -308
     29
```

Step 3: 104 R29 is close to the original estimate, 100, so the answer is reasonable.

Estimate first. Then find the quotient.

1. 78)3,796

2. 51)2,588

3. 38)3,914

4. 37)7,492

5. 46)6,725

6. 62)9,911

7. Is 5,309 ÷ 26 less than 20, greater than 20 but less than 200, or greater than 200?

____

Name ______________________

Practice 5-3

More Dividing Whole Numbers

Estimate first. Then find the quotient.

1. 53)6,324
2. 52)6,348
3. 86)31,309
4. 33)3,455
5. 91)17,496
6. 47)25,214
7. 26)2,312
8. 83)4,895

The Humphrey family decided to fly from San Francisco to New York City, and from there to Rome, New Delhi, and finally Tokyo.

Distances by Plane	
San Francisco to New York	4,140 km
New York to Rome	6,907 km
Rome to New Delhi	5,929 km
New Delhi to Tokyo	5,857 km

9. It took the Humphrey family 6 hours to travel from San Francisco to New York. How many kilometers did they travel per hour?

____

10. During the flight from New Delhi to Tokyo, flight attendants came through with snacks every 600 km. How many times did they come through?

____

11. When the family arrived in New Delhi from Rome, the youngest son asked the pilot how fast he was flying the plane. The pilot told him about 847 km per hour. How many hours did it take the family to fly from Rome to New Delhi?

A 5 h **B** 6 h **C** 7 h **D** 8 h

12. Write a word problem that would require you to use 5,621 ÷ 23.

____

Name ______________________

Reteaching
5-4

Dividing Decimals by a Whole Number

Find 196.8 ÷ 32.

Step 1

Put the decimal in the quotient right above the decimal in the dividend. Divide. Subtract.

```
       6.
32 ) 196.8
    -192
       4
```

Step 2

Bring down the 8. Divide. Subtract.

```
       6.1
32 ) 196.8
    -192↓
       48
      -32
       16
```

Step 3

Annex a zero to the end of the dividend. Bring down the zero. Divide. Subtract.

```
       6.15
32 ) 196.80
    -192↓
       48
      -32↓
       160
      -160
         0
```

Remember, you can use estimation to see if your answer is reasonable: 180 ÷ 30 = 6. You can check your answer using multiplication: 32 × 6.15 = 196.8

Find the quotient.

1.
```
     2.
9 ) 20.7
   -18
     2
```
______

2.
```
     3.
7 ) 22.61
   -21
```
______

3.
```
      $ 3.
12 ) $44.40
     - 36
        8
```
______

4. 11) 93.5

______

5. 30) 1.56

______

6. 8) 412.0

______

7. **Writing to Explain** Destiny said that 0.6 ÷ 2 = 0.3. Is she correct? Explain why or why not.

______

______

Name ______________________

Practice
5-4

Dividing Decimals by a Whole Number

Find the quotient.

1. \$42.78 ÷ 3 ______ **2.** 85.5 ÷ 6 ______ **3.** 3.4 ÷ 10 ______

4. 9 ÷ 900 ______ **5.** 59.6 ÷ 8 ______ **6.** 188.4 ÷ 60 ______

7. \$1.24 ÷ 4 ______ **8.** 231 ÷ 42 ______ **9.** 11.2 ÷ 25 ______

10. Yolanda bought 8 tickets to a concert for \$214. What was the cost of each ticket?

______

11. Algebra Tony bought a 72-ounce box of dog biscuits. How many pounds of dog biscuits did he buy? (Remember: 1 pound = 16 ounces.)

A 4 pounds

B 4.5 pounds

C 90 pounds

D 4,320 pounds

12. Number Sense Vicky uses 42 beads for each necklace she makes. She bought a bag of 500 beads. How many necklaces can she make?

______

13. Writing to Explain In what place is the first digit of the quotient for 12.88 ÷ 4? Tell how you know.

______

______

Name ____________________

Reteaching **5-5**

Dividing Decimals

When you divide by a decimal, you need to rewrite the dividend and the divisor so that you are dividing by a whole number.

Find 2.48 ÷ 0.8.

Step 1: Estimate. Use compatible numbers.

240 ÷ 80 = 3

Step 2: Make the divisor a whole number. Multiply the divisor AND the dividend by the same power of 10.

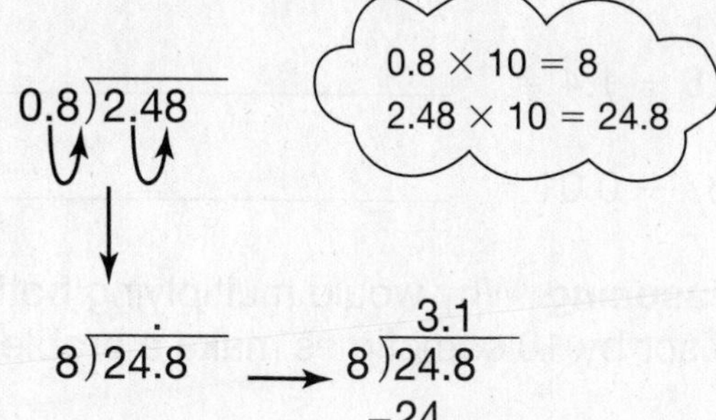

Place the decimal in the quotient.

Step 3: Divide as you would with whole numbers. Remember that sometimes you may need to annex zeros to complete your division.

$$8\overline{)24.8} \rightarrow \begin{array}{r} 3.1 \\ 8\overline{)24.8} \\ -24 \\ \hline 8 \\ -8 \\ \hline 0 \end{array}$$

Step 4: Compare the quotient with your estimate.

Since 3.1 is close to 3, the answer checks.

Find each quotient.

1. $0.2\overline{)1.5}$

Estimate: ____________________

Multiply dividend and divisor by what power of 10? ______

Place the decimal point in the quotient.

Divide. How many zeros do you need to annex? ______

Compare the quotient to your estimate.
Is the answer reasonable? ____________________

2. $0.6\overline{)0.36}$

3. $0.4\overline{)9.6}$

4. $0.75\overline{)0.3}$

5. Draw a Picture Fernando used tenths grids to draw this picture showing 1.6 ÷ 0.4 = 4. Draw a picture to show 1.8 ÷ 0.6. Write the quotient.

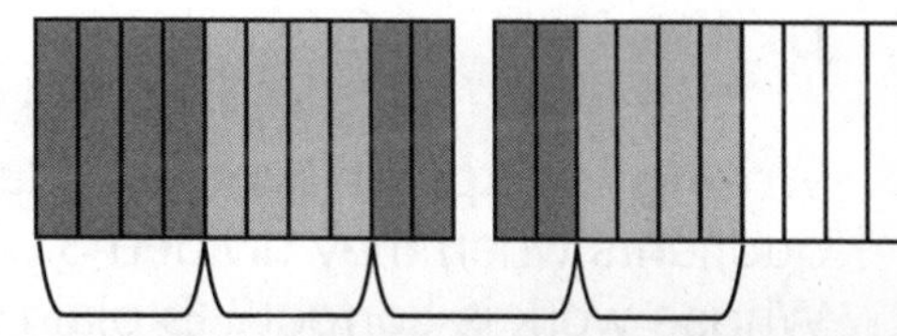

Name ______________________

Practice
5-5

Dividing Decimals

Find each quotient.

1. 8.4 ÷ 0.3 = ________
2. 66.15 ÷ 0.63 = ________
3. 10.5 ÷ 1.5 = ________
4. 86 ÷ 0.4 = ________
5. 72.8 ÷ 1.4 = ________
6. 14.36 ÷ 0.4 = ________
7. 2.87 ÷ 0.01 = ________
8. 78.32 ÷ 0.22 = ________

9. **Reasoning** Why would multiplying both the dividend and the divisor by 10 sometimes make a problem easier to solve?

____

____

For each item, find how many times greater the 2002 cost is than the 1960 cost. Round your answer to the nearest hundredth.

Item	1960 Cost	2002 Cost
Movie admission	$0.75	$8.50
Regular popcorn	$0.25	$3.25
Regular drink	$0.35	$2.75

10. movie admission ________
11. regular popcorn ________
12. regular drink ________

13. Which item has increased the greatest amount of times from its original cost? ________

14. Divide. Round to the nearest hundredth. 250.6 ÷ 1.6

A 156

B 156.6

C 156.61

D 156.63

15. **Writing to Explain** Lynn and Randi got different quotients when they divided 3.60 by 0.12. Whose work is correct? Explain why.

Lynn	Randi
$12\overline{)3.60}$ = 0.30	$12\overline{)360.0}$ = 30.0

____

____

Name ______________________

Reteaching
5-6

Evaluating Expressions with Decimals

To evaluate an expression, follow these steps:

1. Substitute or replace the variable with the value given in the problem.
2. Perform the operation or operations.
3. If there is more than one operation, use the order of operations.

Evaluate $5.1 + 3n$ for $n = 2.6$.

Replace n with 2.6.	$5.1 + 3 \times 2.6$
Multiply first.	$5.1 + 7.8$
Then add.	12.9

The value of the expression is 12.9.

Evaluate $x^2 + 2x - x \div 3$ for $x = 3.3$.

Replace x with 3.3.	$3.3^2 + 2 \times 3.3 - 3.3 \div 3$
Evaluate terms with exponents.	$10.89 + 2 \times 3.3 - 3.3 \div 3$
Then multiply and divide.	$10.89 + 6.6 - 1.1$
Then add and subtract.	16.39

The value of the expression is 16.39.

Evaluate each expression by using substitution.

1. $6n$; $n = 2.3$ ______________ **2.** $3x - 8.1$; $x = 6.4$ ______________ **3.** $r + 53.3 \div r$; $r = 6.5$ ______________

For **4** through **6**, evaluate each expression for $x = 3.1$, $x = 6.2$, and $x = 8.3$.

4. $5x$ ______________ **5.** $8.2 + x \div 2$ ______________ **6.** $2x + 1.5x$ ______________

7. Juan rented a paddle board for $5.75 per hour plus a $17.50 fee. Write an expression that shows how much it will cost Juan to rent the paddle board for x hours. Then solve the expression for 3 hours.

____

8. Writing to Explain Katie is solving the problem $12.6 + 8.3 \div q \times 5$ for $q = 3$. List in order the steps Katie should follow.

____

Name ______________________

Practice
5-6

Evaluating Expressions with Decimals

Evaluate each expression by using substitution.

1. $n \times 8.62$; $n = 8$

____

4. $7s - 4$; $s = 11.7$

____

2. $x \div 3.2$; $x = 28.8$

____

5. $2.94 + h \div 4$; $h = 21.6$

____

3. $5r + (r \div 3)$; $r = 5.1$

____

6. $12.5 - g^2$; $g = 2.5$

____

For **7** through **9**, evaluate each expression for $x = 1.2$, $x = 6$, and $x = 9.6$.

7. $x \div 8$

____

8. $3x + 2.7$

____

9. $4x + 1.4x$

____

10. The table shows how much a frozen yogurt shop charges for its yogurt. Write an expression to show how much it costs to buy a small yogurt with no toppings and a large yogurt with x toppings. Then solve for buying a small yogurt with no toppings and a large yogurt with 3 toppings.

Size of cup	Cost of cup	Cost per topping
Small	$2.85	$0.25
Medium	$3.75	$0.30
Large	$4.65	$0.35

____

11. What is the value of the expression $7.2 + 10.8 \div p$ for $p = 2.4$?

A 7.5 **B** 9 **C** 11.7 **D** 12.5

12. Writing to Explain Explain in words how you would evaluate the expression $5.1 + q \div 3.4$ for $q = 28.9$.

____

____

____

Name ____________________

Reteaching **5-7**

Solving Equations with Decimals

To solve an equation, make the two sides of the equation equal with the variable alone on one side. You can use inverse operations and Properties of Equality.

Inverse operations are operations that "undo" each other. The **Division** and **Multiplication Properties of Equality** say you can multiply or divide both sides of an equation by the same number and the two sides remain equal to each other.

Use division to "undo" multiplication.

With numbers:

$3.2 \times 2.5 = 8$

$3.2 \times 2.5 \div \mathbf{2.5} = 8 \div \mathbf{2.5}$

$3.2 = 3.2$

With variables:

$q \times 1.8 = 10.8$

$q \times 1.8 \div \mathbf{1.8} = 10.8 \div \mathbf{1.8}$

$q = 6$

Use multiplication to "undo" division.

With numbers:

$12.8 \div 3.2 = 4$

$12.8 \div 3.2 \times \mathbf{3.2} = 4 \times \mathbf{3.2}$

$12.8 = 12.8$

With variables:

$r \div 7.2 = 6$

$r \div 7.2 \times \mathbf{7.2} = 6 \times \mathbf{7.2}$

$r = 43.2$

Evaluate each expression by using substitution.

1. $6n$; $n = 2.3$ ____________

2. $3x - 8.1$; $x = 6.4$ ____________

3. $r + 53.3 \div r$; $r = 6.5$ ____________

For **4** through **6**, evaluate each expression for $x = 3.1$, $x = 6.2$, and $x = 8.3$.

4. $5x$ ____________

5. $8.2 + x \div 2$ ____________

6. $2x + 1.5x$ ____________

7. Writing to Explain Explain how you would solve the equation $3.2x = 38.4$ by describing the inverse operation and the property of equality needed.

____

____

Name ______________________

Practice
5-7

Solving Equations with Decimals

Explain how to get the variable alone in each equation.

1. $7n = 6.3$ ______

2. $x \div 3.2 = 8$ ______

3. $67.3 = 3.2q$ ______

For **4** through **9**, solve each equation. Check your answers.

4. $x \div 8 = 5.6$ ______

5. $p \times 3.4 = 7.48$ ______

6. $4z = 50.8$ ______

7. $56 = 1.4t$ ______

8. $n \div 2.1 = 12$ ______

9. $5 = s \div 3.7$ ______

10. Sonja purchased some pens that cost 65 cents each. She spent a total of $9.10. How many pens did she purchase? Write an equation to describe the situation and solve.

______

11. Critical Thinking If $32n = 99.2$, then what is the value of the expression $8n$?

A 3.1 **B** 12.4 **C** 24.8 **D** 32

12. Which equation has the same solution as $m \div 2.6 = 3.5$?

A $m \div 3.5 = 2.6$

B $m \div 9.1 = 2.6$

C $2.6m = 3.5$

D $3.5m = 2.6$

13. Writing to Explain Tell how you would get the variable p alone on one side of the equation $32.4 = 4p$.

______

______

______

Name ______________________

Problem Solving: Multiple-Step Problems

Multiple-step problems often contain hidden questions. Sometimes you cannot answer the problem until you have answered these hidden questions.

James and Raul designed and printed T-shirts for school spirit week. James had 35 T-shirts printed and Raul had 3 times that number printed. It costs $3.25 each to print the T-shirts. How much did it cost altogether for James and Raul to print the T-shirts?

Hidden question: How many T-shirts did Raul have printed?
35 T-shirts × 3 = 105 T-shirts

Solve the problem:
35 + 105 = 140
140 × $3.25 = $455

Answer: It cost $455 to print the T-shirts.

1. The school store offers a discount for purchases made during lunchtime. The usual price of pencils is $0.25. The discount price is $0.15. How much can you save by buying 5 pencils during lunchtime?

____

2. Janine practiced piano for 1.25 hours each day Monday through Friday. Her sister Emily practiced twice as long as Janine on Wednesday, Thursday, and Friday. Who practiced more hours during the week?

____

3. During a week-long dry spell, the water level in a pond decreased by 4 in. per day, except for two days when it decreased by half that amount. How much did the water level decrease in the pond in one week?

____

4. Critical Thinking What hidden questions did you have to answer to solve the above problem?

____

____

____

Name ____________________

Problem Solving: Multiple-Step Problems

1. At a school concert, the orchestra plays 8 songs that are 4.25 min long and 3 songs that are twice as long as each of the others. How long is the concert?

____

2. A shoe store sold 53 pairs of shoes on Monday and 35 pairs on Tuesday. On Wednesday, the store sold as many pairs of shoes as they sold on Monday and Tuesday combined. They sold half as many on Thursday as Wednesday. How many pairs of shoes did the shoe store sell Monday through Thursday?

____

3. **Write a Problem** Use a real-life situation to create a problem in which there is a hidden question. Then identify the hidden question and the answer.

____

____

____

____

4. **Critical Thinking** Jackson is writing a report on California missions. He spent 2 hours researching missions on the Internet and three times as long writing the report. What is the hidden question if you want to find how many total hours Jackson spent on the report?

   A How many hours did he spend researching and writing the report?

   B How many hours did he spend researching the report?

   C How much longer did it take to write the report than research it?

   D How many hours did he spend writing the report?

5. **Writing to Explain** Explain how you can find the hidden questions in problem 2.

____

____

____

____

Name ______________________________

Greatest Common Factor

The greatest number that divides into two numbers is the greatest common factor (GCF) of the two numbers. Here are two ways to find the GCF of 12 and 40.

List the Factors

Step 1: List the factors of each number.

12: 1, 2, 3, 4, 6, 12

40: 1, 2, 4, 5, 8, 10, 20, 40

Step 2: Circle the factors that are common to both numbers.

12: 1, (2), 3, (4), 6, 12

40: 1, (2), (4), 5, 8, 10, 20, 40

Step 3: Choose the greatest factor that is common to both numbers. Both 2 and 4 are common factors, but 4 is greater.

The GCF is 4.

Use Prime Factorization

Step 1: Write the prime factorization of each number.

12: $2 \times 2 \times 3$

40: $2 \times 2 \times 2 \times 5$

Step 2: Circle the prime factors that the numbers have in common.

12: (2) × (2) × 3

40: (2) × (2) × 2 × 5

Step 3: Multiply the common factors.

$2 \times 2 = 4$ The GCF is 4.

Find the GCF for each set of numbers.

1. 10, 70 ________ **2.** 4, 20 ________ **3.** 18, 24 ________

4. 18, 63 ________ **5.** 17, 31 ________ **6.** 14, 28 ________

7. Number Sense Name two numbers that have a greatest common factor of 8.

____

8. Geometry Al's garden is 18 feet long and 30 feet wide. He wants to put fence posts the same distance apart along both the length and width of the fence. What is the greatest distance apart he can put the fence posts?

____

Name ______________________

Practice
6-1

Greatest Common Factor

Find the GCF for each set of numbers.

1. 12, 48 ________ **2.** 20, 24 ________ **3.** 19, 22 ________

4. 24, 100 ________ **5.** 18, 130 ________ **6.** 200, 205 ________

7. **Number Sense** Name three pairs of numbers that have 5 as their greatest common factor. Use each number only once in your answer.

____

8. The bake-sale committee divided each type of item evenly onto plates, so that every plate contained only one type of item and every plate had exactly the same number of items with no leftovers. What is the maximum number of items that could have been placed on each plate?

Bake Sale Donations	
Muffins	96
Bread sticks	48
Rolls	84

____

9. Using this system, how many plates of rolls could the bake-sale committee make? ________

10. Using this system, how many plates of muffins could the bake-sale committee make? ________

11. Which of the following pairs of numbers is correctly listed with its greatest common factor?

A 20, 24; GCF: 4

B 50, 100; GCF: 25

C 4, 6; GCF: 24

D 15, 20; GCF: 10

12. **Writing to Explain** Explain one method of finding the greatest common factor of 48 and 84.

____

____

____

____

Name ____________________

Reteaching
6-2

Least Common Multiple

There are different ways to find the least common multiple (LCM) of two numbers. Here are two ways of finding the LCM of 4 and 5:

List Multiples

Step 1: List multiples of each number.

4: 4, 8, 12, 16, 20, 24, 28, 32, 36, 40, 44, 48…

5: 5, 10, 15, 20, 25, 30, 35, 40, 45, 50…

Step 2: Check the multiples the numbers have in common.

4: 4, 8, 12, 16, (20), 24, 28, 32, 36, (40), 44, 48…

5: 5, 10, 15, (20), 25, 30, 35, (40), 45, 50…

Step 3: Determine which of the common multiples is the least.

20 and 40 are both common multiples, but 20 is the least.

The LCM of 4 and 5 is 20.

Use Prime Factors

Step 1: List the prime factors of each number.

4: 2×2

5: 5

Step 2: Circle the greatest number of times each different factor appears.

4: (2×2)

5: (5)

Step 3: Find the product of the factors you circled.

$2 \times 2 \times 5 = 20$

The LCM of 4 and 5 is 20.

Find the LCM of each set of numbers.

1. 6, 7 ________ **2.** 4, 5 ________ **3.** 10, 11 ________

4. 2, 5 ________ **5.** 6, 11 ________ **6.** 8, 10 ________

7. 3, 10 ________ **8.** 5, 10 ________ **9.** 7, 8 ________

10. Number Sense If you know the LCM of 4 and 5, how could you find the LCM of 40 and 50?

____

____

11. Writing to Explain Peter says the least common multiple of 4 and 6 is 24. Do you agree or disagree? Explain.

____

____

____

Name ______________________________

Practice
6-2

Least Common Multiple

Find the LCM of each set of numbers.

1. 5, 9 ________ **2.** 4, 10 ________ **3.** 8, 12 ________

4. 7, 12 ________ **5.** 4, 11 ________ **6.** 3, 7 ________

7. 7, 8 ________ **8.** 6, 9 ________ **9.** 3, 12 ________

10. At what times of the day between 10:00 A.M. and 5:00 P.M. do the chemistry presentation and the recycling presentation start at the same time?

____

____

Science Museum	
— Show Schedule —	
Chemistry	— Every 10 minutes
Electricity	— Every 20 minutes
Recycling	— Every 6 minutes
Fossils	— Every 45 minutes
The first showing for all shows is at 10:00 A.M.	

11. The museum does shows in schools every Monday and shows in public libraries every fifth day (on both weekdays and weekends). If the museum did both a school show and a library show on Monday, how many days will it be until it does both shows on the same day again?

____

12. Which of the following pairs of numbers is correctly listed with its LCM?

A 5, 10; LCM: 50

B 2, 3; LCM: 6

C 2, 6; LCM: 12

D 7, 9; LCM: 21

13. Writing to Explain What method would you use to find the LCM of a group of four numbers? Explain and give an example.

____

____

____

____

____

Name ______________________________

Reteaching
6-3

Understanding Division of Fractions

Divide a fraction by a whole number.

Find $\frac{1}{8} \div 4$.

Use a model to show $\frac{1}{8}$.

$\frac{1}{8}$	$\frac{1}{8}$	$\frac{1}{8}$	$\frac{1}{8}$	$\frac{1}{8}$	$\frac{1}{8}$	$\frac{1}{8}$	$\frac{1}{8}$

Divide each eighth into 4 equal parts.

$\frac{1}{32}$							

Each section shows $\frac{1}{(8 \times 4)} = \frac{1}{32}$.

$\frac{1}{8} \div 4 = \frac{1}{32}$.

Solve each division sentence. Use a model to help.

1. $3 \div \frac{1}{3} =$ ________

2. $\frac{1}{5} \div 4 =$ ________

3. $16 \div \frac{1}{4} =$ ________

4. $\frac{1}{7} \div 8 =$ ________

Find each quotient. Use a model if you wish.
Simplify if possible.

5. $3 \div \frac{1}{2} =$ ________

6. $\frac{9}{10} \div 10 =$ ________

7. $\frac{1}{5} \div 3 =$ ________

8. $\frac{3}{16} \div 2 =$ ________

9. $5 \div \frac{1}{3} =$ ________

10. $\frac{1}{2} \div 6 =$ ________

11. $8 \div \frac{1}{4} =$ ________

12. $\frac{7}{12} \div 4 =$ ________

13. $\frac{6}{7} \div 7 =$ ________

14. Draw a Picture The square dancing club meets for 3 hours. Every $\frac{3}{4}$ hour, the dancers change partners. How many different partners will each dancer have in one meeting? Draw a picture to show your solution.

____

15. Writing to Explain Explain why the quotient of two fractions less than 1 is always greater than either fraction.

____

Name ______________________

Understanding Division of Fractions

Solve each division sentence using the models provided.

1. $3 \div \frac{1}{3} =$ ________ **2.** $\frac{1}{4} \div 6 =$ ________ **3.** $\frac{5}{6} \div 6 =$ ________

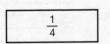

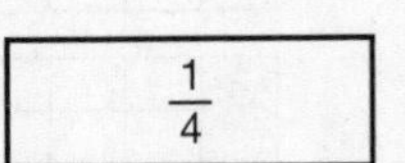

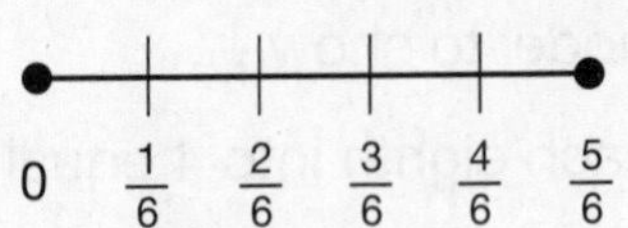

Find each quotient. You can make a model to help. Simplify if possible.

4. $8 \div \frac{1}{4} =$ ________ **5.** $\frac{1}{7} \div 4 =$ ________ **6.** $5 \div \frac{1}{2} =$ ________

7. $\frac{7}{8} \div 8 =$ ________ **8.** $\frac{11}{12} \div 12 =$ ________ **9.** $\frac{1}{12} \div 3 =$ ________

10. $6 \div \frac{2}{3} =$ ________ **11.** $7 \div \frac{1}{3} =$ ________ **12.** $\frac{15}{16} \div \frac{1}{16} =$ ________

13. Draw a Picture Olivia has a piece of ribbon $\frac{1}{2}$ yard long. If she cuts it into 6 equal pieces, what will be the length of each piece, in yards?

____

14. Geometry A regular polygon has a perimeter of 12 units. If each side measures $\frac{3}{4}$ unit, how many sides does the polygon have?

____

15. Which division expression is shown by this model?

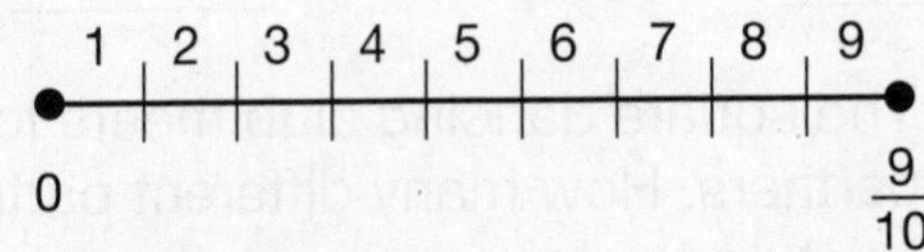

A $\frac{9}{10} \div \frac{1}{10}$ **B** $1 \div \frac{1}{10}$ **C** $\frac{9}{10} \div 1$ **D** $10 \div \frac{9}{10}$

16. Writing to Explain When you divide a whole number by a fraction less than 1, will the quotient be greater than or less than the whole number? Explain, and give an example.

____

____

____

Name ______________________________

Reteaching
6-4

Dividing Whole Numbers by Fractions

To divide a whole number by a fraction, you can multiply the whole number by the reciprocal of the fraction. The reciprocal of a number has the numerator and the denominator reversed. The product of a number and its reciprocal is 1.

Number	×	Reciprocal	=	Product
3	×	$\frac{1}{3}$	=	1
$\frac{1}{8}$	×	$\frac{8}{1}$	=	1
$\frac{2}{3}$	×	$\frac{3}{2}$	=	1

Find $14 \div \frac{4}{7}$.

Step 1

Rewrite the division as multiplication using the reciprocal of the divisor.

The reciprocal of $\frac{4}{7}$ is $\frac{7}{4}$.

$14 \div \frac{4}{7} = 14 \times \frac{7}{4}$

Step 2

Divide out common factors if possible. Then multiply.

$\frac{\overset{7}{\cancel{14}}}{1} \times \frac{7}{\underset{2}{\cancel{4}}} = \frac{49}{2}$

Step 3

If your answer is an improper fraction, change it to a mixed number.

$\frac{49}{2} = 24\frac{1}{2}$

Find the reciprocal of each fraction or whole number.

1. $\frac{5}{7}$ __________ **2.** 11 __________ **3.** $\frac{9}{2}$ __________

Find each quotient. Simplify if possible.

4. $12 \div \frac{4}{5}$ __________ **5.** $2 \div \frac{1}{4}$ __________ **6.** $16 \div \frac{8}{10}$ __________

7. $24 \div \frac{3}{4}$ __________ **8.** $18 \div \frac{8}{9}$ __________ **9.** $25 \div \frac{10}{11}$ __________

10. $36 \div \frac{8}{9}$ __________ **11.** $42 \div \frac{7}{8}$ __________ **12.** $40 \div \frac{4}{5}$ __________

13. Karolyn makes rolls for a friend's dinner party. She uses 3 lb of butter. Each stick of butter weighs $\frac{1}{4}$ lb. How many sticks of butter does Karolyn need to make her rolls?

____

Name ______________________

Practice 6-4

Dividing Whole Numbers by Fractions

Find the reciprocal of each fraction or whole number.

1. $\frac{5}{9}$ ______ **2.** 8 ______ **3.** $\frac{7}{3}$ ______

Find each quotient. Simplify if possible.

4. $8 \div \frac{2}{5} =$ ______ **5.** $4 \div \frac{1}{6} =$ ______ **6.** $18 \div \frac{3}{8} =$ ______

7. $12 \div \frac{1}{2} =$ ______ **8.** $42 \div \frac{7}{9} =$ ______ **9.** $10 \div \frac{5}{6} =$ ______

10. $20 \div \frac{3}{4} =$ ______ **11.** $22 \div \frac{5}{6} =$ ______ **12.** $7 \div \frac{2}{3} =$ ______

13. $9 \div \frac{1}{8} =$ ______ **14.** $15 \div \frac{1}{3} =$ ______ **15.** $6 \div \frac{1}{5} =$ ______

16. Writing to Explain Will the quotient of $5 \div \frac{7}{8}$ be greater than or less than 5? Explain.

____

____

17. Reasoning How many times will you need to fill a $\frac{1}{2}$ cup measuring cup to measure 4 cups of flour?

____

18. Geometry The distance around a circular flower bed is 36 feet. Jasper wants to put stakes every 8 inches ($\frac{2}{3}$ of a foot) around the bed. How many stakes does he need?

____

19. Algebra Which expression is equal to $9 \times \frac{3}{2}$?

A $2 \div \frac{3}{9}$

B $3 \div \frac{9}{2}$

C $9 \div \frac{2}{3}$

D $9 \div \frac{3}{2}$

Name ______________________________

Modeling Division of Fractions

Reteaching **6-5**

You can use fraction strips to divide fractions.

Find $\frac{1}{3} \div \frac{1}{6}$.

Use part of the strip for thirds to show $\frac{1}{3}$.

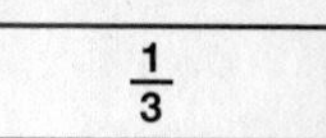

Then place the strip for sixths below the strip for thirds.

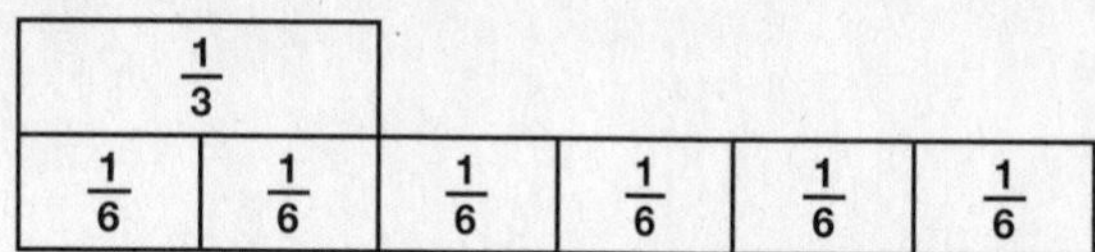

Count how many sixths are as long as the strip for $\frac{1}{3}$.

Two sixths are as long as $\frac{1}{3}$.
So, $\frac{1}{3} \div \frac{1}{6} = 2$.

Use the pictures of the fraction strips to find each quotient.

1. $\frac{1}{2} \div \frac{1}{4} =$ ______

$\frac{1}{2}$			
$\frac{1}{4}$	$\frac{1}{4}$	$\frac{1}{4}$	$\frac{1}{4}$

2. $\frac{3}{4} \div \frac{1}{12} =$ ______

$\frac{1}{4}$		$\frac{1}{4}$		$\frac{1}{4}$							
$\frac{1}{12}$	$\frac{1}{12}$	$\frac{1}{12}$	$\frac{1}{12}$	$\frac{1}{12}$	$\frac{1}{12}$	$\frac{1}{12}$	$\frac{1}{12}$	$\frac{1}{12}$	$\frac{1}{12}$	$\frac{1}{12}$	$\frac{1}{12}$

3. $\frac{4}{5} \div \frac{1}{10} =$ ______

$\frac{1}{5}$		$\frac{1}{5}$		$\frac{1}{5}$		$\frac{1}{5}$			
$\frac{1}{10}$	$\frac{1}{10}$	$\frac{1}{10}$	$\frac{1}{10}$	$\frac{1}{10}$	$\frac{1}{10}$	$\frac{1}{10}$	$\frac{1}{10}$	$\frac{1}{10}$	$\frac{1}{10}$

4. $\frac{1}{4} \div \frac{1}{8} =$ ______

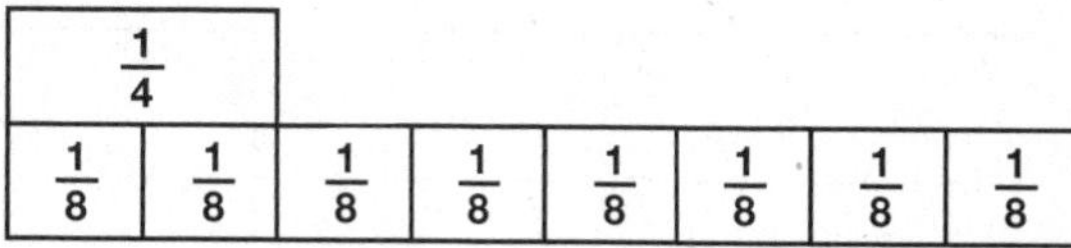

Find each quotient. You can use fraction strips to help.

5. $\frac{2}{3} \div \frac{1}{6} =$ ______

6. $\frac{3}{5} \div \frac{1}{10} =$ ______

7. $\frac{1}{3} \div \frac{1}{12} =$ ______

8. Writing to Explain Why is the quotient of two fractions less than 1 always greater than either fraction? Explain.

____

____

Name ______________________________

Practice
6-5

Modeling Division of Fractions

Solve each division sentence using the models provided.

1. $\frac{5}{6} \div \frac{1}{6} =$ __________

0 $\frac{5}{6}$ 1

2. $\frac{3}{5} \div \frac{1}{10} =$ __________

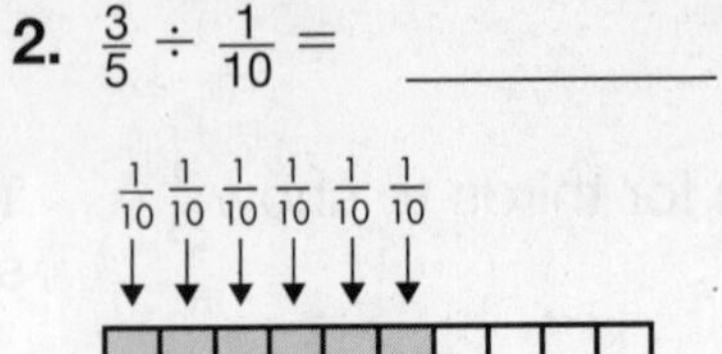

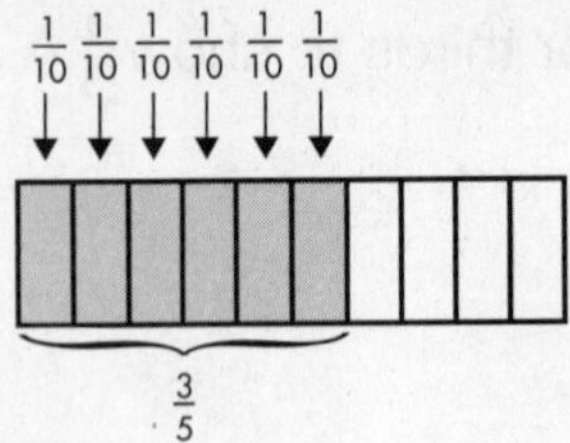

Find each quotient. You can draw a model to help.

3. $\frac{6}{7} \div \frac{2}{7} =$ __________

4. $\frac{3}{4} \div \frac{1}{16} =$ __________

5. $\frac{7}{8} \div \frac{1}{8} =$ __________

6. $\frac{15}{16} \div \frac{1}{16} =$ __________

7. $\frac{11}{12} \div \frac{1}{12} =$ __________

8. $\frac{5}{8} \div \frac{5}{16} =$ __________

9. Draw a Picture Olivia has a piece of ribbon $\frac{1}{2}$ yard long. She will cut it into pieces that are each $\frac{1}{12}$ yard long. How many pieces will Olivia have?

____

10. Writing to Explain Write an explanation for another student telling him or her how to divide $\frac{2}{3}$ by $\frac{1}{6}$.

____

____

____

____

11. Which division expression is shown by the model?

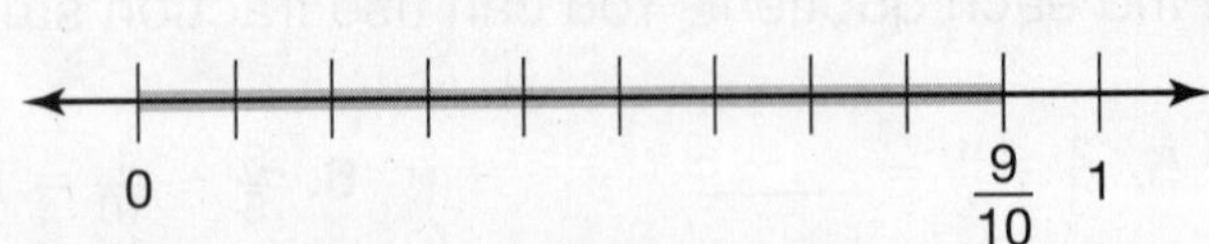

A $\frac{9}{10} \div \frac{1}{10}$ **B** $1 \div \frac{9}{10}$ **C** $\frac{1}{10} \div \frac{9}{10}$ **D** $\frac{1}{10} \div \frac{1}{9}$

12. Algebra Which equation could you use to find the number of $\frac{1}{8}$-inch pieces that can be cut from a piece of string that is $\frac{3}{4}$ of an inch long?

A $\frac{1}{4} \times \frac{8}{5} = n$ **B** $\frac{1}{8} \div \frac{3}{4} = n$ **C** $\frac{5}{8} \times \frac{1}{4} = n$ **D** $\frac{3}{4} \div \frac{1}{8} = n$

Name ____________________

Reteaching
6-6

Dividing Fractions

To divide by a fraction, you can multiply by its reciprocal. The reciprocal of a number has the numerator and the denominator reversed.

Find $\frac{4}{5} \div \frac{3}{10}$.

Step 1

Rewrite the division as multiplication using the reciprocal of the divisor.

The reciprocal of $\frac{3}{10}$ is $\frac{10}{3}$.

$\frac{4}{5} \div \frac{3}{10} = \frac{4}{5} \times \frac{10}{3}$

Step 2

Divide out common factors if possible. Then multiply.

$\frac{4}{\cancel{5}_1} \times \frac{\cancel{10}^2}{3} = \frac{8}{3}$

Step 3

If your answer is an improper fraction, change it to a mixed number.

$\frac{8}{3} = 2\frac{2}{3}$

Find each quotient. Simplify if possible.

1. $\frac{1}{2} \div \frac{1}{4} = \frac{1}{2} \times$ ______ = ______
(Reciprocal of $\frac{1}{4}$)

2. $\frac{4}{7} \div \frac{8}{21} =$ ______ × ______ = ______
(Reciprocal of $\frac{8}{21}$)

3. $\frac{1}{3} \div \frac{1}{2}$ ______

4. $\frac{2}{5} \div \frac{2}{3}$ ______

5. $\frac{5}{8} \div \frac{7}{10}$ ______

6. $\frac{3}{7} \div 3$ ______

7. $\frac{1}{3} \div \frac{8}{9}$ ______

8. $\frac{5}{6} \div \frac{1}{8}$ ______

9. $\frac{5}{9} \div \frac{1}{2}$ ______

10. $\frac{3}{5} \div \frac{3}{4}$ ______

11. $\frac{3}{4} \div \frac{5}{6}$ ______

12. $\frac{9}{10} \div \frac{4}{5}$ ______

13. $\frac{1}{3} \div \frac{3}{8}$ ______

14. $\frac{4}{7} \div \frac{3}{4}$ ______

15. Aaron has $\frac{7}{8}$ gallon of bottled water. How many $\frac{3}{16}$-gallon servings can he pour?

____

16. **Draw a Picture** Show how Rebecca can divide $\frac{3}{4}$ of a cake into 9 pieces. What fraction of the whole cake will each piece be?

____

Name ______________________

Practice
6-6

Dividing Fractions

Find each quotient. Simplify if possible.

1. $\frac{1}{3} \div \frac{5}{6} =$ ______ **2.** $\frac{3}{8} \div \frac{1}{2} =$ ______ **3.** $\frac{7}{8} \div \frac{7}{12} =$ ______

4. $\frac{5}{9} \div 5 =$ ______ **5.** $\frac{6}{7} \div \frac{3}{4} =$ ______ **6.** $\frac{2}{3} \div \frac{3}{4} =$ ______

7. $\frac{1}{2} \div \frac{3}{10} =$ ______ **8.** $\frac{5}{12} \div \frac{2}{3} =$ ______ **9.** $\frac{14}{15} \div \frac{2}{5} =$ ______

10. $\frac{1}{3} \div \frac{3}{4} =$ ______ **11.** $\frac{3}{8} \div 4 =$ ______ **12.** $\frac{9}{10} \div \frac{3}{5} =$ ______

13. Writing to Explain Serena said that by looking for common factors and simplifying the expression, she found that $\frac{4}{10} \div \frac{5}{8} = 1\frac{9}{16}$. Do you agree with Serena? Why or why not?

$$\frac{\cancel{10}^{\,5}}{4} \times \frac{5}{\cancel{8}_{\,4}} = \frac{25}{16} = 1\frac{9}{16}$$

____

____

____

14. A $\frac{5}{6}$-yard piece of fencing is made of boards that are $\frac{1}{12}$ yard wide. How many boards make up the fence?

____

15. Nathan has $\frac{7}{8}$ lb of hummus. How many $\frac{3}{10}$-lb servings does he have?

____

16. Algebra Which equation can you use to find the number of $\frac{1}{4}$–inch pieces that can be cut from a piece of metal $\frac{5}{8}$ of an inch long?

A $\frac{5}{8} \div \frac{1}{4} = n$

B $\frac{1}{4} \div \frac{5}{8} = n$

C $\frac{5}{8} \times \frac{1}{4} = n$

D $\frac{1}{4} \times \frac{8}{5} = n$

Name ______________________________

Estimating Mixed-Number Quotients

When you are working with fractions and mixed numbers, you can estimate using rounding and compatible numbers.

Estimate $23\frac{5}{6} \div 8\frac{3}{7}$.

$23\frac{5}{6} \div 8\frac{3}{7}$ — Round each mixed number to the nearest whole number.

$24 \div 8 = 3$ — Divide.

$23\frac{5}{6} \div 8\frac{3}{7} \approx 3$

Estimate $31\frac{1}{6} \div 4\frac{5}{8}$.

$31\frac{1}{6} \div 4\frac{5}{8}$ — Change $31\frac{1}{6}$ and $4\frac{5}{8}$ to the nearest compatible whole numbers.

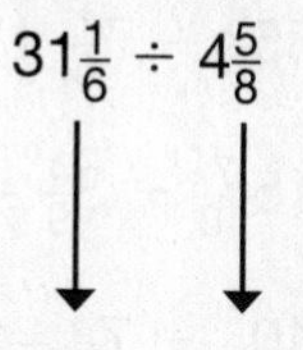

$30 \div 5 = 6$ — Think: $31\frac{1}{6}$ and $4\frac{5}{8}$ are close to 30 and 5.

$31\frac{1}{6} \div 4\frac{5}{8} \approx 6$

Estimate each quotient.

1. $11\frac{1}{2} \div 6\frac{1}{4}$ ________ **2.** $19\frac{1}{3} \div 3\frac{2}{3}$ ________ **3.** $41\frac{7}{9} \div 7\frac{1}{5}$ ________

4. $35\frac{1}{8} \div 5\frac{4}{5}$ ________ **5.** $61\frac{3}{8} \div 8\frac{5}{9}$ ________ **6.** $72\frac{2}{9} \div 7\frac{7}{8}$ ________

7. $86\frac{3}{4} \div 10\frac{5}{6}$ ________ **8.** $26\frac{9}{10} \div 2\frac{5}{8}$ ________ **9.** $11\frac{2}{7} \div 3\frac{3}{5}$ ________

10. $7\frac{9}{10} \div 2\frac{3}{10}$ ________ **11.** $47\frac{6}{10} \div 7\frac{1}{12}$ ________ **12.** $60\frac{5}{12} \div 5\frac{4}{9}$ ________

13. Critical Thinking Which of these two estimates is closer to the actual quotient? How do you know?
Lisa's estimate: $55\frac{1}{2} \div 6\frac{3}{4} \approx 54 \div 6 = 9$
Hayden's estimate: $55\frac{1}{2} \div 6\frac{3}{4} \approx 56 \div 7 = 8$

____

____

14. Patrick uses wire to make wreaths. He has $31\frac{1}{2}$ feet of wire left on a spool. Estimate how many $3\frac{3}{4}$ pieces can he cut from the longer piece of wire.

____

Name ____________________

Practice **6-7**

Estimating Mixed-Number Quotients

Estimate each product.

1. $37\frac{1}{3} \div 5\frac{7}{8} =$ ______
2. $25\frac{1}{2} \div 6\frac{1}{4} =$ ______
3. $49\frac{4}{5} \div 6\frac{1}{2} =$ ______
4. $12\frac{3}{4} \div 5\frac{5}{9} =$ ______
5. $43\frac{2}{3} \div 5\frac{2}{5} =$ ______
6. $8\frac{1}{3} \div 2\frac{9}{10} =$ ______
7. $67\frac{1}{5} \div 7\frac{2}{7} =$ ______
8. $55\frac{5}{9} \div 7\frac{1}{6} =$ ______
9. $19\frac{6}{7} \div 4\frac{1}{8} =$ ______
10. $71\frac{4}{5} \div 7\frac{8}{9} =$ ______
11. $15\frac{7}{10} \div 3\frac{4}{9} =$ ______
12. $79\frac{4}{7} \div 8\frac{5}{8} =$ ______
13. $26\frac{1}{4} \div 2\frac{3}{8} =$ ______
14. $40\frac{8}{9} \div 7\frac{3}{5} =$ ______
15. $58\frac{1}{3} \div 19\frac{5}{6} =$ ______

16. **Number Sense** Tran wants to cut strips of paper that are $2\frac{1}{4}$ in. wide. His sheet of paper is $11\frac{1}{2}$ in. wide. He estimates that $11\frac{1}{2} \div 2\frac{1}{4} = 6$, so he can cut 6 strips from each sheet of paper. Is his estimate an overestimate or an underestimate? Explain.

____

____

17. **Writing to Explain** Eliza uses $2\frac{7}{8}$ feet of yarn in each gift basket she makes. Explain how to estimate how many baskets Eliza can make if she has 22 feet of yarn.

____

____

18. **Geometry** The area of this rectangle is $257\frac{1}{4}$ sq in. What is the best estimate of side length *w*? Remember, $A = \ell \times w$.

$257\frac{1}{4}$ sq in. $10\frac{1}{2}$ in. *w*

A 66,000 in.

B 50 in.

C 25 in.

D 5 in.

19. **Critical Thinking** What estimation method did you use to find the length of side *w* in Problem 18?

____

____

Name ____________________

Reteaching 6-8

Dividing Mixed Numbers

You can follow these steps to find $5\frac{1}{3} \div 1\frac{1}{3}$ and $21 \div 2\frac{1}{3}$.

Step 1	**Step 2**	**Step 3**
First estimate. Then write each number as an improper fraction.	Find the reciprocal of the divisor. Rewrite as a multiplication problem.	Look for common factors. Simplify, then multiply.
Find $5\frac{1}{3} \div 1\frac{1}{3}$. Estimate $5 \div 1 = 5$. $5\frac{1}{3} \div 1\frac{1}{3} =$ ↓ ↓ $\frac{16}{3} \div \frac{4}{3}$	$\frac{16}{3} \div \frac{4}{3} =$ $\frac{16}{3} \times \frac{3}{4}$	$\frac{16}{3} \times \frac{3}{4} =$ $\frac{\overset{4}{\cancel{16}}}{\underset{1}{\cancel{3}}} \times \frac{\overset{1}{\cancel{3}}}{\underset{1}{\cancel{4}}} = \frac{4}{1} = 4$ 4 is close to 5, so the answer is reasonable.
Find $21 \div 2\frac{1}{3}$. Estimate $21 \div 2 = 10\frac{1}{2}$. $21 \div 2\frac{1}{3}$ ↓ ↓ $\frac{21}{1} \div \frac{7}{3}$	$\frac{21}{1} \div \frac{7}{3} =$ $\frac{21}{1} \times \frac{3}{7}$	$\frac{21}{1} \times \frac{3}{7} =$ $\frac{\overset{3}{\cancel{21}}}{1} \times \frac{3}{\underset{1}{\cancel{7}}} = \frac{9}{1} = 9$ 9 is close to $10\frac{1}{2}$, so the answer is reasonable.

Find each quotient. Simplify if possible.

1. $2\frac{2}{3} \div 3\frac{1}{4} =$ ________

2. $1\frac{3}{4} \div 4\frac{1}{8} =$ ________

3. $2\frac{1}{5} \div 2\frac{1}{3} =$ ________

4. $5\frac{1}{4} \div 3 =$ ________

5. $10 \div 3\frac{1}{4} =$ ________

6. $7\frac{1}{4} \div 2\frac{1}{8} =$ ________

7. Writing to Explain Paper needs to be cut for voting ballots. Each piece of paper is $10\frac{1}{2}$ in. long. Each ballot should be $1\frac{3}{4}$ in. long. How many ballots can be cut from one piece of paper?

____

Name ____________________

Practice **6-8**

Dividing Mixed Numbers

Find each quotient. Simplify if possible.

1. $1\frac{1}{2} \div 2\frac{1}{3} =$ ______ **2.** $4\frac{1}{4} \div 3\frac{1}{8} =$ ______ **3.** $2\frac{1}{4} \div 5\frac{1}{2} =$ ______

4. $3\frac{1}{2} \div 2\frac{1}{4} =$ ______ **5.** $3\frac{3}{4} \div 2 =$ ______ **6.** $1\frac{1}{2} \div 2\frac{1}{4} =$ ______

7. $8 \div 2\frac{3}{4} =$ ______ **8.** $2\frac{1}{2} \div 1\frac{3}{8} =$ ______ **9.** $4\frac{2}{3} \div 1\frac{3}{4} =$ ______

10. **Reasoning** Is it possible to divide 15 by a mixed number and get a quotient that is greater than 15? Explain.

____

____

Room	Gallons of Paint
Kitchen	$2\frac{1}{2}$
Bedroom	$3\frac{3}{4}$
Living room	$4\frac{1}{3}$

Max is painting the inside of an apartment complex. The table shows how many gallons of paint are needed to paint each type of room.

11. How many kitchens can Max paint with 20 gal? ______

12. How many living rooms can Max paint with 26 gal? ______

13. How many bedrooms can Max paint with 60 gal? ______

14. Find $4\frac{1}{2} \div 2\frac{1}{4}$.

A 1

B 2

C 3

D 4

15. **Writing to Explain** Explain how you would find $4\frac{1}{5} \div 2\frac{1}{3}$.

____

____

____

Name ______________________________

Reteaching **6-9**

Evaluating Expressions with Fractions

To evaluate expressions with fractions, follow the same steps as evaluating expressions with whole numbers.

- Replace with the variable with the given value.
- Follow the order of operations to solve.

Evaluate $n \times \frac{6}{7} - \frac{2}{7}$, if $n = 5$.

Replace n with 5. $5 \times \frac{6}{7} - \frac{2}{7}$

Solve. $\frac{30}{7} - \frac{2}{7} = \frac{28}{7}$

Simplify the fraction. $\frac{28}{7} = 4$

Substitute to evaluate the expressions. Simplify if possible.

1. $3a + \frac{3}{6}$, if $a = \frac{1}{4}$ ________

2. $\frac{5}{9} \div y + 6$, if $y = \frac{7}{12}$ ________

3. $\frac{3}{4}f \div \frac{6}{10}$, if $f = \frac{4}{5}$ ________

4. $6 + 8(y - \frac{3}{5})$, if $y = \frac{8}{9}$ ________

5. $\frac{1}{2} \div (c - \frac{3}{4})$, if $c = \frac{13}{16}$ ________

6. $d + \frac{1}{5} \times 3$, if $d = 1\frac{2}{3}$ ________

7. $\frac{5}{12} \div s + (\frac{2}{3} - \frac{1}{4})$, if $s = \frac{5}{6}$ ________

8. $\frac{7}{10} - \frac{2}{5} + s \times s$, if $s = \frac{3}{4}$ ________

9. $11g + (g \div 3)$, if $g = \frac{2}{5}$ ________

10. $1\frac{3}{4} \times b \div 2$, if $b = \frac{2}{3}$ ________

11. Persevere Margaret is ordering mosaic tiles to cover a table top from an online store. She has narrowed her selection to two different types of tiles. Tile A is $1\frac{3}{8}$ inches wide and $2\frac{5}{8}$ inches long. Tile B is $1\frac{6}{7}$ inches wide and $2\frac{1}{2}$ inches long. Margaret wants to order the tile with the greater area. Using the expression $l \times w$ to find area, which tile should she order? Show your work.

____

____

____

Name ______________________

Practice
6-9

Evaluating Expressions with Fractions

Evaluate each expression by substituting the value. Simplify if possible.

1. $j + \frac{3}{8}$, if $j = \frac{3}{4}$ ________

2. $8 - g \div \frac{7}{8}$, if $g = \frac{5}{6}$ ________

3. $3m \div \frac{2}{5}$, if $m = \frac{2}{3}$ ________

4. $w + (\frac{11}{12} - \frac{2}{3}) \times 4$, if $w = \frac{3}{4}$ ________

5. $\frac{9}{10} \times h - 1\frac{1}{4}$, if $h = 2\frac{1}{2}$ ________

6. $m + m \times \frac{4}{5}$, if $m = 1\frac{3}{7}$ ________

7. $6\frac{1}{2} \div r + 4\frac{1}{2}$, if $r = \frac{3}{5}$ ________

8. $c \times c + 2\frac{3}{5}$, if $c = 1\frac{1}{3}$ ________

9. Evaluate the expression for values of h and complete the table.

	$h = \frac{4}{5}$	$h = \frac{2}{3}$	$h = 4\frac{1}{5}$	$h = \frac{7}{8}$
$3h - \frac{1}{3}$				

10. Algebra Sally has 20 feet of ribbon. She is going to cut the ribbon into equal-sized lengths to make bracelets. She wants to compare how many bracelets she can make if she uses different lengths. Write an algebraic expression that Sally can use to figure out how many bracelets she can make if she cuts the ribbon into $7\frac{1}{2}$-inch or $6\frac{3}{4}$-inch lengths.

____

____

11. Writing to Explain How would Sally change her expression if she wants to figure out how many feet of ribbon she needs to make 100 bracelets?

____

____

____

____

Name ______________________

Reteaching

6-10

Solving Equations with Fractions

To solve an equation with a fraction, you need to isolate the variable.

Solve $\frac{8}{10}f = \frac{1}{4}$.

Step 1

Divide each side of the equation by $\frac{8}{10}$.

$\frac{8}{10}f \div \frac{8}{10} = \frac{1}{4} \div \frac{8}{10}$

Step 2

Solve for *f*. Remember to use the reciprocal.

$f = \frac{1}{4} \times \frac{10}{8}$

$f = \frac{10}{32}$

Step 3

Simplify if possible.

$f = \frac{5}{16}$

Solve each equation. Simplify if possible.

1. $3a = \frac{5}{6}$ ________

2. $g \div \frac{5}{8} = \frac{2}{3}$ ________

3. $\frac{2}{3}h = 23$ ________

4. $d \div \frac{3}{5} = \frac{1}{2}$ ________

5. $y \div 6 = \frac{4}{5}$ ________

6. $\frac{7}{8}z = \frac{9}{10}$ ________

7. $8\frac{1}{2}m = 4$ ________

8. $n \div \frac{2}{3} = \frac{3}{10}$ ________

9. $b \div 2\frac{1}{2} = 1\frac{3}{4}$ ________

10. Geometry Helen wants to paint a rectangle with an area of 35 square feet on her wall. If the height of the rectangle is $3\frac{3}{4}$ feet, what is the width of the rectangle? (Remember, area = length × width.) Write an equation and solve.

____

Name ______________________

Practice

6-10

Solving Equations with Fractions

Solve each equation. Simplify if possible.

1. $j \div 6 = \frac{9}{10}$ ________

2. $d \div 12 = \frac{1}{6}$ ________

3. $4v = 3\frac{2}{3}$ ________

4. $4\frac{2}{5} \times b = 1\frac{5}{6}$ ________

5. $\frac{2}{5}h = \frac{3}{4}$ ________

6. $3\frac{1}{3} \times s = 20$ ________

7. $t \div \frac{3}{8} = \frac{3}{4}$ ________

8. $c \div 2\frac{1}{3} = \frac{1}{4}$ ________

9. Peggy worked $20\frac{2}{3}$ hours over three days last week. She worked the same number of hours each day. How many hours did Peggy work each day? Write an equation and solve.

____

10. Writing to Explain The children's room at a local library has a square-shaped floor with an area of 400 feet. How can you find the length and width of the room without knowing either measurement?

____

____

____

____

11. Reasoning Which equation do you think has the greater solution: $1\frac{4}{5}h = 3\frac{1}{3}$ or $3\frac{1}{3}g = 2$? Explain your thinking. Then, solve to check your prediction.

____

____

____

Name ____________________

Reteaching
6-11

Problem Solving: Look for a Pattern

Sometimes you can solve a problem by identifying a pattern.
Here are two types of patterns.

Patterns in sets of numbers

$\frac{15}{4}, \frac{13}{4}, \frac{11}{4}, \frac{9}{4}, \frac{7}{4}, \frac{5}{4}, \frac{3}{4}$

Ask yourself:
Are the numbers increasing?
Are they decreasing?
Do they change by the same amount each time?
Do you add, subtract, multiply, or divide to find the next number?

Patterns in groups of figures

Ask yourself:
How is the first figure modified to make the second figure?
How is the second figure modified to make the third?

Remember: Once you have identified a possible number pattern, check at least two other consecutive numbers to make sure that the pattern is true for all of the numbers.

Find the missing numbers. Describe the pattern.

1. $\frac{3}{4}$, 1, $1\frac{1}{4}$, $1\frac{1}{2}$, ______, ______, ______, ______, $2\frac{3}{4}$ ______________

2. 89, 78, 67, ______, ______, ______, ______, 12, 1 ______________

3. $\frac{1}{5}, \frac{4}{5}, \frac{7}{5}, \frac{10}{5}$, ______, ______, ______, ______, $\frac{25}{5}$ ______________

4. Draw the next figure in the pattern below.

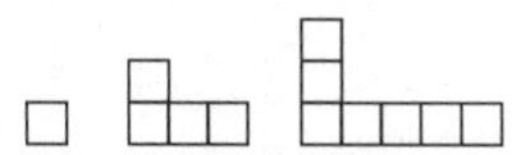

5. **Number Sense** The table below shows the number of cells in a culture. How many cells will there be at 4:30?

Time	1:00	1:30	2:00	2:30	3:00
Number of Cells	1	2	4	8	16

____

Name ______________________________

Problem Solving: Look for a Pattern

Find the missing numbers. Describe the pattern.

1. $\frac{1}{8}, \frac{6}{8}, \frac{11}{8}, \frac{16}{8}$, ______, ______, ______, ______, $\frac{41}{8}$ ______________

2. $\frac{1}{4}, \frac{1}{2}$, 1, ______, ______, ______, ______, 32, 64 ______________

3. 1.1, 1.1, 2.2, 6.6, ______, ______, ______, ______ ______________

4. $14\frac{1}{2}, 12\frac{3}{4}$, 11, ______, ______, ______, ______, $2\frac{1}{4}, \frac{1}{2}$ ______________

5. 27, 9, 3, 1, $\frac{1}{3}$, ______, ______, ______, ______ ______________

6. 3, 5, 9, 15, ______, ______, ______, ______, 75 ______________

7. **Number Sense** In the figure, the sum of each row forms a pattern. What is the sum of the seventh row?

   ____

1
2 2
3 3 3
4 4 4 4
5 5 5 5 5

8. Which figure completes this pattern?

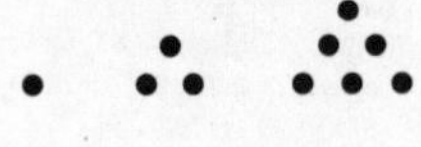

A

B

C

D

9. **Writing to Explain** How can you find the answer to exercise **7** without finding the sum of the numbers in a row?

____

____

Name ______________________________

Understanding Integers

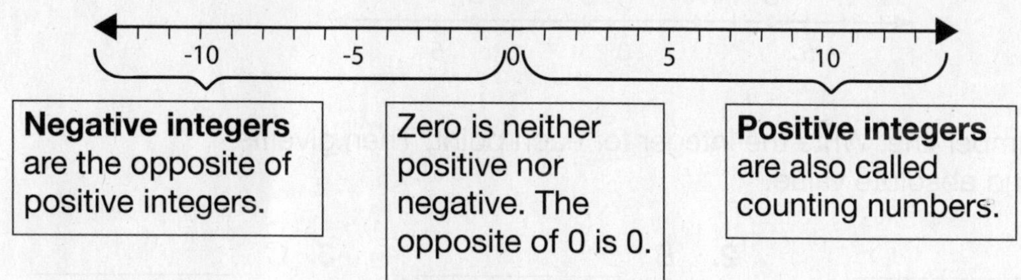

The **absolute value** of an integer is the distance from that integer to zero on the number line. Distance is always a positive measure, so the absolute value of any integer is positive.

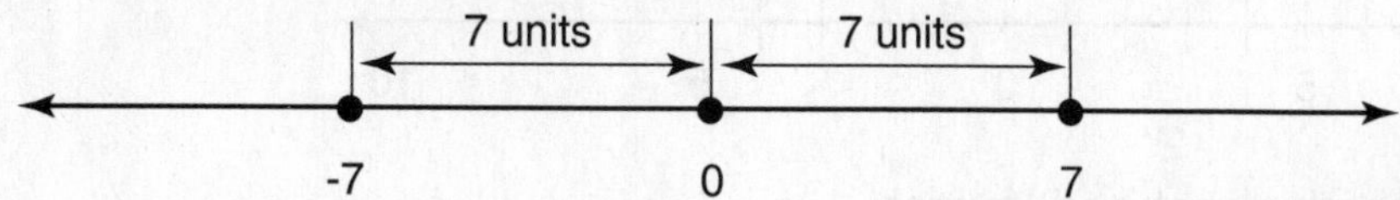

The distance from 0 to 7 is 7 units, so $|7| = 7$.

The distance from 0 to -7 is 7 units, so $|-7| = 7$.

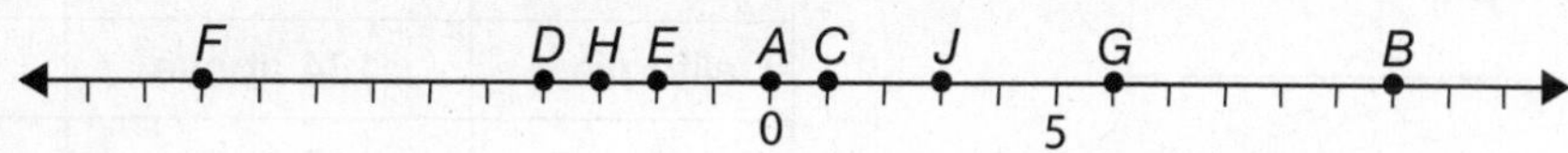

Use the number line above. Write the integer for each point. Then write its opposite and absolute value.

1. *A* ____________ **2.** *B* ____________

3. *C* ____________ **4.** *D* ____________

5. *E* ____________ **6.** *F* ____________

7. *G* ____________ **8.** *H* ____________

9. *J* ____________

10. Number Sense John borrowed $6 from Adam. The next week John borrowed $15 more from Adam. Write an integer that represents John's total debt to Adam. ________

11. Reasoning What is the opposite of the opposite of negative nine? ________

Name ______________________

Understanding Integers

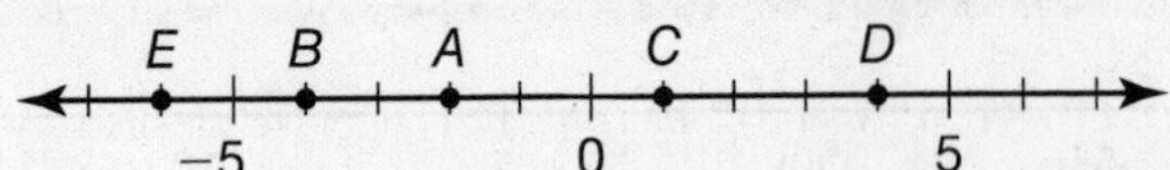

Use the number line. Write the integer for each point. Then give its opposite and absolute value.

1. *A* ____________ **2.** *B* ____________ **3.** *C* ____________

4. *D* ____________ **5.** *E* ____________

6. On the number line, graph the points −8, 3, −4, 2, and −1.

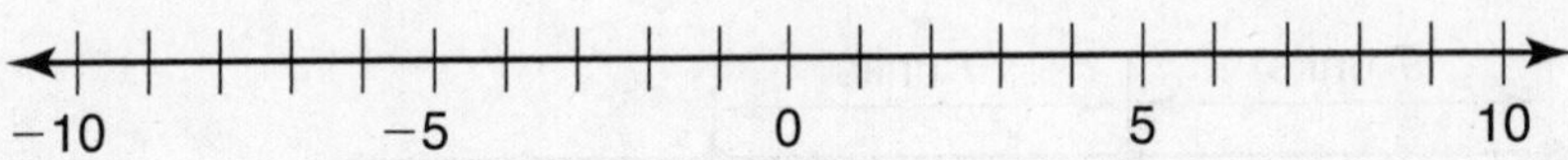

The table gives the highest and lowest temperatures for some states in the United States. Use integers to describe the two temperatures for each state.

Record Temperatures (in degrees, relative to zero)

State	Highest	Lowest
Alabama	112 above	27 below
Delaware	110 above	17 below
California	134 above	45 below
Colorado	118 above	61 below

7. Delaware ____________

8. California ____________

9. Colorado ____________

10. Alabama ____________

11. Which is an integer?

A −0.5

B −5

C 5.5

D $5\frac{4}{5}$

12. Writing to Explain In your own words, tell what is meant by "the absolute value of an integer."

____

____

____

Name ______________________________

Comparing and Ordering Integers

When comparing two integers on a number line, the integer that is farther to the right is greater. The integer that is farther to the left is less.

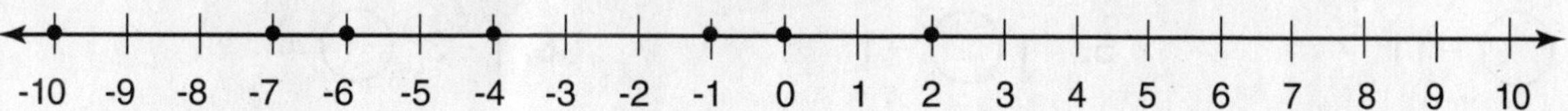

Compare -6 and -10.

Because -6 is farther to the right than -10, it is greater. So, $-6 > -10$.

Compare -1 and 2.

Because 2 is farther to the right than -1, it is greater. So, $2 > -1$.

Order -4, 0, and -7 from least to greatest.

Because -7 is the farthest to the left, it is the least. 0 is farther to the right than -4, so -4 is the next least. So, the numbers in order from least to greatest are -7, -4, and 0.

Use $>$, $<$, or $=$ to compare.

1. -5 ◯ 3 **2.** 15 ◯ -4 **3.** 0 ◯ 27

4. 52 ◯ $|-52|$ **5.** -9 ◯ $|-9|$ **6.** -6 ◯ -7

7. 13 ◯ 12 **8.** -17 ◯ -15 **9.** -8 ◯ -8

Order the numbers from least to greatest.

10. 9, -1, -4, 2 ______________

11. 1, $|-2|$, -8, 6 ______________

12. 15, -7, -12, 0, $|5|$ ______________

13. Manuel dug holes to plant an oak tree, a rosebush, lantana, and prairie grass. The table shows the depths of the holes. You can think of ground level as 0, so the holes closest to ground level are not as deep as the holes farthest from ground level. Which plant hole is closest to ground level? Which is farthest? Compare the depths of their holes.

Plant	Hole (inches)
Lantana	-8
Prairie Grass	-6
Oak Tree	-22
Rosebush	-15

____

14. Reasoning Write 3 integers less than -27. ______________________________

Name ______________________________

Practice
7-2

Comparing and Ordering Integers

Use <, >, or = to compare.

1. 6 ◯ −8 **2.** −12 ◯ −11 **3.** 2 ◯ $|-2|$

4. 12 ◯ −11 **5.** 11 ◯ −1 **6.** $|-3|$ ◯ 4

Order from least to greatest.

7. −6, 4, 7, 0, −9

8. −1, −5, 5 , 7, −8

9. −7, −8, −2, 6, $|-11|$, −11, −9, 4, 5

____

10. Reasoning Can any negative integer be greater than a positive integer? Explain.

____

____

____

Kyle kept track of the number of points he scored each time he played a video game. Sometimes the score is less than zero.

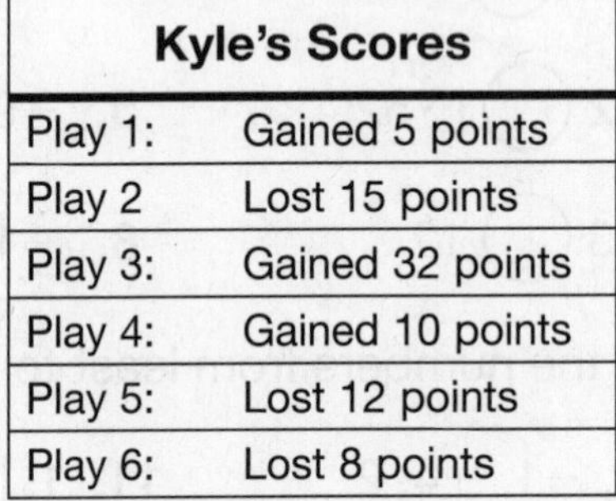

Kyle's Scores	
Play 1:	Gained 5 points
Play 2	Lost 15 points
Play 3:	Gained 32 points
Play 4:	Gained 10 points
Play 5:	Lost 12 points
Play 6:	Lost 8 points

11. Order the negative plays from least to greatest.

____

12. Order the positive plays from greatest to least.

____

13. Which integer is greatest?

A 1 **B** −10 **C** 9 **D** 3

14. Writing to Explain Explain how to find the greatest integer plotted on a number line.

____

____

Name ______________________________

Reteaching
7-3

Absolute Value

The absolute value of a number is its distance from 0 on a number line. You can use a number line to help you compare and order the absolute values of numbers.

Order the values from least to greatest: |−4|, |−1|, |3|.

Plot each number on the number line, and then look at each point's distance from 0.

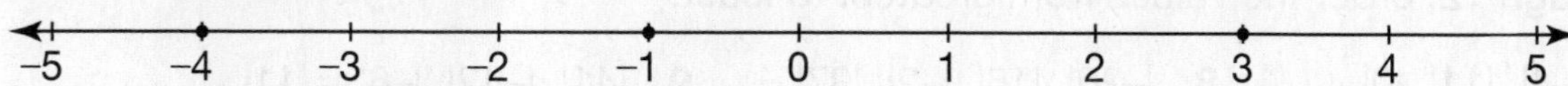

Since −1 is the point closest to 0, |−1| is the least value.

Since 3 is the next closest point to 0, |3| is the next greater value.

Since −4 is the point farthest from 0, |−4| is the greatest value.

The order of the values from least to greatest is |−1|, |3|, |−4|.

For **1** through **6**, use < or > to compare. You can use the number line to help you.

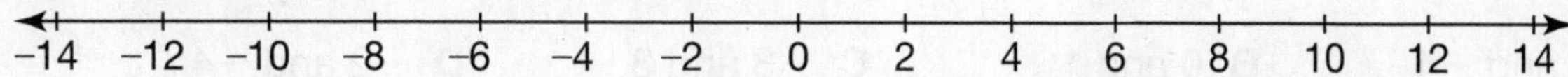

1. |3| ◯ |−4| **2.** |−5| ◯ |0| **3.** |1| ◯ |−2|

4. |13| ◯ |−12| **5.** |−10| ◯ |−9| **6.** |6| ◯ |−14|

For 7 through 12, order the values from least to greatest. You can use the number line to help you.

7. |−4|, |−2|, |11| ____________ **8.** |−9|, |0|, |−2| ____________ **9.** |4|, |−5|, |−7| ____________

10. |−1|, |−8|, |2| ____________ **11.** |−14|, |0|, |−6| ____________ **12.** |8|, |−11|, |−6| ____________

13. Writing to Explain How do you know that |8| and |−8| are the same distance from 0? Do they have the same absolute value? Explain.

____

____

14. Number Sense Name two numbers that are not located the same distance from 0. What are their absolute values?

____

Name ______________________

Absolute Value

For **1** through **6**, use $<$ or $>$ to compare.

1. $|-22|$ ◯ $|-12|$ **2.** $|45|$ ◯ $|-46|$ **3.** $|13|$ ◯ $|-2|$

4. $|48|$ ◯ $|-39|$ **5.** $|-55.5|$ ◯ $|55|$ **6.** $|21\frac{1}{3}|$ ◯ $|-21\frac{1}{2}|$

For 7 through 12, order the values from greatest to least.

7. $|-6|, |-4|, |11|, |0|$ ______ **8.** $|-20|, |16|, |-2|, |37|$ ______ **9.** $|41|, |-42|, |-63|, |11|$ ______

10. $|4|, |-3|, |-18|, |-3.18|$ ______ **11.** $|0|, |-27|, |-32|, |6|$ ______ **12.** $|-\frac{1}{2}|, |-\frac{2}{3}|, |-\frac{1}{10}|, |0|$ ______

13. Which pair of numbers are located the same distance from 0 on the number line?

A 5 and -4 **B** 0 and 1 **C** -3 and 3 **D** -2 and -4

14. A stock's price gained 3% in April and 5% in May, and then lost 4% in June and 1% in July. During which month did the stock's price change the most?

______

15. Max starts on the 20th floor of a building and takes the elevator 4 floors down. Then he takes the elevator up 3 floors, and then down another 5 floors. Write the absolute value of the greatest change in floors that Max made.

______

16. Writing to Explain The table shows the daily change in high temperature for several days. Explain how you can order the days from least to greatest amount of temperature change.

Day	Temperature Change
Monday	+3°F
Tuesday	−4°F
Wednesday	−1°F
Thursday	+2°F

______

______

______

Name ______________________

Rational Numbers on a Number Line

When comparing and ordering rational numbers on a number line, it helps to change all of the numbers to fractions and mixed numbers or to decimals.

How do you compare rational numbers?

Compare -1.33 and $-\frac{9}{5}$.

Convert $-\frac{9}{5}$ to a decimal so that both numbers are in the same form.
$-\frac{9}{5} = -9 \div 5 = -1.8$

Place the numbers on a number line.

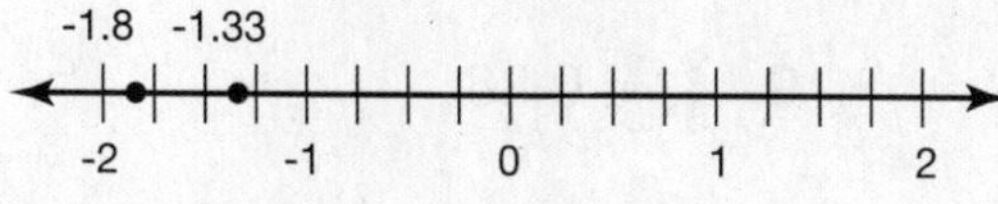

-1.33 is to the right of -1.8.

So, $-1.33 > -9/5$.

How do you order rational numbers?

Order 0.3, $-\frac{5}{6}$ and $\frac{5}{8}$ from least to greatest.

Convert 0.3 to a fraction so that all of the numbers are in the same form.

$0.3 = \frac{3}{10}$

Place the numbers on a number line.

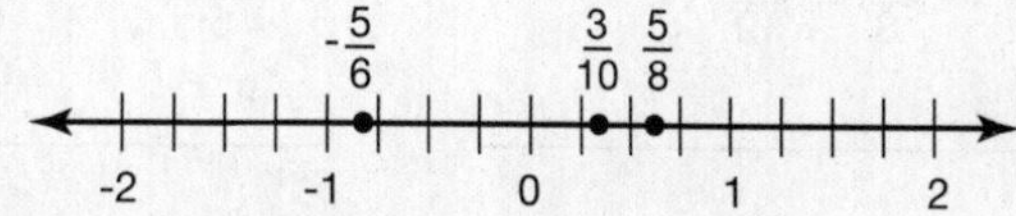

$\frac{3}{10}$ is to the right of $-\frac{5}{6}$ and $\frac{5}{8}$ is to the right of 0.3.

So, the numbers in order from least to greatest are $-\frac{5}{6}$, 0.3, $\frac{5}{8}$.

Write < or > in the circle.

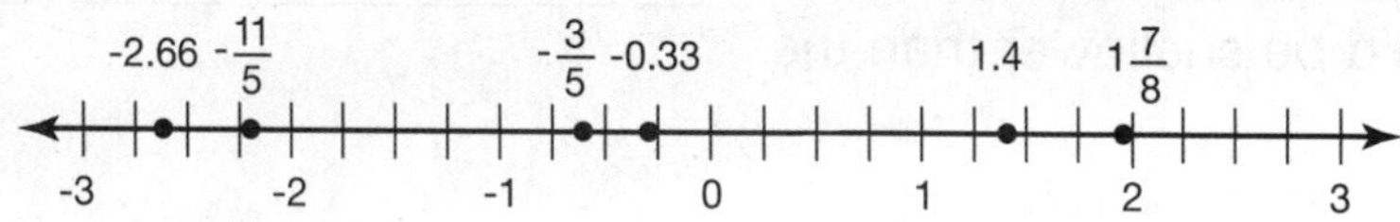

1. $-\frac{3}{5}$ ◯ -0.33
2. $1\frac{7}{8}$ ◯ 1.4
3. -2.66 ◯ $-\frac{11}{5}$
4. $-2\frac{1}{3}$ ◯ -2.8
5. -1.1 ◯ $-1\frac{4}{5}$
6. 1.15 ◯ $\frac{11}{8}$

Write the numbers in order from least to greatest.

7. 0.15, $-\frac{2}{3}$, -0.1 ______________
8. $-\frac{11}{5}$, -2.5, $-2\frac{2}{3}$ ______________
9. 1.6, $\frac{15}{8}$, $1\frac{2}{5}$ ______________

10. **Reasoning** The rainfall in a city was $-\frac{3}{8}$ in. below average in June and -0.45 in. below average in July. Which month is closest to the average?

____

Name ______________________

Practice
7-4

Rational Numbers on a Number Line

Write < or > in the circle.

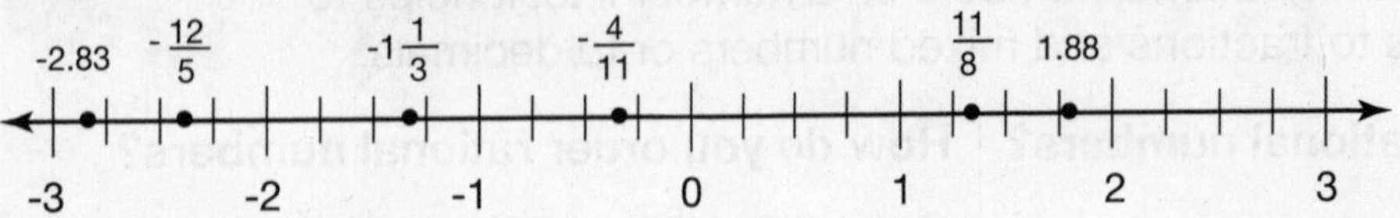

1. $-1\frac{1}{3}$ ◯ $-\frac{12}{5}$ **2.** $\frac{11}{8}$ ◯ 1.88 **3.** -2.83 ◯ $-1\frac{1}{3}$

4. $-\frac{4}{11}$ ◯ -0.19 **5.** 1.6 ◯ $\frac{4}{3}$ **6.** $-\frac{1}{6}$ ◯ -0.1

Write the numbers in order from least to greatest.

7. 0.66, $-\frac{1}{3}$, $-\frac{5}{12}$ **8.** $-\frac{12}{5}$, -1.35, $-1\frac{7}{9}$ **9.** $\frac{3}{8}$, $\frac{2}{5}$, 0.38

______________ ______________ ______________

Use the table for **10** and **11**.

10. A scientist is testing lake water at different depths. Order the samples of lake water from greatest depth to least depth.

____

Day	Feet Below the Lake Surface
Monday	$-1\frac{3}{8}$
Tuesday	-0.4
Wednesday	-1.55
Thursday	$-\frac{9}{16}$

11. Number Sense At what depth could the scientist take a new sample that would be shallower than the shallowest sample?

____

12. Which rational number is least?

A 0.66

B $-\frac{4}{5}$

C $-\frac{6}{7}$

D -0.6

13. Writing to Explain Lauren says that -3.5 is greater than $-3\frac{1}{3}$. Do you agree? Explain.

____

Name ________________________________

Comparing and Ordering Rational Numbers

When ordering rational numbers on a number line, the number that is farther to the right is greatest. The number farthest to the left is least.

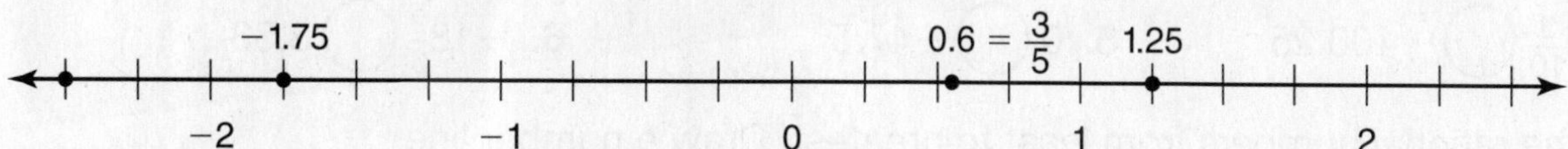

Order $\frac{3}{5}$, 1.25, and −1.75 from least to greatest.

One Way

Use number sense and the number line to order the rational numbers.

- −1.75 is negative, so it is farthest to the left.
- $\frac{3}{5}$ is between 0 and 1.
- 1.25 is greater than 1.

Another Way

Convert rational numbers to a common form to order them.

- Use division to convert $\frac{3}{5}$ to a decimal. $\frac{3}{5} = 0.6$
- −1.75 is to the left of 0.6.
- 0.6 is to the left of 1.25.

Place these numbers on the number line.
Write the order: −1.75, 0.6, 1.25.

Use >, <, or = to compare.

1. $-4.875 \bigcirc 2\frac{1}{3}$ **2.** $10\frac{3}{4} \bigcirc -30.5$ **3.** $-6\frac{1}{2} \bigcirc -6.5$

Order the rational numbers from greatest to least.

4. 7.25, −8.9, 0 ____________

5. $12\frac{1}{2}$, −22.1, 11.9 ____________

6. $-\frac{3}{2}$, $-\frac{3}{4}$, 0.375 ____________

Order the rational numbers from least to greatest.

7. 0.56, $-\frac{5}{6}$, $\frac{6}{5}$ ____________

8. 15.5, $-15\frac{1}{2}$, $-\frac{15}{2}$ ____________

9. 0, 1.1, $-27\frac{9}{10}$ ____________

10. Leslie, Anthony, and Pam are playing a game with rational numbers. The chart shows the number they add to their score for each roll of a number cube. Order the points they could get from a roll of a number cube from greatest to least.

Roll	Points
1 or 2	$-1\frac{5}{6}$
3	2.7
4	−1.56
5 or 6	$2\frac{3}{4}$

____

Name ____________________

Practice 7-5

Comparing and Ordering Rational Numbers

Use <, >, or = to compare.

1. $6\frac{5}{6}$ ◯ -9.9

2. $-1\frac{2}{5}$ ◯ -1.25

3. -17.5 ◯ $-17\frac{1}{2}$

4. $10\frac{3}{10}$ ◯ -100.25

5. 0 ◯ -47.5

6. $-18\frac{2}{3}$ ◯ 3.33

Order the rational numbers from least to greatest. Draw a number line to help you.

7. $7\frac{1}{4}$, 0, -6.25, 7.14 ____________________

8. 13.35, $-\frac{3}{2}$, $13\frac{3}{5}$, -1.3 ____________________

Order the rational numbers from greatest to least. Draw a number line to help you, if necessary.

9. $4\frac{7}{10}$, -8.875, 4.75, $-8\frac{9}{10}$ ____________________

10. -2.4, $\frac{9}{8}$, $-2\frac{3}{8}$, 1.9 ____________________

11. Reasoning Omar says that -9.5 is greater than 1.75 because 9.5 is greater than 1.75. Do you agree with him? Explain.

____

____

____

12. Two scientists compared measurements they took during different experiments. The first scientist had 0.375, -1.5, and 1.4 written down. The second scientist wrote down $\frac{3}{4}$, $-1\frac{5}{8}$, and $1\frac{3}{5}$. Order their measures from least to greatest.

____

13. Which rational number is the greatest?

A $20\frac{3}{8}$ **B** -25.95 **C** 20.25 **D** 20.4

14. Writing to Explain Explain how to find the least rational number plotted on a number line.

____

____

Name ______________________________

Problem Solving: Use Reasoning

After he bought a meal for $7.72 and a new DVD for $22.95, Eric had $13.84 in his pocket. How much money did he start with?

You can solve the problem by using reasoning.

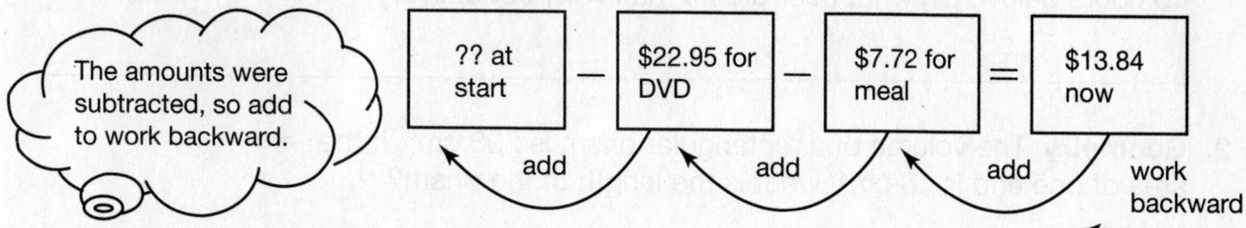

$13.84 + $7.72 + $22.95 = $44.51
Eric started with $44.51.

1. Elana spent 45 minutes at the library, half an hour at the grocery store, 20 minutes visiting a friend, and arrived home at 4:10 P.M. What time did she leave home?

____

2. The football team gained 13 yards, lost 5 yards, gained 8 yards, and gained another 11 yards to end on their 47-yard line. At what yard line did they start?

____

3. Scott has $82.50 in his checking account after he wrote checks to pay bills for $37.96, $52.00, $12.26, and $97.36. How much was in his checking account before he paid his bills?

____

4. Vince helped the Pep Club make sandwiches to raise money. He put two sandwiches in each of 30 bags and 5 sandwiches in 26 family bags, and he has 17 sandwiches left over. How many sandwiches did they make to start with?

____

5. Kimo divided a number by 3, subtracted 6, multiplied by 3.6 and added 12 to get 282. What number did he start with?

____

Name ______________________

Practice
7-6

Problem Solving: Use Reasoning

1. The delivery person stopped on the 14th floor to talk to a friend. Before stopping, he had just made a delivery 4 floors above. Before that he made a delivery 6 floors below. Before that he had made a delivery 9 floors above. Before that he had made a delivery 15 floors below. On what floor did he make his first delivery?

____

2. **Geometry** The volume of a rectangular prism is 208 cm^3. If the area of one end is 16 cm^2, what is the length of the prism?

____

3. On one day, a store sold 16 boxes of rice, restocked the shelf with 22 boxes, sold 27 boxes, restocked with 30 boxes, and sold 15 boxes. There are now 21 boxes of rice on the shelf. How many boxes were on the shelf at the start of the day?

____

4. At the end of the day, Brooke had $138.75 in her checking account. She had made a deposit of $115.07 and written checks totaling $176.94. How much did she have in her checking account at the beginning of the day?

A –$76.88

B $76.88

C $200.62

D $430.76

5. **Writing to Explain** The football team gained 7 yards, gained 4 yards, lost 5 yards, gained 21 yards, lost 2 yards, and gained 4 yards to their 43 yard line. Explain how you solved this problem. Then find the yard line where the team began.

____

____

____

Name ___________________________

Reteaching **8-1**

Integers on the Coordinate Plane

Parts of a coordinate plane:

x-axis: a horizontal number line
y-axis: a vertical number line
origin: the place where the two number lines meet
quadrants: the four sections created by the two number lines

A point in a coordinate plane is represented by an **ordered pair.** (4, −3)

x-coordinate y-coordinate

To locate point (4, −3), start at the origin.
Move to 4 on the x-axis. Then move to −3 on the y-axis.

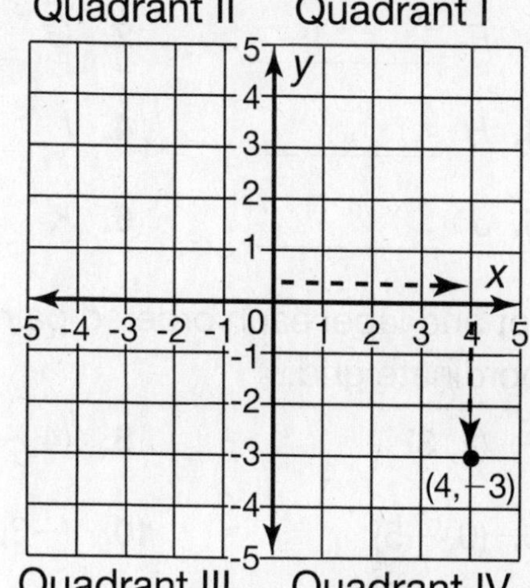

Graph and label these points on the coordinate plane.

1. (4, 1) **2.** (−3, 3)

3. (2, 0) **4.** (4, −2)

5. (−2, 4) **6.** (−3, −4)

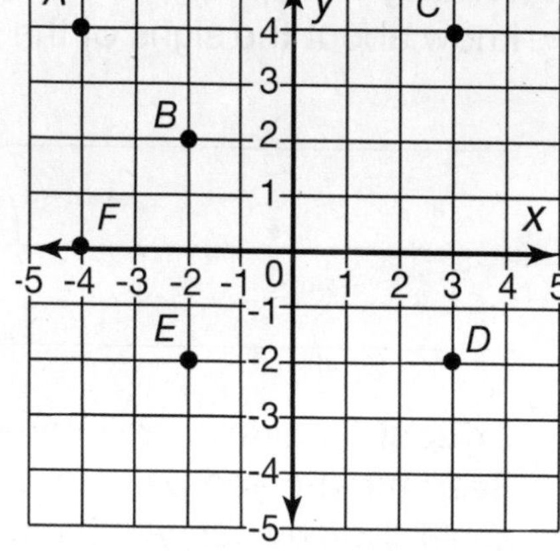

Write the ordered pair for each point.

7. *A* __________ **8.** *B* __________

9. *D* __________ **10.** *E* __________

11. Writing to Explain How would you plot the point (−8, 10) on the coordinate plane?

____

____

____

12. Reasoning In what quadrant will a point with a negative x-coordinate and a positive y-coordinate (negative number, positive number) be located?

____

Name ______________________

Integers on the Coordinate Plane

Write the ordered pair for each point.

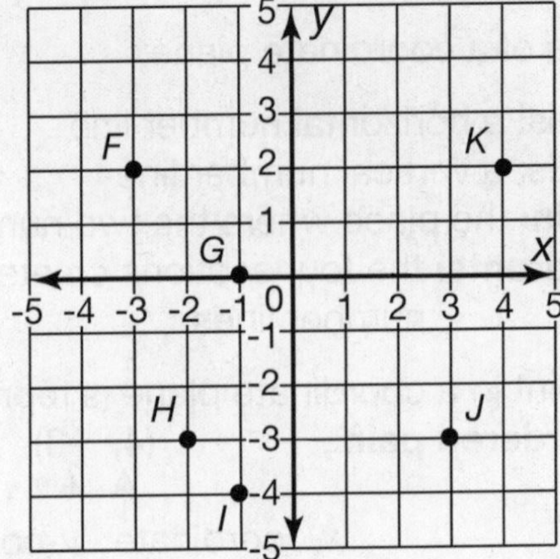

1. *F* ______ **2.** *G* ______

3. *H* ______ **4.** *I* ______

5. *J* ______ **6.** *K* ______

Plot and label each ordered pair on the coordinate grid.

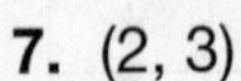

7. (2, 3) **8.** (4, −4)

9. (0, −5) **10.** (−3, −3)

11. (−4, 4) **12.** (−5, 0)

13. Writing to Explain A point is located in Quadrant IV. What do you know about the signs of the coordinates for the point? Explain.

____

____

____

14. Critical Thinking Draw three lines that are parallel to the *x*-axis. Read the ordered pairs for points on each line. What generalization can you make about the ordered pairs for lines parallel to the *x*-axis?

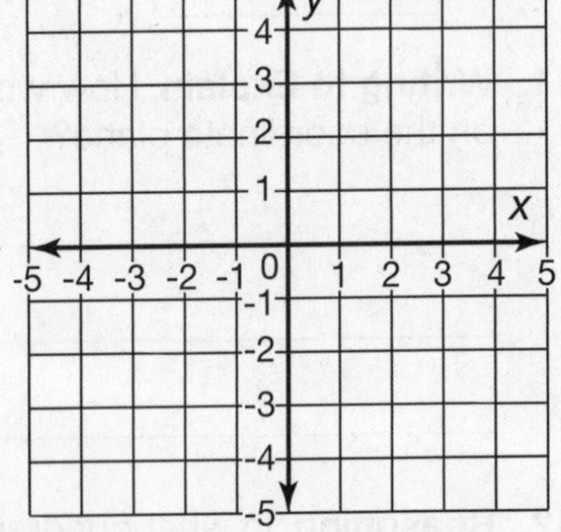

____

____

15. Geometry Which ordered pair is located in Quadrant III?

A (−1, −1)

B (−4, 0)

C (−2, 2)

D (0, 5)

Name ______________________________

Rational Numbers on the Coordinate Plane

The coordinate grid has an ***x*-axis**, a ***y*-axis**, an **origin (0, 0)**, and four **quadrants**.

Ordered pairs of rational numbers can be plotted just like ordered pairs of integers. Plot $(-2, -1\frac{1}{2})$ on the grid.

To locate point $(-2, -1\frac{1}{2})$, start at the origin. Move 2 units to the left on the *x*-axis. Then move down $1\frac{1}{2}$ units on the *y*-axis.

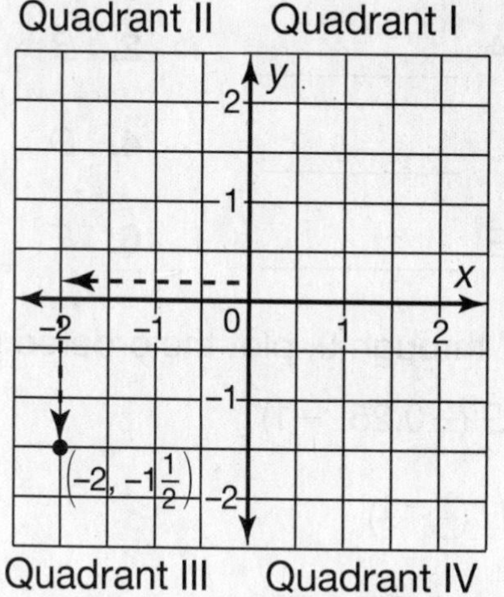

Graph and label these points on the coordinate plane.

1. $(-1.5, 1.5)$
2. $(0, -1.5)$
3. $(1\frac{1}{2}, -1\frac{1}{2})$
4. $(-2\frac{1}{2}, 0)$
5. $(1.5, 2)$
6. $(-1\frac{1}{2}, -2\frac{1}{2})$

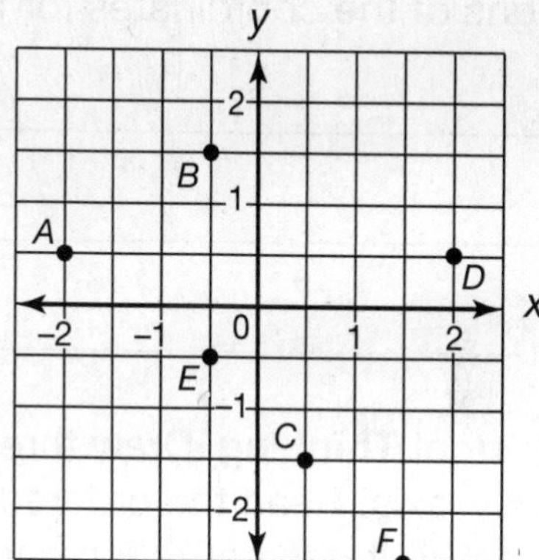

Write the ordered pair for each point, using fractions or decimals.

7. *A* ______________________________
8. *B* ______________________________
9. *C* ______________________________
10. *D* ______________________________
11. *E* ______________________________
12. *F* ______________________________

13. **Reasoning** In which quadrant will both the *x*-coordinate and *y*-coordinate of a point be negative?

____

Name ____________________

Practice
8-2

Rational Numbers on the Coordinate Plane

Write the ordered pair for each point.

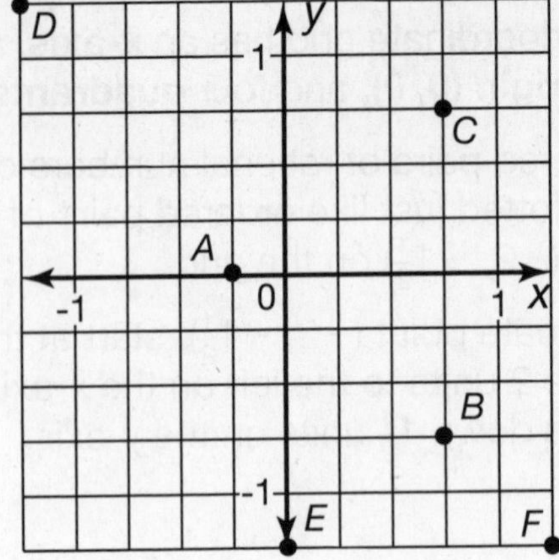

1. *A* ________ **2.** *B* ________

3. *C* ________ **4.** *D* ________

5. *E* ________ **6.** *F* ________

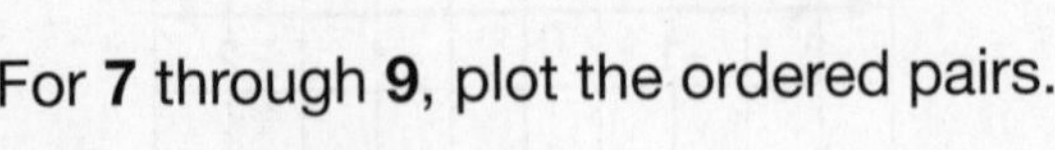

For **7** through **9**, plot the ordered pairs.

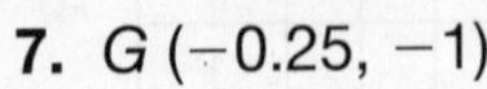

7. *G* (−0.25, −1)

8. *H* $\left(\frac{3}{4}, 1\frac{1}{4}\right)$

9. *I* (−0.75, 0.75)

10. Writing to Explain A point is located in Quadrant II. What do you know about the signs of the coordinates for the point? Explain.

____

____

____

11. Critical Thinking Draw three lines that are parallel to the *y*-axis. Read the ordered pairs for points on each line. What generalization can you make about the ordered pairs for lines parallel to the *y*-axis?

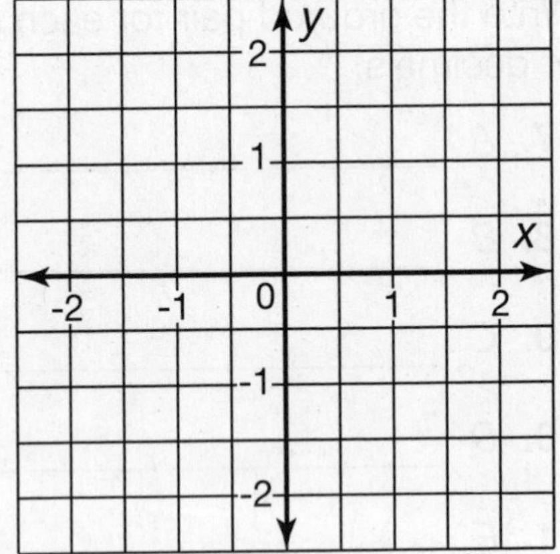

____

____

____

12. Reason In which quadrants do the *x*-coordinate and the *y*-coordinate of a point have the same sign? Explain.

____

____

____

Name ____________________

Distance on the Coordinate Plane

Find the distance between (−3, 5) and (4, 5).

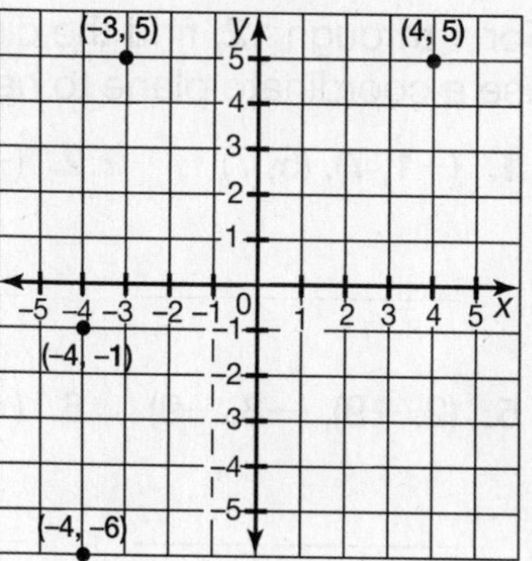

Use absolute value. Look at the *x*-coordinates. Since the points are in different quadrants, add the absolute values.

$|-3| + |4| = 3 + 4 = 7.$

The points are 7 units apart.

Find the distance between (−4, −1) and (−4, −6).

Use absolute value. Look at the *y*-coordinates. Since the points are in the same quadrant, subtract the absolute values.

$|-6| + |-1| = 6 - 1 = 5.$

The points are 5 units apart.

Use the coordinate plane for **1** through **3.**

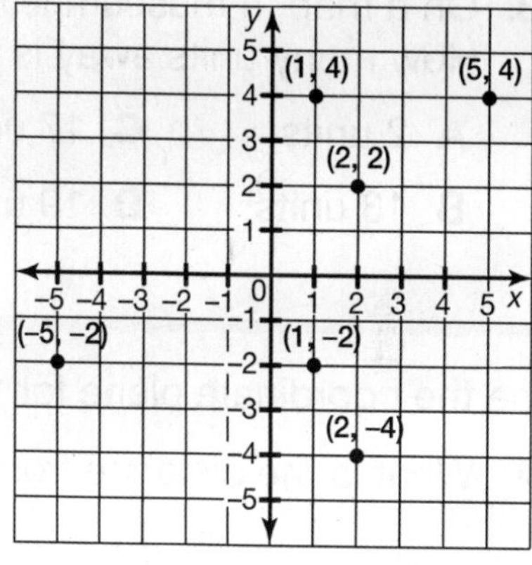

1. What is the distance between (1, 4) and (5, 4)?

A 1 unit

B 3 units

C 4 units

D 6 units

2. Find the distance between (2, 2) and (2, −4).

____

____

3. Writing to Explain How can you find the distance between (−5, −2) and (1, −2)?

____

____

____

Name ______________________

Practice
8-3

Distance on the Coordinate Plane

For **1** through **12,** find the distance between the ordered pairs. You can use a coordinate plane to help.

1. (−1, 7), (5, 7) **2.** (−3, −9), (−3, −1) **3.** (−2, −6), (−2, 0) **4.** (12, −2), (12, 12)

5. (2, −9), (−3, −9) **6.** (−1, 5), (5, 5) **7.** (0, −1), (0, 16) **8.** (15, −9), (15, −6)

9. (−8, −4), (3, −4) **10.** (−7, −9), (−7, 8) **11.** (13, −3), (−3, −3) **12.** (−16, −9), (−16, −11)

13. On a map, a museum is located at (15, 17). A library is located at (15, −2). How many units away is the museum from the library?

A 2 units **C** 17 units

B 13 units **D** 19 units

Use the coordinate plane for **14** and **15.**

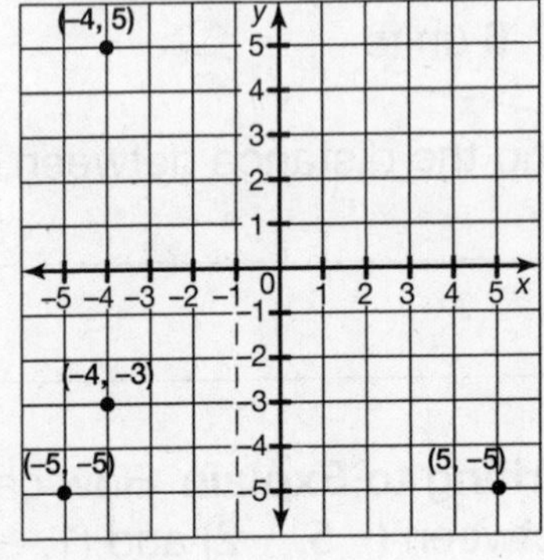

14. What is the distance from (5, −5) to (−5, −5)?

15. Kendra walks from a park located at (−4, −3) to her house at (−4, 5). How far did she walk?

16. Reason On a map, Jorge is standing at (11, −11). His friend Leslie is standing at (1, −11). If Jorge walks 10 units to the right, will he be standing with Leslie? Explain.

Name ____________________

Reteaching 8-4

Polygons on the Coordinate Plane

How can you find the perimeter of a polygon on the coordinate plane?

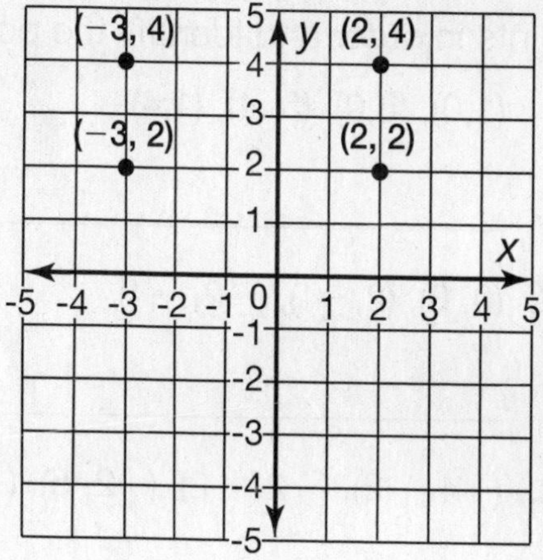

Remember, perimeter is the distance around a figure. So, find the distance between each pair of points by counting or using absolute value.

Top side: (−3, 4) to (2, 4): 5 units

Right side: (2, 4) to (2, 2): 2 units

Bottom side: (2, 2) to (−3, 2): 5 units

Left side: (−3, 2) to (−3, 4): 2 units

$5 + 2 + 5 + 2 = 14$.

So, the perimeter is 14 units.

In **1** through **4**, list the coordinates of each point.

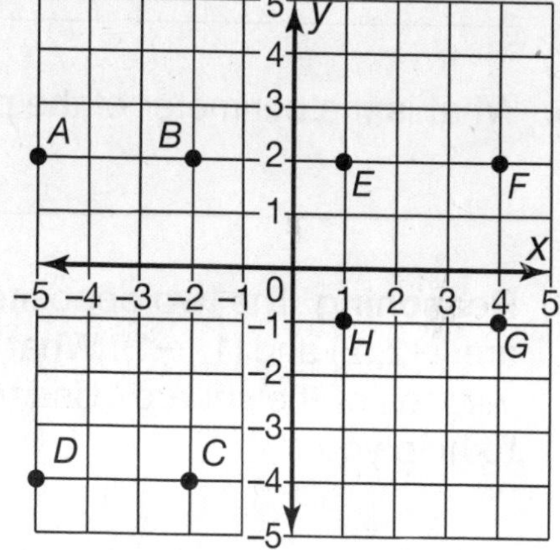

1. *A* ____________ **2.** *B* ____________

3. *C* ____________ **4.** *D* ____________

5. Find the length of each side of the polygon. What is the perimeter of rectangle *ABCD*?

____

In **6** through **10**, list the coordinates of each point.

6. *E* ____________ **7.** *F* ____________

8. *G* ____________ **9.** *H* ____________

10. Find the length of each side. What is the perimeter of polygon *EFGH*?

____

11. Geometry What type of quadrilateral is polygon *EFGH*? Be as specific as possible.

____

Name ______________________________

Practice
8-4

Polygons on the Coordinate Plane

For **1** through **3**, graph the ordered pairs. Connect the points in order and identify the polygon you drew.

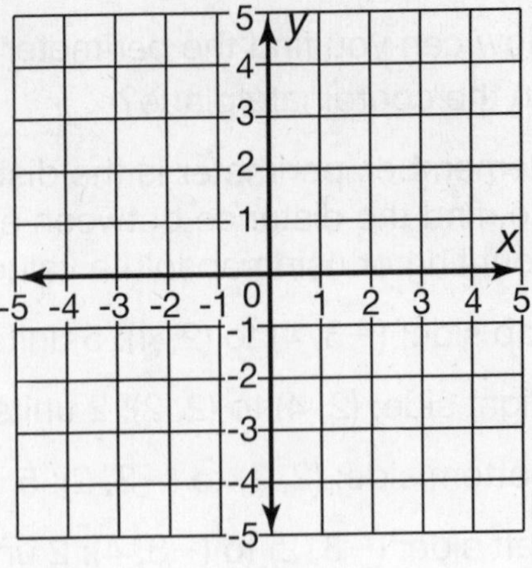

1. (1,0), (5,0), (5, 4), (1,4)

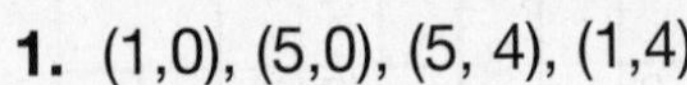

____

2. (0, 0), (2, −4), (−2, −4)

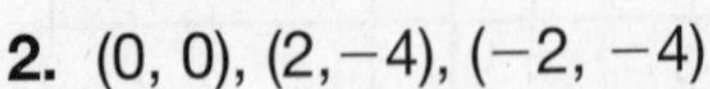

____

3. (−4, −2), (−2, −2), (−2, 5), (−4, 5)

____

4. What is the perimeter of the polygon you drew in **1** above?

____

5. What is the perimeter of the polygon you drew in **3** above?

____

6. Reasoning The two opposite vertices of a square are (−2, 2) and (1, −1). What are the other two vertices of the square? Use the coordinate grid to help you.

____

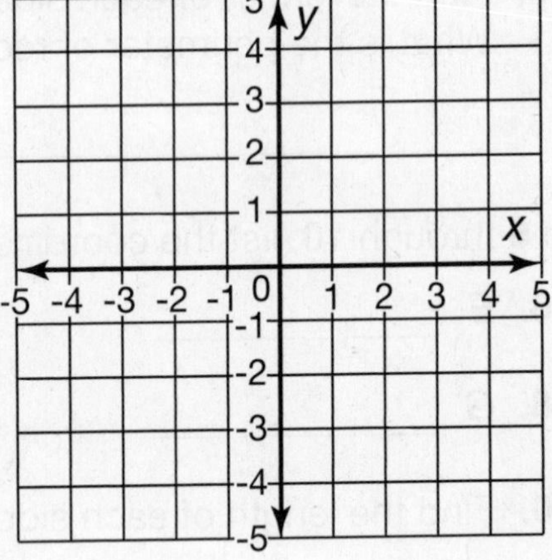

7. Geometry Which set of ordered pairs can be connected in order to form a right triangle?

A (−1, 3), (−1, −1), (2, −1)

B (−4, 0), (0, 1), (1, −2)

C (2, 2), (2, −2), (−2, −2), (−2, 2)

D (0, 5), (−3, 3), (3, −3)

Name ___________________________

Reteaching
8-5

Graphing Equations

How to graph equations:

Graph the equation $y = x - 3$.

First make a T-table like the one at the right.

Use at least 3 values for x.

x	y
3	0
4	1
5	2

Graph each ordered pair onto the coordinate plane, then draw a line connecting the points. Every point on this line meets the condition that $y = x - 3$.

Because the graph of this equation is a straight line, it is called a linear equation.

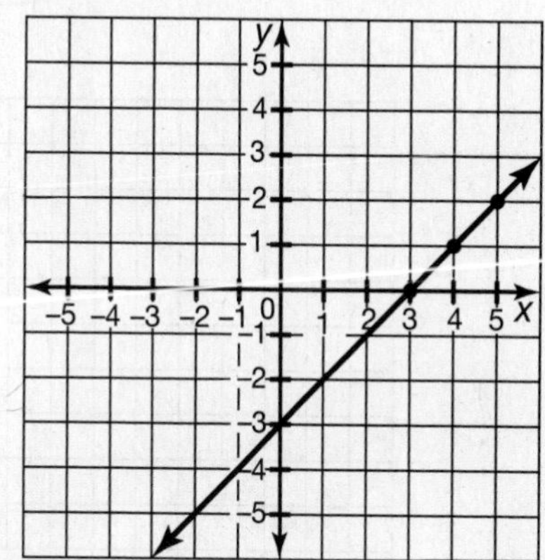

Complete each T-table. Then graph each equation.

1. $y = x + 1$

x	y
1	
2	
3	

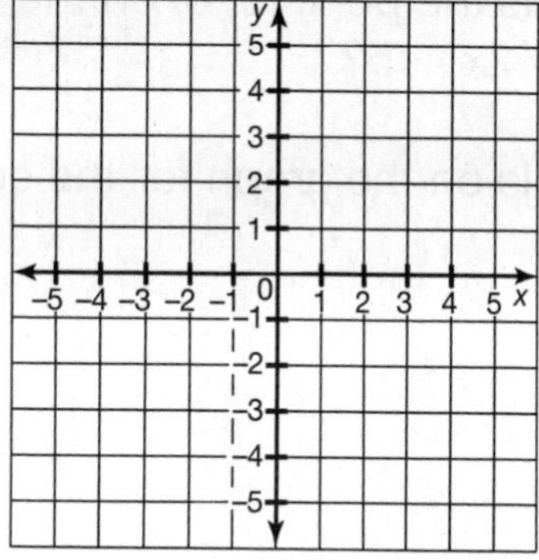

2. $y = 3 - x$

x	y
0	
2	
3	

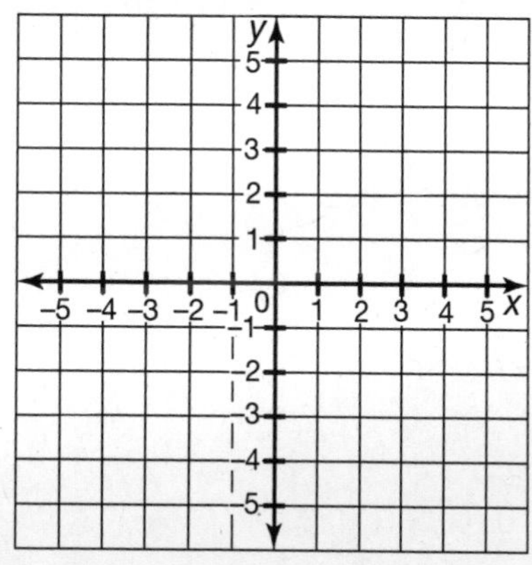

Name ______________________________

Practice
8-5

Graphing Equations

For **1** and **2,** make a T-table. Then graph each equation.

1. $y = x - 3$

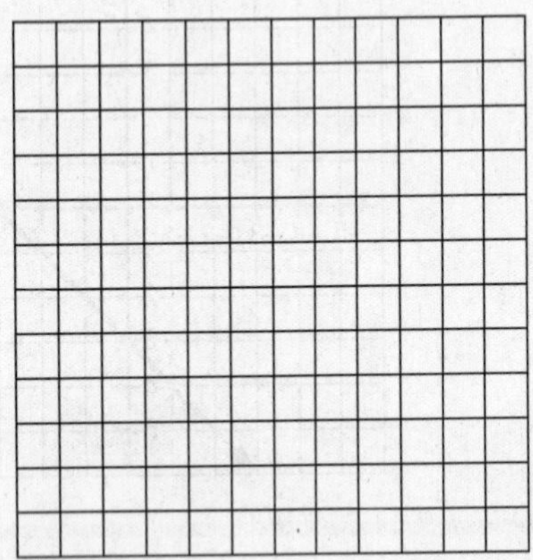

2. $y = 2x$

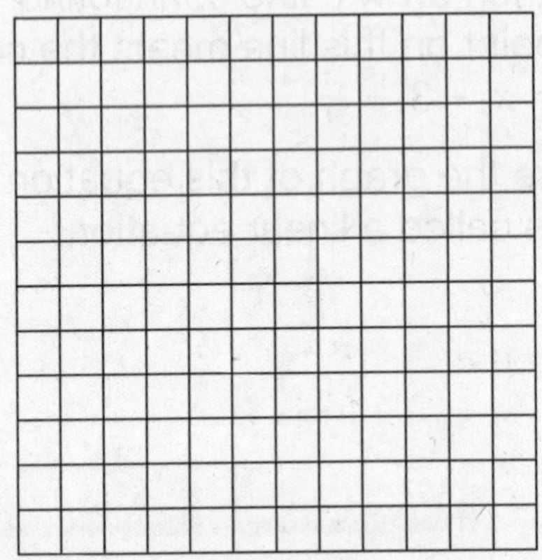

3. Reasoning Is the point (5, 6) on the graph for the equation $y = 2x + 5$? ______________

4. Which point is on the graph for the equation $y = x + 14$?

A (2, 17)

B (5, 20)

C (10, 24)

D (7, 23)

5. Writing to Explain Explain how making a T-table helps you graph an equation.

____

____

Name ______________________________

More Graphing Equations

Reteaching **8-6**

Use the same steps to graph an equation with more than one operation as you used to graph an equation with only one operation.
Graph $y = 2x - 4$.

Step 1: Make a T-table. Use at least three number pairs in the table.

x	y
2	0
3	2
4	4

Ordered Pairs
→ (2, 0)
→ (3, 2)
→ (4, 4)

Step 2: Graph each ordered pair on a coordinate plane. Connect the points.

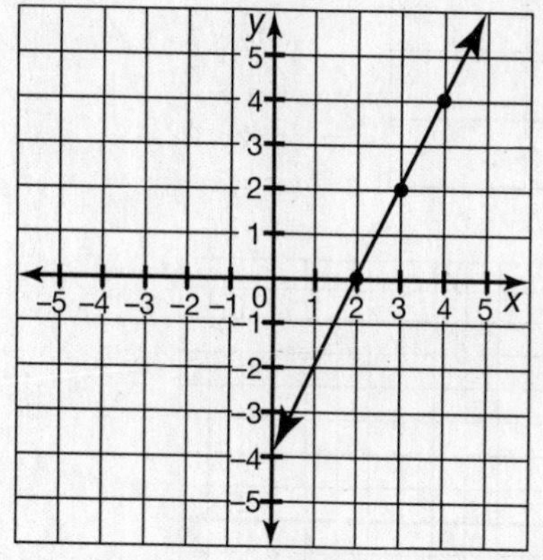

1. Complete the T-table and graph the equation.
$y = 4x - 8$

x	y	Ordered Pairs
2		
3		
4		

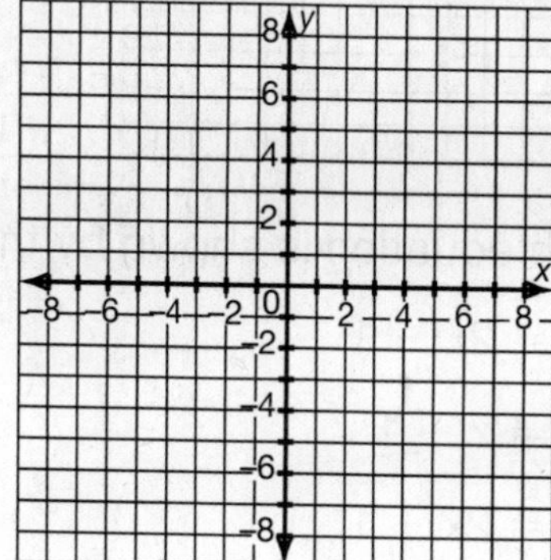

Graph $y = 6 - 2x$ at the right. Use it to answer **2** through **4**.

2. At what point does the equation $y = 6 - 2x$ cross the y-axis? __________

3. If $x = 2$, what is the value of y? __________

4. Writing to Explain Plot point (0, 4) on the grid. Is (0, 4) a solution to $y = 6 - 2x$? Explain.

____

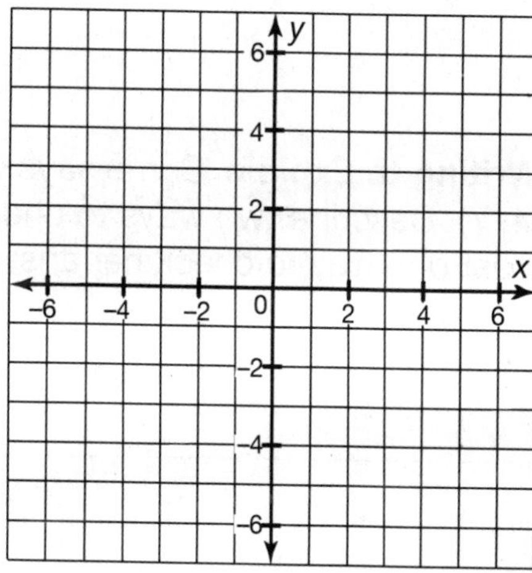

Name ____________________

More Graphing Equations

For **1** and **2,** make a T-table and graph each equation.

1. $y = 3x - 5$

x	*y*

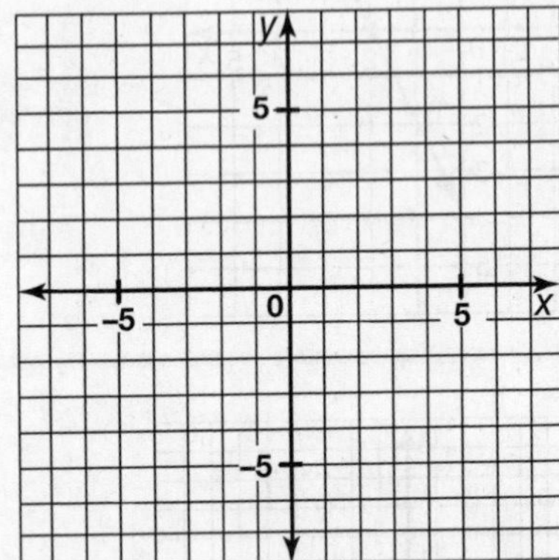

2. $y = 2x + 2$

x	*y*

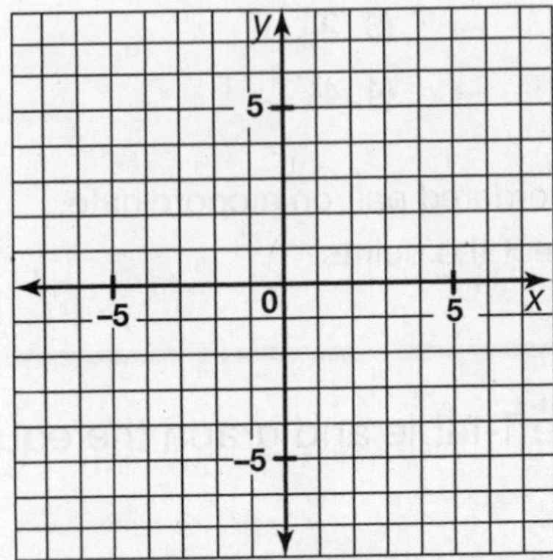

3. Which equation is shown by the graph?

A $y = 2x - 1$

B $y = x - 1$

C $y = 2x + 1$

D $y = x + 1$

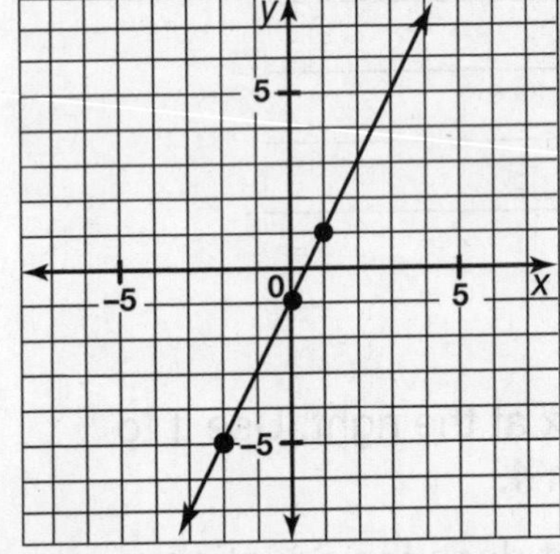

4. Writing to Explain Carrie says that one solution to $y = 3x - 5$ is (4, 7). Describe two ways to check if her statement is true. Use at least one way to check her answer.

____

____

Name ______________________

Reteaching
8-7

Problem Solving: Multiple-Step Problems

Some word problems have hidden questions that must be answered before you can solve the problem.

A paved trail is 8 miles long. Rita runs $\frac{3}{8}$ of the length of the trail and walks the rest of the way. How many miles of the trail does Rita walk?

What do you know? Rita runs $\frac{3}{8}$ of an 8-mile trail.

What are you asked to find? How many miles of the trail that Rita walks.

How can you find the distance that Rita walks? Subtract the distance Rita ran from the length of the trail.

What is the hidden question? The hidden question will help you find data you need to solve the problem. How many miles did Rita run? To answer, find $\frac{3}{8} \times 8 = 3$.

Use the data to solve: $8 - 3 = 5$, so Rita walked 5 of the 8 miles.

Write and answer the hidden question(s) in each problem. Then solve the problem.

1. April surfed for $\frac{1}{3}$ of the 6 hours she was at the beach. She spent the rest of the time building a sand castle. How many hours did she spend building the castle?

Hidden question: ______________________

Solution: ______________________

2. Bill put gasoline in 2 of his 5-gallon cans and 4 of his 2-gallon cans. He filled all the cans to the exact capacity. How many gallons of gasoline did he buy?

Hidden question 1: ______________________

Hidden question 2: ______________________

Solution: ______________________

3. It costs Le Stor \$20 to buy a shirt. The store sells the shirt for $2\frac{1}{2}$ times its cost. What is the profit for 100 of these shirts? Hint: Profit equals sales minus cost.

Hidden question 1: ______________________

Hidden question 2: ______________________

Solution: ______________________

Name ____________________

Practice
8-7

Problem Solving: Multiple-Step Problems

Write and answer the hidden question(s) in each problem. Then solve the problem.

1. Tiwa spent $1\frac{1}{2}$ hours setting up her computer. It took her 3 times as long to install the software. How long did it take Tiwa to set up the computer and install software?

Hidden question(s): ____________________

Solution: ____________________

2. Lon bought 40 ounces of sliced ham. He used $\frac{3}{4}$ of the ham to make sandwiches for his friends and $\frac{1}{5}$ of the ham in an omelet. How many ounces of ham were left?

Hidden question(s): ____________________

Solution: ____________________

3. Lionel cut off $\frac{1}{6}$ of a 48-inch piece of rope. Marsha cut off $\frac{1}{4}$ of a 36-inch piece of rope. They compared their cut pieces. Whose piece is longer? How much longer?

Hidden question(s): ____________________

Solution: ____________________

4. Melanie bought 3 CDs. The country music CD cost \$15. The rock music CD cost $\frac{2}{3}$ as much as the country music CD. The platinum edition CD cost twice as much as the rock CD. What was the cost of the three CDs?

Hidden question(s): ____________________

Solution: ____________________

5. Writing to Explain Choose one of the problems above. Explain how you determined the hidden question and why it was necessary to answer that question in order to solve the problem.

____

____

____

Name ______________________________

Understanding Ratios

A ratio is a pair of numbers that compares two quantities.

Count to find the ratio of squares to circles.

↓ ↓
4 to 3

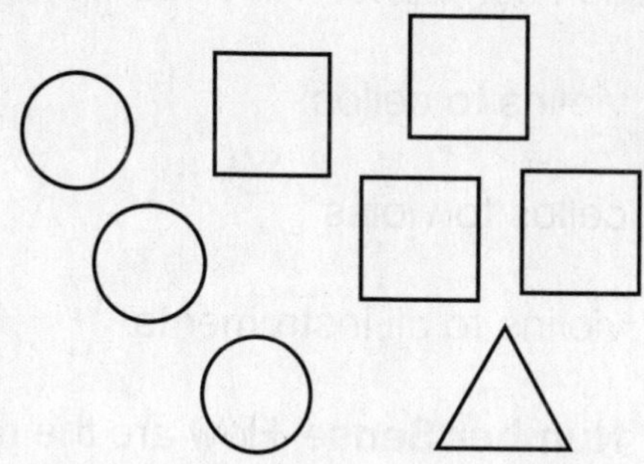

The ratio 4 to 3 can also be written as 4:3 or $\frac{4}{3}$.

The order of the numbers in a ratio is important.
4:3 is the ratio of squares to circles.
3:4 is the ratio of circles to squares.

Use the picture above for exercises **1** through **6.** Write a ratio for each comparison in three ways.

1. The number of triangles to the total number of shapes

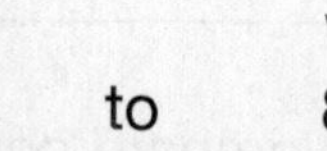

1 to 8 ______________

2. The number of squares to the number of triangles ______________

3. The number of triangles to the number of squares ______________

4. The number of triangles to the number of circles ______________

5. The number of circles to the total number of shapes ______________

6. The total number of shapes to the number of squares ______________

7. There are 14 boys and 16 girls in Mr. Allen's class. What is the ratio of girls to the total number of students in the class? Write the ratio 3 ways.

____

8. **Writing to Explain** At a cat and dog hospital, 9 of the patients were cats, 17 were dogs. Use this fact to write two ratios. Explain what each ratio means.

____

Name ______________________

Practice
9-1

Understanding Ratios

A string quartet consists of 2 violins, 1 viola, and 1 cello. Write a ratio for each comparison in three ways.

1. violins to cellos ______________

2. cellos to violas ______________

3. violins to all instruments ______________

4. **Number Sense** How are the ratios in Exercises 1 and 2 different from the ratio in Exercise 3?

____

____

____

Midland Orchards grows a large variety of apples. The orchard contains 12 rows of Granny Smith trees, 10 rows of Fuji trees, 15 rows of Gala trees, 2 rows of Golden Delicious trees, and 2 rows of Jonathan trees. Write each ratio in three ways.

5. rows of Granny Smith trees to rows of Golden Delicious trees ______________

6. rows of Fuji trees to the total number of rows of trees ______________

7. A grade school has 45 students who walk to school and 150 students who ride the bus. The other 50 students are driven to school. Which shows the ratio of students who walk to school to the total number of students in the school?

A 45:50 **B** 45:195 **C** 45:150 **D** 45:245

8. **Writing to Explain** Steve said it does not matter which term is first and which term is second in a ratio, since ratios are different than fractions. Is he correct? Explain why or why not.

____

____

____

Name ____________________

Reteaching **9-2**

Equivalent Ratios

You can find equivalent ratios just like you find equivalent fractions.

Find ratios equivalent to $\frac{30}{40}$.

Multiply both terms by the same number.

$\frac{30 \times 2}{40 \times 2} = \frac{60}{80}$

Divide both terms by the same number. To find the simplest form ratio, divide by the greatest common factor (GCF) of the two numbers.

The GCF of 30 and 40 is 10.

$\frac{30 \div 10}{40 \div 10} = \frac{3}{4}$

Two equivalent ratios form a proportion. The units must be the same in both ratios.

Do the ratios 24 ft:16 seconds and 36 ft:24 seconds form a proportion?

First check the units.

Both ratios compare feet to seconds, so the units are the same.

Then write each ratio in simplest form.

$\frac{24 \text{ ft}}{16 \text{ seconds}} = \frac{3 \text{ ft}}{2 \text{ seconds}}$

$\frac{36 \text{ ft}}{24 \text{ seconds}} = \frac{3 \text{ ft}}{2 \text{ seconds}}$

Compare the simplest form ratios. They are the same, so the ratios form a proportion.

Write three ratios that are equivalent to the ratio given.

1. $\frac{3}{5}$ ____________ 2. $\frac{4}{8}$ ____________ 3. $\frac{6}{18}$ ____________

4. 8:10 ____________ 5. 6:8 ____________ 6. 10:12 ____________

7. 12 to 18 ____________ 8. 16 to 18 ____________ 9. 5 to 25 ____________

Write the ratios in simplest form.

10. $\frac{10}{15}$ ____________ 11. 21 to 14 ____________ 12. 15:25 ____________

Write = if the ratios form a proportion; if they do not form a proportion, write ≠.

13. $\frac{15}{18}$ ◯ $\frac{10}{12}$ 14. 20:24 ◯ 24:30 15. 16 to 20 ◯ 28 to 35

16. **Number Sense** Dale says that the ratios 3:5 and 2:10 are equivalent. Is he correct? Explain.

____

Name ______________________

Practice
9-2

Equivalent Ratios

Write three ratios that are equivalent to the ratio given.

1. $\frac{8}{10}$ ________ **2.** $\frac{2}{3}$ ________ **3.** $\frac{3}{4}$ ________

4. 21 to 18 ________ **5.** 5 to 4 ________ **6.** 1 to 3 ________

7. 14:16 ________ **8.** 2:4 ________ **9.** 2:5 ________

Write = if the ratios form a proportion; if they do not form a proportion, write ≠.

10. 3:12 ◯ 6:24 **11.** $\frac{14}{16}$ ◯ $\frac{7}{4}$ **12.** 4 to 20 ◯ 1 to 4

Find the number that makes the ratios equivalent.

13. $\frac{8}{9} = \frac{}{36}$ **14.** 15:18 = 5:________ **15.** ________ to 7 = 9 to 21

Write the ratios in simplest form.

16. $\frac{42}{28}$ ________ **17.** 21 to 36 ________ **18.** 15:45 ________

19. $\frac{35}{25}$ ________ **20.** 60 to 30 ________ **21.** 10:40 ________

22. Writing to Explain Tell why you cannot multiply or divide by zero to find equivalent ratios.

____

23. Geometry Is the ratio of length to width for these two rectangles proportional? Tell how you know.

14 in.
7 in.
21 in.
15 in.

____

____

24. Algebra Which value for *x* would make the ratios equivalent?
$\frac{3}{8} = \frac{x}{32}$

A $x = 4$

B $x = 6$

C $x = 8$

D $x = 12$

Name ______________________________

Modeling Ratios

You can use a diagram to solve problems about ratios.

A zoo has 3 zebras for every 2 giraffes. How many giraffes does the zoo have if it has 12 zebras? Draw a diagram to solve the problem.

Draw rectangles to model the ratio 3 zebras to 2 giraffes.

Divide the number of zebras into 3 equal parts to find how many animals each part represents. $12 \div 3 = 4$

zebras

giraffes

12 zebras

4	4	4

4	4

? giraffes

Then multiply the number of parts for the giraffes times 4 animals per part to find the number of giraffes.

$4 \times 2 = 8$

The zoo has 8 giraffes.

Draw a diagram to help you solve each problem.

1. One exhibit at the zoo has 7 birds for every 2 mammals. If there are 10 mammals in the exhibit, how many birds are there?

____

2. There are 5 children for every 3 adults who visit the zoo. If there are 30 children at the zoo, how many adults are there?

____

3. The monkeys get fed 6 buckets of vegetables for every 2 buckets of cereal. How many buckets of vegetables do the monkeys get fed if they get 8 buckets of cereal?

____

4. It takes 8 minutes for the train to fill 3 cars with people from the zoo. How long does it take the train to fill 18 cars of people from the zoo?

____

5. Writing to Explain Arlen buys 2 small cups of food for the animals for 5 tokens. Explain how to use a diagram to find how many cups of food Arlen could buy for 20 tokens.

____

____

Name ___

Practice
9-3

Modeling Ratios

In **1** through **8**, draw a diagram to solve the problem.

1. Sam puts 3 tulips and 4 lilacs in each vase. How many lilacs does Sam use if he puts 36 tulips into vases?

___

2. Seven students ride the bus to school for every 2 students who walk. If there are 105 students who ride the bus, how many students walk?

___

3. A golf store is having a special, giving away 10 free golf tees for every box of 3 golf balls a customer buys. If a customer buys 24 golf balls, how many golf tees does she get?

___

4. Sarah's family has an apple orchard. The family sells 8 baskets of apples for every 3 jars of applesauce. How many baskets of apples do they sell if they sell 120 jars of applesauce?

___

5. Martin enjoys hiking on rural trails near his home in Michigan. He can hike 6 miles in 2 hours. How long would it take Martin to hike 24 miles?

___

6. The coach mixes 15 scoops of powder with 2 gallons of water to make a sports drink for his team. How many scoops of powder does the coach need to mix with 10 gallons of water?

___

7. A 4-pound bag of potatoes costs $3.16. How much would 32 pounds of potatoes cost?

___

8. Ali packs 54 cans into 3 boxes to ship. How many boxes of the same size will Ali need to ship 324 cans?

___

9. **Algebra** Which value of *p* makes the ratios equivalent?

$\frac{5}{7} = \frac{p}{56}$

A 8 **B** 13 **C** 40 **D** 64

10. **Writing to Explain** There are 4 girls to every 3 boys on the school's track team. Explain how to use a diagram to find how many members are on the track team if there are 16 girls on the team.

___

___

Name ______________________________

Using Ratio Tables

A ratio table showing equivalent ratios can be used to solve a proportion.

Ross uses 11 skeins of yarn to make 4 scarves. How many scarves can he make from 66 skeins of yarn?

Write a proportion. Use x for the number of scarves.

$$\frac{4 \text{ scarves}}{11 \text{ skeins}} = \frac{x \text{ scarves}}{66 \text{ skeins}}$$

Make a ratio table. Multiply or divide to find equivalent ratios. Find ratios equivalent to $\frac{4}{11}$ by multiplying both terms of the ratio by the same number until you find 66 skeins.

Number of scarves	4	8	12	16	20	24
Number of skeins	11	22	33	44	55	66

$$\frac{4 \text{ scarves}}{11 \text{ skeins}} = \frac{24 \text{ scarves}}{66 \text{ skeins}}$$

So, Ross can make 24 scarves from 66 skeins of yarn.

Answer the question and complete each ratio table.

1. $\frac{\$25}{\square \text{ min}} = \frac{\$200}{1{,}000 \text{ min}}$

Number of dollars	200	100	50	25
Number of minutes	1,000			

2. $\frac{\square \text{ batteries}}{9 \text{ flashlights}} = \frac{12 \text{ batteries}}{3 \text{ flashlights}}$

Number of batteries				
Number of flashlights				

3. $\frac{\square \text{ ft}}{800 \text{ h}} = \frac{9 \text{ ft}}{8 \text{ h}}$

Number of ________				
Number of ________				

4. $\frac{4 \text{ carts}}{16 \text{ horses}} = \frac{\square \text{ carts}}{64 \text{ horses}}$

Number of ________				
Number of ________				

5. Laine was practicing her free throws. She shot nine times and made five baskets. At this ratio, how many times will she need to shoot to make 35 baskets?

____

6. Hiram said that he can use the same ratio table to solve the two proportions below. Do you agree or disagree with Hiram?

$\frac{8 \text{ cows}}{2 \text{ pigs}} = \frac{c \text{ cows}}{10 \text{ pigs}}$ $\frac{2 \text{ pigs}}{8 \text{ cows}} = \frac{10 \text{ pigs}}{c \text{ cows}}$

____

Name ______________________________

Practice
9-4

Using Ratio Tables

Complete the ratio table. Add columns if needed.

1. $\frac{3 \text{ hops}}{5 \text{ jumps}} = \frac{\square \text{ hops}}{15 \text{ jumps}}$

Number of hops		
Number of jumps		

____

2. $\frac{\$60}{2 \text{ weeks}} = \frac{\$240}{\square \text{ weeks}}$

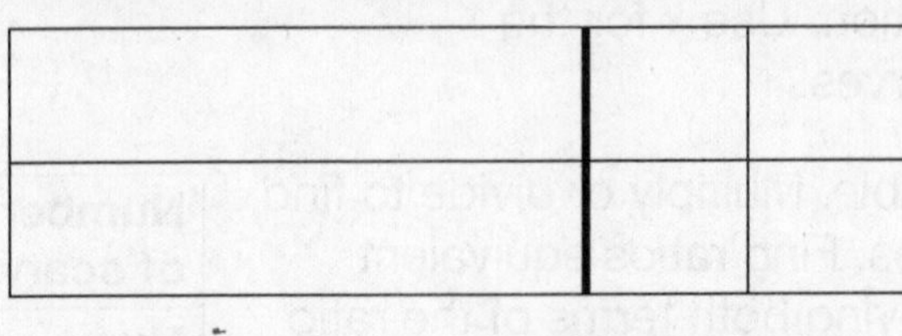

____

3. $\frac{12 \text{ cans}}{7 \text{ bottles}} = \frac{60 \text{ cans}}{\square \text{ bottles}}$

____

4. How many cups of loam are needed to make 66 c of potting soil? ______

5. How many cups of humus are needed to make 11 c of potting soil? ______

6. Sondra uses 78 c of loam to make potting soil. How many cups of humus did she use ? ______

Potting Soil for Ferns (Makes 22 c)
6 c sand
6 c loam
9 c peat moss
3 c humus
1 c dried cow manure

7. It takes Renaldo 8 hours to make 7 carvings. How many hours will it take him to make 63 carvings?

A $7\frac{7}{8}$ hours

B 9 hours

C 56 hours

D 72 hours

8. Writing to Explain Find three sets of values for x and y to make $\frac{x \text{ mi}}{y \text{ min}} = \frac{4 \text{ mi}}{32 \text{ min}}$ a proportion. Explain how you found the values.

____

____

Name ____________________

Ratios and Graphs

You can make or complete a table of equivalent ratios and graph the values on a coordinate grid.

Complete the table to show equivalent ratios for $\frac{3}{4}$.

3	6	9	12
4			

To complete the table, find fractions that are equal to $\frac{3}{4}$ that have numerators of 6, 9, and 12.

$\frac{3 \times \mathbf{2}}{4 \times \mathbf{2}} = \frac{6}{8}$ $\quad \frac{3 \times \mathbf{3}}{4 \times \mathbf{3}} = \frac{9}{12}$ $\quad \frac{3 \times \mathbf{4}}{4 \times \mathbf{4}} = \frac{12}{16}$

The missing values in the table are the denominators of the equal fractions. The values are: 8, 12, and 16.

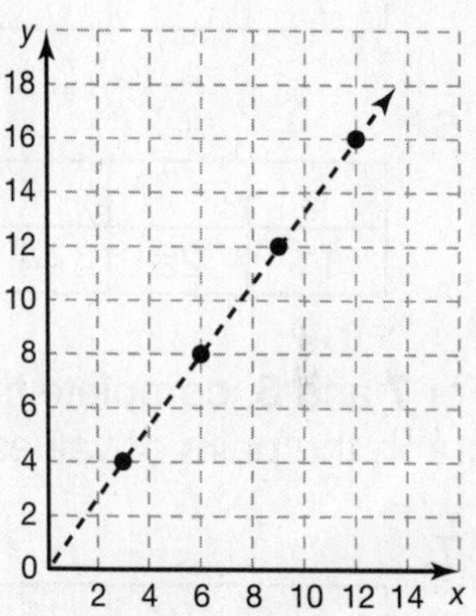

Graph the equivalent ratios on a coordinate grid. Use an appropriate scale for the *x* and *y* axes.

Plot the points for each ratio, *x* to *y*. Draw a dashed line from (0, 0) through the points extending through the final point.

Complete the table to show equivalent ratios. Graph the set of equal ratios on a coordinate grid.

1.

2	4	6	8	10
3				

2.

1	2	3	4	5
2				

3.

3	6	9	12	15
5				

4.

2	6	12	18	24
7				

5.

4	12	16	48	60
12				

6.

6	18	24	36	48
9				

7.

5	15	25	35	45
8				

8.

1	5	8	10	15
7				

Name ______________________________

Practice
9-5

Ratios and Graphs

For **1** through **6**, complete the table to show equivalent ratios.

1.

4				
3	6	9	12	15

2.

4	2	8	12	16
6				

3.

10	20	30	40	70
7				

4.

3				
2	4	8	12	24

5.

6				
11	22	44	88	110

6.

12	4	24	36	48
3				

For **7** and **8**, complete the table to show equivalent ratios, and graph the pairs of values on the coordinate grid.

7.

5	10	15	25	40
4				

8.

5				
2	4	6	10	14

y
45
40
35
30
25
20
15
10
5
0
5 10 15 20 25 30 35 40 45
x

9. Writing to Explain How are the graphs of the ratios in Exercises 7 and 8 alike, and how are they different?

____

____

____

10. A birdwatcher counted 7 robins for every 4 sparrows. Complete the table to show how many robins she counted if she counted 24 sparrows in a weekend. On a separate piece of graph paper, graph the values on a coordinate grid.

4	8	12	16	20	24
7					

Name ________________________________

Reteaching
9-6

Problem Solving: Draw a Picture

Veronica is celebrating her birthday by having a skating party. As part of a birthday special, Veronica paid for 10 tickets and 2 guests received free admission. What fraction of the people at Veronica's party were not charged for admission?

Read and Understand

What do you know? There were 10 paid admissions and 2 free admissions.
What are you trying to find? The fraction of people attending Veronica's party that were admitted at no charge.

Plan and Solve

What strategy will you use? Draw a picture to show the 10 paid admissions and the 2 free admissions.
Count the boxes. There were 12 people admitted. Since 2 of the 12 people were admitted at no charge, the fraction is $\frac{2}{12}$, or $\frac{1}{6}$ in simplest form.

Paid admission	■	■	■	■	■	■	■	■	■	■
Free admission	■	■								

Look Back and Check

Is your answer reasonable? Yes. The picture shows 2 out of 12 boxes, which is $\frac{2}{12}$, or $\frac{1}{6}$.

Draw or use a picture to solve each problem.

One afternoon, the ratio of black shirts sold to white shirts sold at The Clothes Horse was 2:1. Complete the picture to show the ratio.

Black shirts sold	■	■							
White shirts sold									

1. How many boxes are shaded in all? ________

2. What fraction of the shirts sold were black? ________

3. The Clothes Horse sold 12 shirts that afternoon. How many black shirts were sold? HINT: YOU CAN ADD TO THE PICTURE UNTIL THERE ARE 12 SHADED BOXES TO REPRESENT THE PROBLEM. ________

4. Ilene earns $20. She saves $2 for every $8 that she spends. How much of the $20 will she save? ________

Name ______________________

Problem Solving: Draw a Picture

Draw a picture to solve each problem.

For **1** through **3**, Pamela walks 1 mile and runs 4 miles during her daily workout.

1. What is the ratio of miles walked to miles ran during each of Pamela's workouts? ________

2. What is the ratio of miles walked to total miles in each of Pamela's workouts?

3. Pamela ran 20 miles last week. How many days did she workout? ________

4. There are 5 pens with blue ink, 3 pens with red ink, and 2 pens with purple ink in each package. What fraction of the pens has blue ink?

A 5

B $\frac{5}{5}$

C $\frac{5}{8}$

D $\frac{1}{2}$

5. There are 18 baseballs and basketballs in one gym storage locker. There are 3 baseballs for every 6 basketballs in the locker. How many basketballs are in the locker? ________

6. Writing to Explain Rasheed takes photographs with a digital camera. He estimates that for each photograph he prints, he has 5 photographs that he never prints. How many photographs has Rasheed taken if he makes 4 prints? Explain how drawing a picture can help you solve the problem. Then solve.

____

____

____

Name ____________________

Reteaching **10-1**

Understanding Rates

A rate is a ratio in which the two terms are measured in different units.

Example: 18 bracelets for 3 girls.
$\frac{\text{18 bracelets}}{\text{3 girls}}$

In a unit rate, the second number is 1.

Example: 6 bracelets for 1 girl.
$\frac{\text{6 bracelets}}{\text{1 girl}}$

Remember that the fraction bar shows division.
If you know a rate, you can divide to find the unit rate.

Example: 17 goals in 5 games is written as $\frac{\text{17 goals}}{\text{5 games}}$.

$5\overline{)17.0}$ = 3.4   The unit rate is 3.4 goals per game. (Per means "for each".)

Write the rate and the unit rate.

1. 25 flowers for 5 vases

2. 32 games in 8 weeks

3. 144 pencils in 12 packages

4. 252 students in 9 classes

5. $13.20 for 6 pounds

6. 34 minutes for 8 pages

7. Number Sense If a car travels 350 miles in 7 hours, what is its rate per hour?

8. Estimation Bare root plum trees are on sale at 3 for $40. To the nearest dollar, what is the cost per tree?

Name ______________________

Practice

10-1

Understanding Rates

Write the rate and the unit rate.

1. 42 bricks laid in 2 hours

2. 15 points scored in 4 quarters

3. 225 chairs in 15 rows

4. 24 trees pruned in 5 days

5. 480 miles in 12 hours

6. $6.50 for 10 pounds

7. 72 plants in 9 square feet

8. 357 miles on 14 gallons

9. **Estimation** Over 5 days, 8,208 people visited an amusement park. About how many people visited the park per day?

10. **Writing to Explain** Explain how you could convert a rate of 18,000 miles per hour to miles per second.

11. **Critical Thinking** Matt makes 5 bookcases in 8 days. What is his unit rate?

12. A space shuttle orbits Earth 1 time in 90 minutes. How many times does it orbit Earth in 6 hours?

13. Which is the unit rate for 39 people in 3 vans?

A 39 people per van

B 13 vans per person

C 13 people per van

D 3 people per van

Name ____________________

Reteaching **10-2**

Comparing Rates

Use unit rates to compare two rates that have the same units of measurement.

Daniel painted 9 planks in 6 minutes. Meredith painted 22 planks in 11 minutes. Who painted at a faster rate?

Write each rate as a unit rate.

Daniel's Rate: $\frac{9 \text{ planks}}{6 \text{ min}} = \frac{9 \text{ planks} \div 6}{6 \text{ min} \div 6} = \frac{1.5 \text{ planks}}{1 \text{ min}}$

Meredith's Rate: $\frac{22 \text{ planks}}{11 \text{ min}} = \frac{22 \text{ planks} \div 11}{11 \text{ minutes} \div 11} = \frac{2 \text{ planks}}{1 \text{ min}}$

Since 2 is greater than 1.5, Meredith is the faster painter. The faster rate is 22 planks in 11 min.

Find each unit rate and determine which rate is greater.

1. 51 hits on Jon's website in 3 h or 96 hits on Shana's website in 6 h

____

____

2. 330 mi on 15 gal or 240 mi on 10 gal

____

3. 90 breaths in 6 min or 112 breaths in 8 min

____

4. 660 miles traveled on 20 gallons of gas or 850 miles traveled on 25 gallons of gas

____

5. **Writing to Explain** Earl and Mia danced in a charity fundraiser. Earl raised $275 when he danced for 5 hours. Mia raised $376 when she danced for 8 hours. Which dancer earned more for each hour danced? Explain how you found your answer.

____

____

Name ____________________

Comparing Rates

Find each unit rate and determine which rate is greater.

1. 250 mi per 10 gal or 460 mi per 20 gal

____

2. 1,000 words in 20 min or 2,475 words in 45 min

____

3. 6 in. of rain in 4 h or 8 in. of rain in 5 h

____

4. 120 tees in 4 boxes or 198 tees in 6 boxes

____

5. 108 labels on 9 sheets or 225 labels on 15 sheets

____

6. 5 oz of insect repellant for 7 days or 14 oz of insect repellant for 21 days

____

7. Alejandro makes 154 widgets for each 7-hour shift that he works. Which shift makes more widgets per hour than Alejandro?

   A 120 in a 6-hour shift

   B 160 in an 8-hour shift

   C 72 in a 3-hour shift

   D 81 in a 4-hour shift

8. **Writing to Explain** Montel and Ellie each need to finish 15 history questions. Montel says that he can finish 10 questions in 2 hours. Ellie says that she can finish all 15 questions in 3 hours. Which friend will finish first? Use unit rates to support your answer.

____

____

Name ______________________________

Reteaching
10-3

Unit Rates

A unit rate is a special ratio that compares one quantity to one unit of another quantity. You can use unit rates to solve proportions.

Geraldo makes 100 watches in 4 hours. If he works 7 hours at the same rate, how many watches will he make?

Write a proportion. Use *d* for watches made. $\frac{100 \text{ watches}}{4 \text{ h}} = \frac{d \text{ watches}}{7 \text{ h}}$

Find the unit rate. Divide the first term by the second term.

$100 \div 4 = 25$ watches

The unit rate is $\frac{25 \text{ watches}}{1 \text{ h}}$.

Think: Find an equal ratio with 1 as the second term. $\frac{100 \div 4}{4 \div 4} = \frac{25}{1}$

Multiply by the unit rate. $\frac{25 \text{ watches}}{1 \text{ h}} \times 7\text{h} = 175$ watches

So, $\frac{100 \text{ watches}}{4 \text{ h}} = \frac{75 \text{ watches}}{7 \text{ h}}$. Geraldo will make 175 watches when he works 7 hours.

Use unit rates to solve each proportion. Estimate to check reasonableness.

1. $\frac{\square \text{ g}}{2 \text{ kg}} = \frac{30\text{g}}{15 \text{ kg}}$

Unit Rate: __________

Multiply: __________

2. $\frac{120 \text{ mi}}{3 \text{ gal}} = \frac{\square \text{ mi}}{5 \text{ gal}}$

Unit Rate: __________

Multiply: __________

3. $\frac{8 \text{ in.}}{2 \text{ wk}} = \frac{\square \text{ in.}}{5 \text{ wk}}$

Unit Rate: __________

Multiply: __________

4. $\frac{24 \text{ books}}{3 \text{ wk}} = \frac{\square \text{ books}}{10 \text{ wk}}$

5. $\frac{\square \text{ oz}}{7 \text{ packs}} = \frac{64 \text{ oz}}{8 \text{ packs}}$

6. $\frac{200 \text{ stamps}}{2 \text{ rows}} = \frac{\square \text{ stamps}}{9 \text{ rows}}$

7. Wes used 49 quarts of oil when he changed the oil in 7 cars. Complete and solve the proportion to find how many quarts of oil he would use to change the oil in 20 cars, assuming that all cars need the same quantity of oil.

$\frac{49 \text{ quarts}}{7 \text{ cars}} =$ ______________________________

8. Writing to Explain A café served 180 pickles with 60 sandwiches. If the ratio of sandwiches to pickles is always constant, explain how you can use unit rates and proportions to find how many pickles are needed to serve 32 sandwiches.

____

Name ______________________

Practice **10-3**

Unit Rates

Use unit rates to solve each proportion. Estimate to check for reasonableness.

1. $\frac{a \text{ ft}}{6 \text{ h}} = \frac{20 \text{ ft}}{4 \text{ h}}$ ______
2. $\frac{36 \text{ oz}}{6 \text{ lb}} = \frac{b \text{ oz}}{4 \text{ lb}}$ ______
3. $\frac{c \text{ players}}{10 \text{ teams}} = \frac{27 \text{ players}}{3 \text{ teams}}$ ______
4. $\frac{d \text{ c}}{20 \text{ tsp}} = \frac{60 \text{ c}}{12 \text{ tsp}}$ ______
5. $\frac{e \text{ m}}{12 \text{ cm}} = \frac{63 \text{ m}}{9 \text{ cm}}$ ______
6. $\frac{16 \text{ adults}}{2 \text{ children}} = \frac{f \text{ adults}}{5 \text{ children}}$ ______
7. $\frac{g \text{ m}}{30 \text{ seconds}} = \frac{20 \text{ m}}{8 \text{ seconds}}$ ______
8. $\frac{12 \text{ mL}}{6 \text{ pt}} = \frac{h \text{ mL}}{40 \text{ pt}}$ ______
9. $\frac{33 \text{ meals}}{11 \text{ days}} = \frac{k \text{ meals}}{365 \text{ days}}$ ______

10. It takes DeShawn 30 min to paint 90 feet of fence. If he paints at the same rate, how many feet of fence can he paint in 45 min? ______

11. Inez types 280 words in 7 minutes. If she types at the same rate, how many words will she type in 1 hour? ______

12. **Algebra** Explain how you can tell that $\frac{20 \text{ pens}}{2 \text{ packages}} = \frac{30 \text{ pens}}{3 \text{ packages}}$ using mental math?

____

____

13. Darryl was looking at the speeds of different airplanes. When he wrote a proportion to compare the speeds, he forgot to write one term. If the proportion is correct, which is the term he forgot?

$\frac{45 \text{ mi}}{\square} = \frac{135 \text{ mi}}{12 \text{ min}}$

A 4 mi **C** 36 mi

B 4 min **D** 36 min

14. **Writing to Explain** Jeanette estimates that she mails 2 letters for every 50 e-mails that she sends. She has mailed 9 letters this week. To find how many e-mails she has sent, Jeanette wrote the proportion $\frac{2 \text{ letters}}{50 \text{ e-mails}} = \frac{9 \text{ letters}}{e \text{ e-mails}}$. Tell how she can use unit rates to solve the proportion. Tell how many e-mails she sent.

____

____

____

____

Name ______________________________

Unit Price

A unit price is a unit rate that gives the price of one item. You can use unit prices to find the best buy.

Write each price as a unit rate to find the best buy.

Super O Cereal $= \frac{\$3.52}{16 \text{ oz}} = \frac{\$3.52 \div 16}{16 \text{ oz} \div 16} = \frac{\$\,0.22}{1 \text{ oz}}$

Crunchy O's Cereal $= \frac{\$4.80}{24 \text{ oz}} = \frac{\$4.80 \div 24}{24 \text{ oz} \div 24} = \frac{\$0.20}{1 \text{ oz}}$

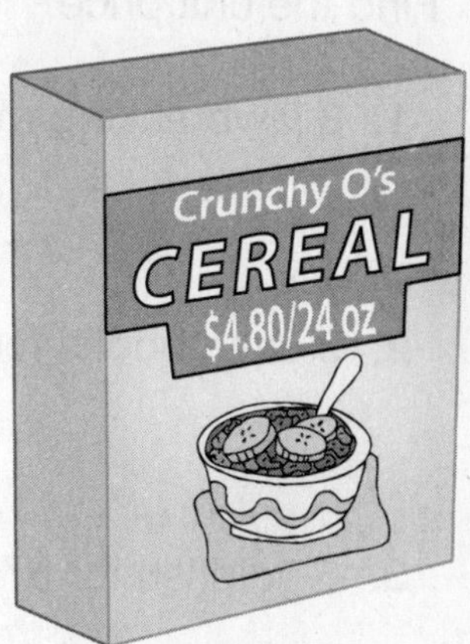

Since $0.20 is less than $0.22, Crunchy O's Cereal is the better buy.

Find each unit price and determine which is a better buy.

1. 20 gallons of gas for $66.00 or 25 gallons of gas for $81.25

2. 24 slices of cheese for $7.44 or 90 slices of cheese for $28.80

3. 32 oz of orange juice for $7.04 or 20 oz of orange juice for $4.80

4. Writing to Explain A bowling alley rents lanes for $24.00 for 3 hours on weekends and $45.00 for the whole day on weekdays. If Ryan would like to rent a lane for 6 hours, and he can come any day of the week, should he come on a weekend or a weekday? Explain how you found your answer.

____

____

____

____

____

Name ______________________

Practice
10-4

Unit Price

Find the unit price.

1. 8 jawbreakers for $4.00

2. 5 used books for $9.45

3. 6 goldfish for $7.38

Find each unit price and determine which is a better buy.

4. 1 lb of apples for $2.15 or 3 lb of apples for $5.76

5. 8 bungee cords for $10.00 or 20 bungee cords for $22.00

6. 5 oz of insect repellant for $6.95 or 14 oz of insect repellant for $19.60

7. Fritz earns $75.60 for each 7-hour shift that he works. Which shift pays a higher hourly wage than the wage Fritz earns?

A $60.30 for a 6-hour shift

B $80.00 for an 8-hour shift

C $36.30 for a 3-hour shift

D $40.40 for a 4-hour shift

8. **Writing to Explain** Shaunda said that buying 4 towels for $17 was a better buy than buying 2 towels for $9. She found her answer by doubling the terms in the ratio $\frac{9}{2}$ and comparing the first terms in the ratio. Is she correct? Use unit prices to support your answer.

____

____

____

Name ______________________________

Constant Speed

The formula $d = r \times t$ uses symbols to relate the quantities for distance (d), constant rate of speed (r), and time (t).

Example 1

How long will it take a car moving at 50 mph to travel 70 mi?

Substitute what you know into the formula $d = r \times t$. $70 \text{ mi} = 50 \text{ mph} \times t$

Solve the equation. $\frac{70 \text{ mi}}{50 \text{ mph}} = \frac{50 \text{ mph} \times t}{50 \text{ mph}}$

$1.4 \text{ h} = t$

It will take 1.4 h to travel 70 mi at 50 mph.

Example 2

A car travels 325 mi in 5 h. What is its rate of speed?

Substitute what you know into the formula $d = r \times t$. $325 \text{ mi} = r \times 5 \text{ h}$

Solve the equation. $\frac{325 \text{ mi}}{5 \text{ h}} = \frac{r = 5 \text{ h}}{5 \text{ h}}$

$65 \text{ mph} = r$

The rate of speed of a car that travels 325 mi in 5 h is 65 mph.

---

1. An airplane flies at 250 mph. How far will it travel in 5 h at that rate of speed?

Substitute the information you know into the formula $d = r \times t$:	Solve the equation.	Write the answer with the correct units.
$d =$ ____________	____________	____________

Find the missing variable.

2. Distance = 60 km time = 4 h rate = ________

3. Distance = 24 cm time = 12 sec rate = ________

4. Distance = 56 yd time = ________ rate = 8 yd/min

5. Distance = ________ time = 25 d rate = 160 m/d

6. Writing to Explain A storm is 15 mi from Lodi. If the storm travels at 6 mph towards the city, how many hours will it take for the storm to get to Lodi? Show your work.

____

Name ___________________________

Constant Speed

Find the missing variable.

1. Distance = 15 mi   time = 2h   rate = __________
2. Distance = 56 km   time = 4 h   rate = __________
3. Distance = 72 yd   time = __________   rate = $\frac{12 \text{ yd}}{\text{min}}$
4. Distance = 27 cm   time = __________   rate = $\frac{3 \text{ cm}}{\text{sec}}$
5. Distance = __________   time = 2 d   rate = $\frac{5{,}000 \text{ m}}{\text{d}}$
6. Distance = __________   time = 6 wk   rate = $\frac{80 \text{ ft}}{\text{wk}}$
7. The California Speedway hosts automobile races. Which rate of speed is higher: a car completing a 500-mi race in about $3\frac{1}{3}$ h or a car completing a 300-mi race in about $2\frac{1}{2}$ h? __________
8. A train traveled 250 mi in 2 h. If it traveled at the same rate of speed, how long would it take the train to travel 600 mi? __________
9. The space shuttle travels 4,375 mi in 15 min as it orbits the earth. Estimate its constant rate of speed during that time to the nearest hundred.

   A About 400 mi per min

   B About 300 mi per min

   C About 60,000 mi per min

   D About 70,000 mi per min

10. **Writing to Explain** Kevin drove his scooter 62 km in 2 h. Explain how to find how far he drives if he drives at the same rate for 3 h.

____

____

____

Name ______________________

Reteaching
10-6

Converting Customary Units

Units of Length

1 foot (ft) = 12 in.
1 yard (yd) = 3 ft
= 36 in.
1 mile (mi) = 5,280 ft
= 1,760 yd

Units of Capacity

1 cup (c) = 8 fluid ounces (fl oz)
1 pint (pt) = 2 c
1 quart (qt) = 2 pt
1 gallon (gal) = 4 qt

Units of Weight

16 ounces (oz) = 1 pound (lb)
2,000 pounds = 1 ton (T)

How to change from one unit of measurement to another:

To change from larger units to smaller units, you have to multiply.

120 yd = ________ ft
1 yd = 3 ft
120 × 3 = 360
120 yd = 360 ft

To change from smaller units to larger ones, you have to divide.

256 fl oz = ________ c
1 c = 8 fl oz
256 ÷ 8 = 32
256 fl oz = 32 c

Complete.

1. 36 in. = ________ ft

2. 4 qt = ________ c

3. 5 lb = ________ oz

4. 39 ft = ________ yd

5. 1.5 mi = ________ ft

6. 3.5 gal = ________ qt

7. 2 T = ________ lb

8. 16 pt = ________ qt

9. 64 oz = ________ lb

10. 3 yd = ________ in.

11. 4 gal = ________ pt

12. 55 yd = ________ ft

13. 6.5 lb = ________ oz

14. 20 pt = ________ gal

15. 4.5 qt = ________ c

16. 205 yd = ________ ft

17. **Reasoning** A vendor at a festival sells soup for $1.25 per cup or $3.75 per quart. Which is the better buy?

____

Name ____________________

Practice 10-6

Converting Customary Units

Complete.

1. 3.5 ft = __________ in.
2. 17 yd = __________ ft
3. 1.5 gal = __________ c
4. 4 mi = __________ ft
5. 160 fl oz = __________ qt
6. 72 in. = __________ ft
7. 3 mi = __________ yd
8. 12 pt = __________ qt
9. 180 ft = __________ yd
10. 2 gal = __________ fl oz

11. How many tons are in 35,000 lb? __________

12. **Number Sense** Brian pole vaulted over a bar that was 189 in. high. How many more inches would he need to vault to go over a bar that was 16 ft high?

____

A paving company was hired to make a 4 mile section of the highway. They need 700 tons of concrete to complete the job.

13. How many yards of highway do they need to repave?

____

14. How many pounds of concrete will they need to repave the highway?

____

15. Gary's cat weighs 11 lb. How many ounces is that?

A 132 **B** 144 **C** 164 **D** 176

16. **Writing to Explain** The average car manufactured in the United States in 2001 could drive 24.5 mi on 1 gal of gas. Explain how to find the number of yards the car can travel on 1 gal of gas.

____

____

____

Name ______________________________

Reteaching **10-7**

Converting Metric Units

Changing from one metric unit to another:

To change from a larger unit to a smaller unit, multiply by a power of ten.

3.8 L = ________ mL

A liter is a larger unit than a milliliter. To change from liters to milliliters, multiply.

1 L = 1,000 mL

3.8 × 1,000 = 3,800

3.8 L = 3,800 mL

To change from a smaller unit to a larger unit, divide by a power of ten.

100 m = ________ km

The meter is a smaller unit than the kilometer. To change from meters to kilometers, divide.

1,000 m = 1 km

100 ÷ 1000 = 0.1

100 m = 0.1 km

Name the most appropriate metric unit for each measurement.

1. mass of a cow ________

2. length of a carrot ________

3. capacity of a thimble ________

Complete.

4. 45 g = ________ mg

5. 3450 mL = ________ L

6. 4.5 m = ________ mm

7. 1.68 L = ________ mL

8. 28 cm = ________ mm

9. 7,658 g = ________ kg

10. 600 cm = ________ m

11. 5,000 mg = ________ g

12. 5.1 km = ________ m

13. 1.780 L = ________ mL

14. 0.780 L = ________ mL

15. 4,300 m = ________ km

16. 9,000 cm = ________ m

17. 8,000 mg = ________ g

18. Reasoning It is recommended that people have 1 g of calcium each day. How many milligrams of calcium is that?

____

Name ____________________

Practice **10-7**

Converting Metric Units

Name the most appropriate metric unit for each measurement.

1. mass of a paperclip ________

2. capacity of a water cooler ________

3. width of a sheet of paper ________

Complete.

4. 2.7 m = ________ cm

5. 1.6 kg = ________ g

6. 9 L = ________ mL

7. 14 m = ________ mm

8. 1.6 cm = ________ mm

9. 5,400 g = ________ kg

10. 1,840 mL = ________ L

11. 32 km = ________ m

12. **Number Sense** The chemist needs 2,220 mL of potassium chloride to complete an experiment. He has 2 L. Does he have enough to complete the experiment? Explain.

____

13. A computer floppy disk has a mass of 20 g. How many would you need to have a total mass of 1 kg? ________

14. A battery is 5 cm long. How many batteries would you need to line up to get 3 m? ________

15. Which would you do to convert 25 cm to millimeters?

A Divide by 10

B Divide by 100

C Multiply by 10

D Multiply by 100

16. **Writing to Explain** A banana has a mass of 122 g. Explain how to find the mass of the banana in milligrams.

____

____

____

Name____

Reteaching
10-8

Problem Solving: Writing to Explain

In a chess club, 1 out of every 4 members is in sixth grade. There are 24 members in the chess club. How many members are in the sixth grade? Explain your solution.

Gerry's explanation:

6 members are in the sixth grade.
Use reasoning: I multiplied 4 members by 6 to get 24 members, so I multiplied 1 by 6 to get 6 members in the sixth grade.
Then I checked to see if the ratios were proportional.

$$\frac{\text{1 sixth grader}}{\text{4 members}} = \frac{\text{6 sixth graders}}{\text{24 members}}$$

Since the ratios are proportional, the answer is correct.

- Use words, numbers, symbols, pictures, diagrams, or tables. If the problem includes pictures, diagrams, or tables that provide information or give details, refer to these.
- Describe the steps and operations you used. Show your work.

Explain your solution. Show your work.

1. Ms. Chin's class recorded the weather conditions for 14 days. The weather was cloudy 3 days out of every 7 days. Ms. Jensen's class recorded the weather for the next 10 days. The weather was cloudy 4 days out of every 5 days. Which class recorded more cloudy days?

____

____

____

____

____

____

2. Lynette earns $5 by delivering newspapers. She saves $3 and she spends the rest. If she saved $27 one month, how much did she spend?

____

____

Name ___________________________

Practice
10-8

Problem Solving: Writing to Explain

Explain your solution. Show your work.

1. A fundraiser is being held to raise money for a new school playground. Of every \$20 raised, \$16 will be spent on playground equipment. If the goal of the fundraiser is \$320.00 for playground equipment, how much total money will it need to raise?

2. Stephan is planning a hiking trip at Kings Canyon National Park. He plans to hike 14 miles every 2 days. If he hikes 42 miles, how many days will he hike?

3. A rental store at the beach has 56 umbrellas and 24 surfboards. Which ratio describes the relationship of surfboards to umbrellas?

A 56:24 **B** 7:3 **C** 3:8 **D** 3:7

4. Writing to Explain Kara can run 3 miles in 25.5 minutes. At this rate, how long would it take her to run 2 miles? *Diana's answer: If I subtract 1 mile from 3 miles, I get 2 miles, so if I subtract 1 minute from 25.5 minutes, I get 24.5 minutes. Kara takes 24.5 minutes to run 2 miles.* Is Diana's answer correct? Explain.

Name ______________________________

Understanding Percent

A percent is a ratio that compares a part to a whole.
The second term in the ratio is always 100.
The whole is 100%.
The grid has 60 of 100 squares shaded.

$\frac{60}{100} = 60\%$

So, 60% of the grid is shaded.

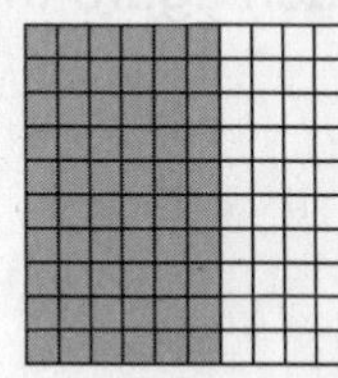

When the second term of a ratio is not 100, you can write an equivalent ratio with a denominator of 100 or use a proportion to find the percent shown by the part.

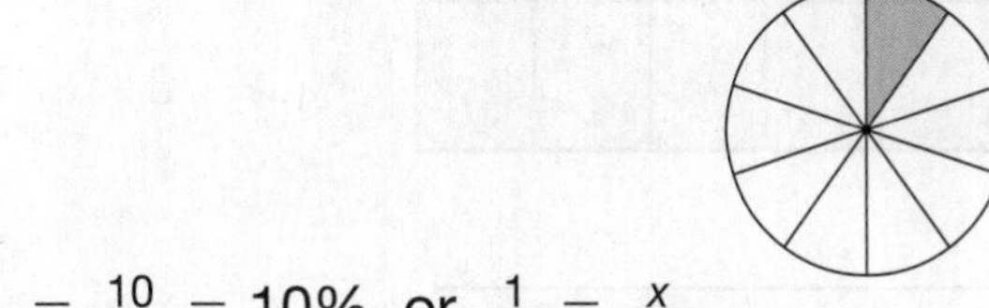

$\frac{1}{10} = \frac{10}{100} = 10\%$ or $\frac{1}{10} = \frac{x}{100}$

$10x = 100$

$x = 10$

So, 10% of the circle is shaded.

The line segment represents 100%. What percent is shown by Point *A*?

0   *A*   100

$\frac{2}{5} = \frac{40}{100} = 40\%$ or $\frac{2}{5} = \frac{x}{100}$

$5x = 200$

$x = 40$

So, 40% of the line segment is shaded.

Write the percent of each figure that is shaded.

1. 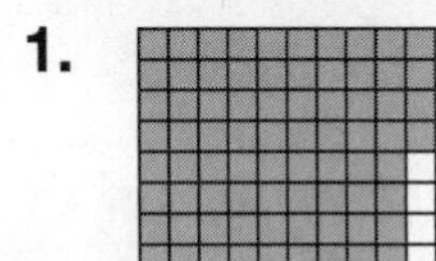 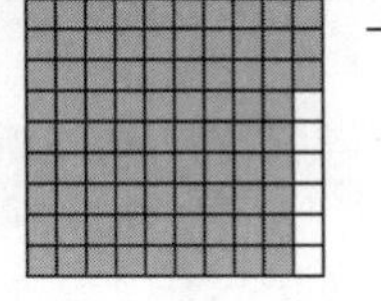 ______

2. 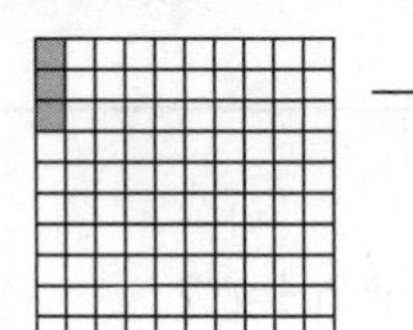 ______

3. 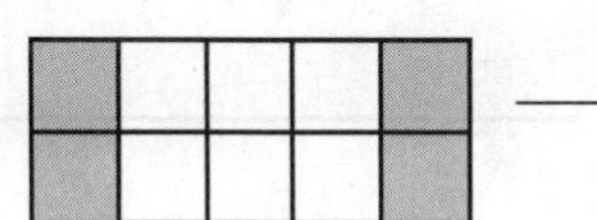 ______

4. 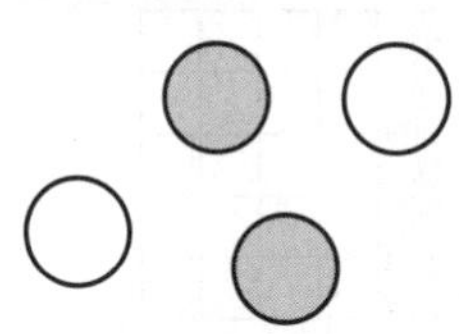 ______

5. 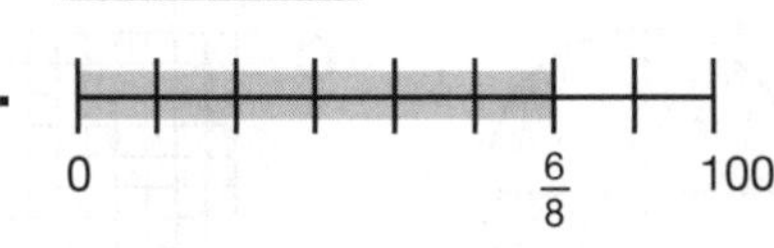

______

6. 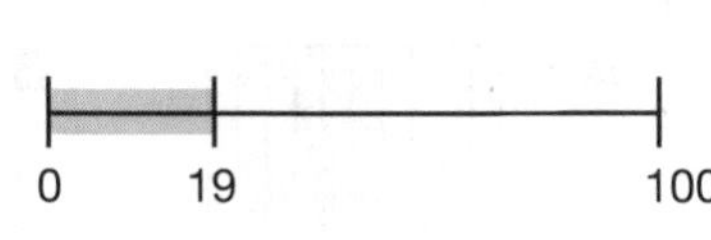

______

7. **Number Sense** Jana divided a sheet of paper into 5 equal sections and colored 2 of the sections red. What percent of the paper did she color? ______

8. **Writing to Explain** Shade each model to show 100%. Explain how you knew how many parts to shade.

____

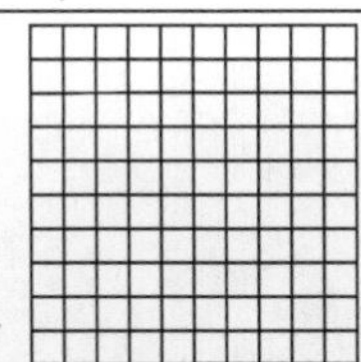

0   100

Name ___

Understanding Percent

Practice **11-1**

Write the percent of each figure that is shaded.

1. 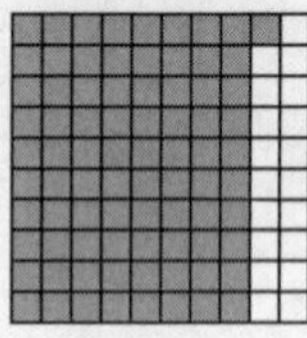

2. 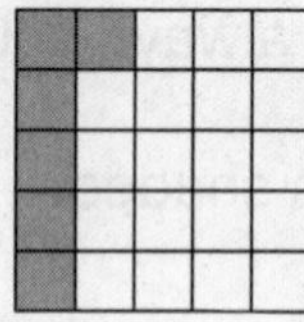

___

3. 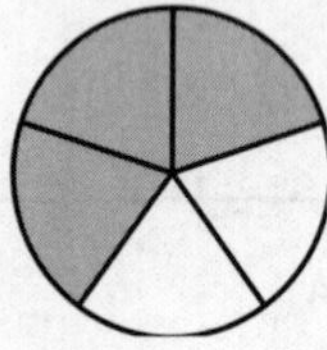

4. 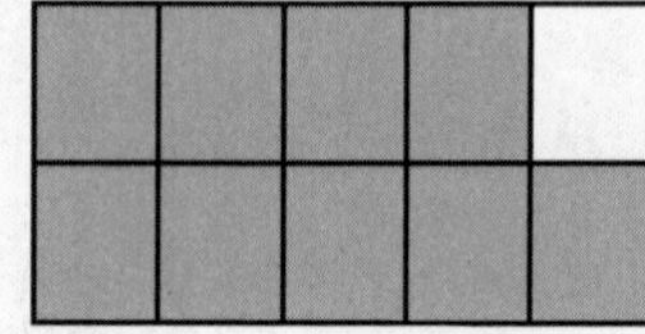

___ ___

5. Number Sense What percent of line segment *AB* is equal to 50% of line segment *CD*?

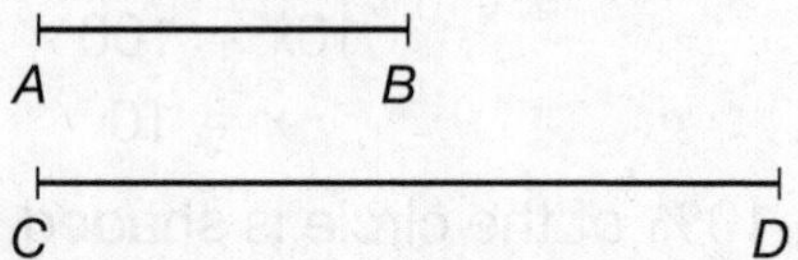

___

6. The line segment below shows 100%. Show 25%, 50%, and 75% of the segment.

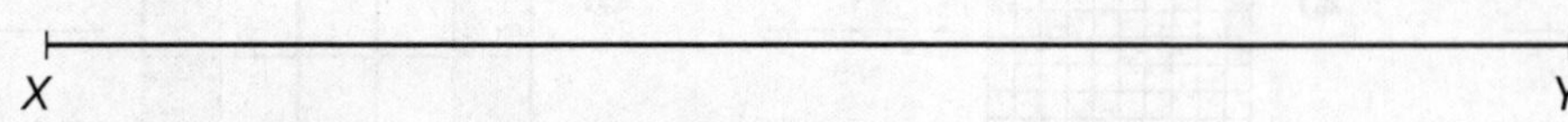

7. Which of the following figures is 60% shaded?

A 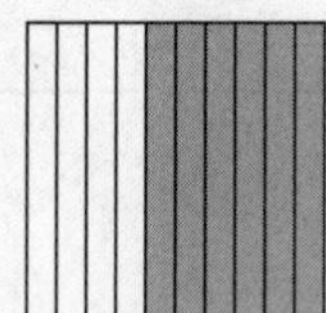

B 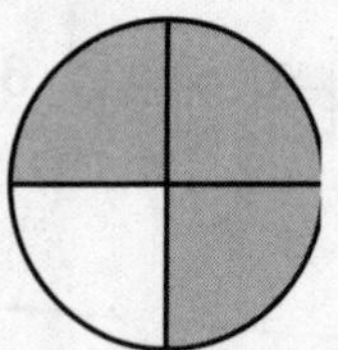

C 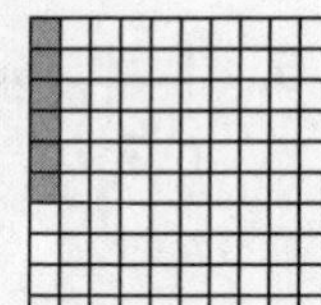

D 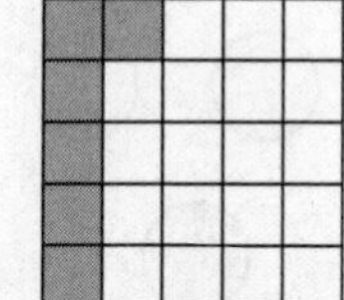

8. Writing to Explain You are thirsty, so a friend has offered to give you 50% of his water. What information must you have in order to find out how much water your friend will give you?

___

___

Name ____________________

Fractions, Decimals, and Percents

Fractions, decimals, and percents all name parts of a whole.
Percent means per hundred, so 15% means 15 parts per hundred.
The grid to the right has 72 out of 100 squares shaded. The shaded part can be represented with a fraction, $\frac{72}{100}$ ($\frac{18}{25}$ in simplest form), by a decimal, 0.72, and by a percent, 72%.

Write 36% as a fraction in simplest form and as a decimal.

$36\% = \frac{36}{100} = 0.36$

Simplify the fraction:

$\frac{36}{100} = \frac{36 \div 4}{100 \div 4} = \frac{9}{25}$

So, $36\% = \frac{9}{25} = 0.36$.

Write 0.47 as a fraction in simplest form and as a percent.

$0.47 = \frac{47}{100} = 47\%$

Write $\frac{3}{4}$ as a decimal and as a percent.

You can use a proportion or divide to help you.

Use a proportion:

$\frac{3}{4} = \frac{n}{100}$

$4n = 300$

$n = 75$

Use division:

```
   0.75
4)3.00
  2 8
    20
    20
     0
```

So, $\frac{3}{4} = \frac{75}{100} = 0.75 = 75\%$.

Write each number in two other ways. Write fractions in simplest form.

1. $\frac{2}{100}$ __________; __________
2. $\frac{71}{100}$ __________; __________
3. $\frac{9}{10}$ __________; __________
4. 17% __________; __________
5. 48% __________; __________
6. 60% __________; __________
7. 0.04 __________; __________
8. 0.22 __________; __________
9. **Writing to Explain** Jamal said that he could write a percent as a decimal by moving the decimal point two places to the left and deleting the percent sign. Is he correct? How do you know?

____

10. **Number Sense** Two stores sell their goods at the manufacturers' suggested retail prices, so their prices are the same. Which store has the greatest markdown from their original prices?

GOODS 2 GO	BUY AND BYE
$\frac{1}{4}$ off original prices!	30% off original prices!

____

Name ___________________________

Practice
11-2

Fractions, Decimals, and Percents

Describe the shaded portion of each as a fraction, decimal, and percent.

1. 

2. 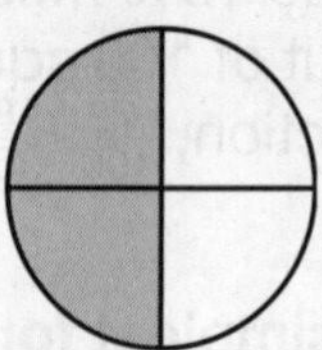

___________________ ___________________

Write each in two other ways.

3. 64% **4.** 0.09 **5.** $\frac{12}{50}$ **6.** 37%

7. $\frac{4}{250}$ **8.** 0.023

The table at the right shows the number of states in the United States at different times in history. There are currently 50 states in the United States. Use the information to answer the questions.

Year	States
1792	15
1817	20
1836	25
1848	30
1863	35
1889	40
1896	45
1959	50

9. In what year were there 0.5 as many states as today?

____

10. What percent of the current number of states had joined the United States by the year 1863?

____

11. In what year were there about $\frac{2}{3}$ as many states as in 1896? ________

12. Which of the following is equivalent to 98%?

A 0.49 **B** $\frac{100}{98}$ **C** 0.98 **D** $\frac{49}{100}$

13. Writing to Explain Explain how you would write $\frac{5}{6}$ as a percent.

____

Name ______________________________

Percents Greater Than 100 or Less Than 1

All percents can be written as fractions in simplest form and as decimals. Percents greater than 100% represent amounts greater than one whole and can be written as improper fractions and as decimals greater than 1. Percents less than 1% represent amounts less than $\frac{1}{100}$ of the whole.

Write 275% as a fraction in simplest form and as a decimal.

Since percent is parts per hundred, write the percent as a fraction with a denominator of 100. $\frac{275}{100}$

Simplify the fraction. $\frac{275}{100} = \frac{275 \div 25}{100 \div 25} = \frac{11}{4} = 2\frac{3}{4}$

To write the number as a decimal, divide the numerator by the denominator. $275 \div 100 = 2.75$

So, $275\% = 2\frac{3}{4} = 2.75$

Write $\frac{1}{5}$% as a fraction in simplest form and as a decimal.

Write the fraction in the percent as a decimal. $\frac{1}{5}\% = 0.2\%$

Write the percent as a fraction with a denominator of 100. $\frac{0.2}{100}$

Write the numerator as a whole number. $\frac{0.2}{100} = \frac{0.2 \times 10}{100 \times 10} = \frac{2}{1{,}000}$

Simplify the fraction. $\frac{2}{1{,}000} = \frac{2 \div 2}{1{,}000 \div 2} = \frac{1}{500}$

Divide the fraction to write the number as a decimal. $\frac{1}{500} = 0.002$

So, $\frac{1}{5}\% = \frac{1}{500} = 0.002$.

Write each percent as a fraction and as a decimal. Write fractions in simplest form.

1. 137% ______________; ______

2. 115% ______________; ______

3. 222% ______________; ______

4. 500% ______________; ______

5. 182% ______________; ______

6. 450% ______________; ______

7. $0.4\% = \frac{\square}{100} = \frac{\square \times 10}{100 \times 10} = \frac{\square}{\square}$; Simplify: $\frac{\square}{\square}$; Decimal: ______

8. $\frac{3}{4}\% = \frac{0.75}{100} = \frac{\square \times 100}{100 \times 100} = \frac{\square}{\square}$ Simplify: $\frac{\square}{\square}$; Decimal: ______

9. **Writing to Explain** Caryn and Alfonso bought school supplies. Caryn spent 130% of the amount Alfonso spent. She said that she spent 1.3 times the amount that Alfonso spent. Is Caryn correct? Explain.

____

Name ______________________

Practice
11-3

Percents Greater Than 100 or Less Than 1

Write a fraction in simplest form, a decimal, and a percent to name each shaded part.

1.

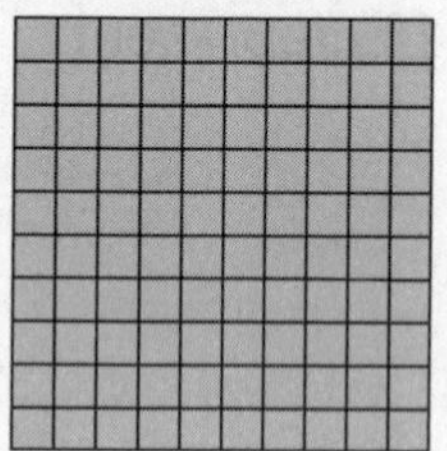

2.

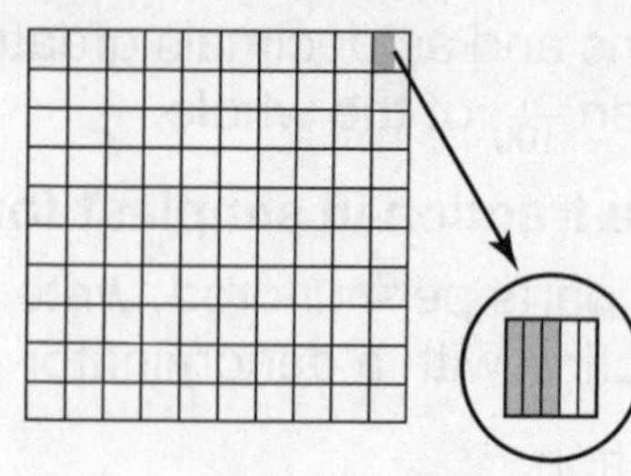

______________________ ______________________

Write each percent as a fraction and as a decimal. Write fractions in simplest form.

3. 188% ________; ________
4. 145% ________; ________
5. 261% ________; ________
6. 350% ________; ________
7. 275% ________; ________
8. 420% ________; ________
9. 400% ________; ________
10. $\frac{1}{5}\%$ ________; ________
11. 0.7% ________; ________
12. $\frac{1}{4}\%$ ________; ________

13. The land area of Yosemite National Park is 3079 km^2. This is about 189% of the land area of Sequoia National Park. Write 189% as a fraction in simplest form and as a decimal.

A $\frac{100}{189}$, 0.53 (rounded)
B $\frac{189}{100}$, 1.89
C $\frac{189}{100}$, 18.9
D $\frac{3079}{189}$, 16.29

14. **Writing to Explain** Nathan wanted to save $400 for a new bicycle. He saved 110% of his goal amount. Write 110% as a fraction in simplest form and as a decimal. Has he saved enough money to buy the bicycle? Explain how you know.

____

____

____

____

Name ______________________

Reteaching **11-4**

Estimating Percent

Estimate 8% of 300,000.

Round the percent.
8% ≈ 10%

Think of the equivalent decimal.
10% = 0.1

Multiply.
0.1 × 300,000 = 30,000

Estimate 27% of 297.

Round both numbers.
27% ≈ 30% 297 ≈ 300

Think of an equivalent decimal.
30% = 0.3

Multiply.
0.3 × 300 = 90

To multiply by 0.1, move the decimal point one place to the left.

0.1 × 50 = 5 0.1 × 4700 = 470 0.1 × 3,659 = 365.9

To multiply by a multiple of 0.1, such as 0.3, break apart the number.
0.3 = 0.1 × 3

Multiply one step at a time.
0.1 × 300 = 30 30 × 3 = 90

Round each percent, then write the equivalent decimal.

1. 41% ______ **2.** 88% ______ **3.** 76% ______

4. 22% ______ **5.** 37% ______ **6.** 59% ______

Break apart each decimal so the numbers are easier to multiply.

7. 0.4 ______ **8.** 0.9 ______ **9.** 0.6 ______

Estimate each percent.

10. 9% of 20 ______ **11.** 21% of 31 ______ **12.** 31% of 37 ______

13. 38% of 49 ______ **14.** 49% of 101 ______ **15.** 61% of 19 ______

16. 59% of 304 ______ **17.** 70% of 471 ______ **18.** 84% of 149 ______

19. Number Sense What is another way to estimate 51% of 42?

____

20. Reasoning If 10% of a number is 100, what is 15% of that number? Explain how you determined your answer.

____

____

Name ______________________

Practice **11-4**

Estimating Percent

Estimate.

1. 35% of 102 ________ **2.** 42% of 307 ________ **3.** 79% of 13 ________

4. 84% of 897 ________ **5.** 13% of 97 ________ **6.** 28% of 95 ________

7. 61% of 211 ________ **8.** 19% of 489 ________ **9.** 48% of 641 ________

10. 21% of 411 ________ **11.** 77% of 164 ________ **12.** 51% of 894 ________

13. 39% of 306 ________ **14.** 62% of 522 ________ **15.** 48% of 341 ________

16. **Number Sense** Which would you need to estimate to find an answer, 45% of 200 or 46% of 97?

17. The school store sold 48 items on Monday. Of those items, 60% were pens. About how many pens were sold on Monday? ________

18. The school cafeteria workers cooked 52 lb of pasta on Thursday. Of that, 90% was sold on Thursday, and 10% was stored in the refrigerator. About how much pasta was stored in the refrigerator? ________

19. On a rainy day, 76% of the students in the school brought umbrellas. There are 600 students in the school. About how many students brought umbrellas? ________

20. Which of the following is the best estimate for 68% of 251?

A 150

B 175

C 204

D 210

21. **Writing to Explain** Explain how you would estimate 79% of 389.

____

____

____

____

____

Name ______________________________

Finding the Percent of a Number

Find 77% of 240.

First estimate.
$77\% \approx 75\% = \frac{3}{4}$
$\frac{3}{4} \times 240 = 180$

Use a decimal.
Change the percent to a decimal.
$77\% = 0.77$

Multiply.
$0.77 \times 240 = 184.8$

The answer 184.8 is close to the estimate 180.

Use a proportion.

Write the percent as a fraction.
$77\% = \frac{77}{100}$

Write the proportion and solve.
$\frac{x}{240} = \frac{77}{100}$
$100x = 18{,}480$
$\frac{100x}{100} = \frac{18{,}480}{100}$
$x = 184.8$

Find the percent of each number.

1. 25% of 24 ________ **2.** 50% of 72 ________ **3.** 72% of 88 ________

4. 18% of 97 ________ **5.** 66% of 843 ________ **6.** 46% of 388 ________

7. 89% of 111 ________ **8.** 0.7% of 392 ________ **9.** 110% of 640 ________

10. Geometry Ava's aquarium is 10 in. tall, 15 in. long, and 8 in. wide. The aquarium is 95% filled with water. How many cubic inches of water are in the aquarium?

____

11. DeWayne used his music club membership card to get 15% off the cost of a CD. If the regular price of the CD was $15.95, how much did DeWayne pay?

____

12. Marla bought a dress priced at $89.99. She used a 20% off coupon. How much did she pay for the dress?

____

13. Writing to Explain Tell how you could use a proportion to find 125% of 500. Why is the solution greater than the original number?

____

Name ____________________

Practice

11-5

Finding the Percent of a Number

Find the percent of each number.

1. 42% of 800 ______ **2.** 5.6% of 425 ______ **3.** 85% of 15 ______

4. $33\frac{1}{3}$% of 678 ______ **5.** 12% of 65 ______ **6.** 58% of 324 ______

7. 98% of 422 ______ **8.** 32% of 813.5 ______ **9.** 78% of 219 ______

10. 13% of 104 ______ **11.** 24% of 529 ______ **12.** 4.5% of 82 ______

13. 64% of 912 ______ **14.** 128% of 256 ______ **15.** 63% of 1,368 ______

16. About 42% of the flag of the United States is red. On a flag that is 9 feet tall and 15 feet wide, how many square feet are red? ______

17. Estimation Estimate 68% of 32, then find the actual answer. Which is greater? ______

______

______

For **18** and **19**, round your answer to the nearest whole number.

18. An adult has 206 bones. Of those, approximately 2.9% are found in the inner ear. About how many bones in the human body are found in the inner ear?

______

19. Approximately 12.6% of the bones are vertebrae in the human back. About how many bones in the human body are vertebrae?

______

20. 45 is 12% of which number?

A 540 **B** 450 **C** 375 **D** 5.4

21. Writing to Explain Without calculating, tell which is greater, 52% of 3,400 or 98% of 1,500. Explain.

______

______

Name ______________________________

Finding the Whole

You can draw a number line model to help you solve this problem:

Darlene spent 10% of her allowance and saved the rest. The amount she spent was 50 cents. How much is Darlene's allowance?

In the problem, 50 cents is the part and 10% is the percent. You need to find Darlene's allowance, *a*.

The model shows 10% as the percent, 50 cents as the part, and *a*, the whole you are trying to find.

A proportion can also help you find the whole.

$\frac{10}{100} = \frac{50}{a}$

Think: 10 times what number equals 50? Since $10 \times 5 = 50$, then multiply 100×5 to get 500.

$a = 500$

500 cents = \$5.00

Darlene's allowance is \$5.00.

For **1** through **3**, draw a number line model to help you solve the problem.

1. Li rode her bike 25% of the way to school. She rode 5 blocks. How many blocks does Li live from school?

____

2. Bob brought 40% of the collected canned goods to the food pantry. If Bob brought 160 cans to the pantry, how many cans were collected?

____

3. Sid memorized 60% of his lines for the class play. He memorized 60 lines. How many lines long was Sid's part in the play?

____

Name ______________________________

Practice **11-6**

Finding the Whole

In **1** through **4**, use the number lines and write a proportion to solve.

1. 10% of what number is 30?

____

2. 150% of what number is 75?

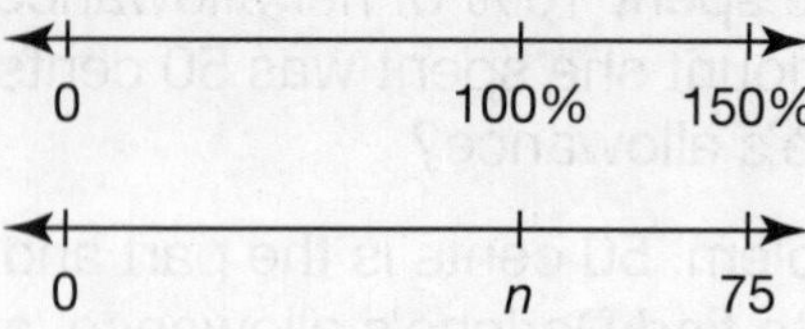

____

3. 70% of what number is 280?

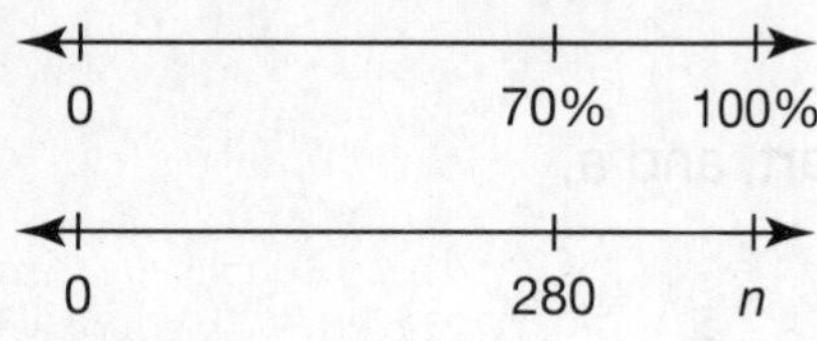

____

4. 56% of what number is 84?

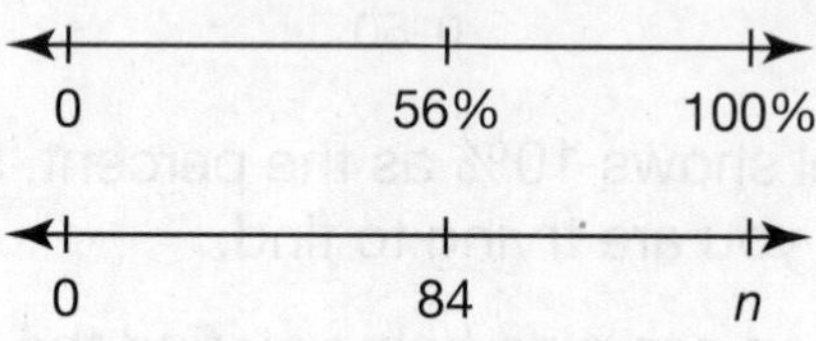

____

For **5** through **8**, find each whole.

5. 60% of what number is 12? ______________________________

6. 100% of what number is 61? ______________________________

7. 40% of what number is 5? ______________________________

8. 14% of what number is 7? ______________________________

9. Only 5% of the total attendees for a concert have arrived. If 105 people have arrived, how many attendees are expected?

A 2,100 **B** 2,025 **C** 1,950 **D** 1,800

10. Writing to Explain You want to solve 11% of what number is 22. Explain how you can do this using a proportion

____

____

____

Name ______________________________

Problem Solving: Reasonableness

After solving a problem, look back and check that your answer is reasonable and that you answered the correct question.

Terrell bought a skateboard on sale for 20% off the original price. He also had a coupon for 10% off. The original price was $80. How much did Terrell pay for the skateboard before tax?

Answer: Terrell paid $24 for the skateboard.

Is my answer reasonable?

Since the discount is about 30% off, Terrell will pay about 70% of the original cost of the skateboard.

70% of $80 is $56.

The answer is not reasonable because the price of the skateboard should be about 70% of the original price, or $56.

Ask yourself:

Did I use the correct operation(s) to solve the problem?

Is all of my work correct?

Is the actual answer close to my estimate?

Did I answer the correct question?

Yes. The question asks for the sale price of the skateboard.

Ask yourself:

What am I asked to find?

Look back and check. Tell if the answer given is reasonable. Explain why or why not.

1. Marita bought some toys for her cat at the pet store. The pet store is having a storewide discount of 15% on all pet toys. How much will Marita pay for the toys if the total price before the discount is $42?
Answer: The discount price is $35.70.

____

____

2. Frankie paid a total of $53.50 for some fish for his aquarium. The price includes a coupon for 7% off. What was the cost of the fish?
Answer: The fish cost $50.00.

____

____

Name ______________________________

Practice
11-7

Problem Solving: Reasonableness

Look back and check. Tell if the answer given is reasonable. Explain why or why not.

1. A shipment of 200 games is 20% video games, 50% board games, and 30% puzzles. How many board games are chess if 25% of the board games are chess?
Answer: The number of chess games is 50.

____

____

2. A DVD player costs \$199. How much will it cost if it is 15% off?
Answer: The cost of the DVD player will be \$169.15.

____

____

3. Write a Problem An ad in the newspaper is offering 25% off ski lift tickets at Big Bear. The original tickets cost \$60. Write a problem using the information from the ad. Then give an answer for someone to look back and check for reasonableness.

____

____

4. Students at Warm Springs Middle School are going on a field trip to Orange County. If 60% of the 120 students signed up for the field trip are girls, and 25% of the girls are in sixth grade, how many sixth grade girls are going on the field trip?

A 18 **B** 25 **C** 43 **D** 102

5. Writing to Explain Bailey paid \$42 for a backpack that was 40% off the original price. Is \$56 a reasonable price for the original cost of the backpack? Explain.

____

____

Name ______________________________

Area of Rectangles

Find the area of a rectangle that is 8 inches long and 3 inches wide.

Use Counting
Draw the rectangle on grid paper. Let each square represent 1 square inch.

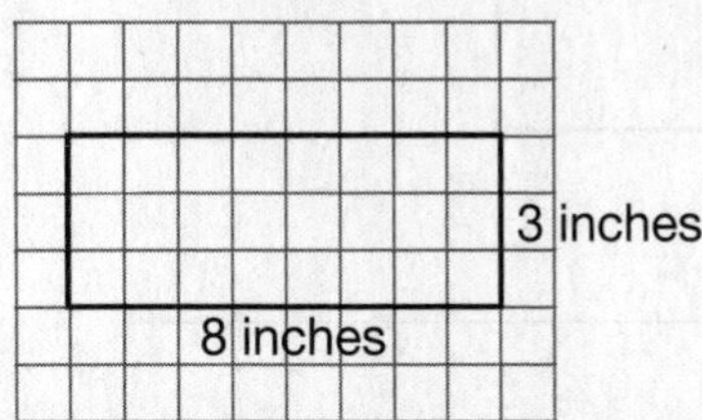

Count the squares inside the rectangle. There are 24 squares, so the area is 24 sq in.

Use a Formula
Use the formula for area. To find area, multiply length times width.

$A = \ell \times w$ ℓ = length, w = width
$A = 8 \times 3$ $\ell = 8$, $w = 3$
$A = 24$

The area of the rectangle is 24 in^2.

A garden measures 8 ft by 7 ft. What is the area of the garden?

Use Counting
Draw the figure on grid paper. Let each square represent 1 square foot.

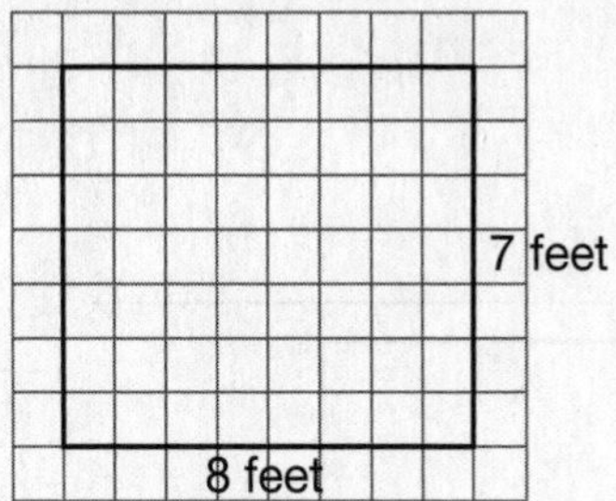

Count the squares inside the garden. There are 56 squares, so the area is 56 sq ft.

Use a Formula
Find the area of the rectangular garden by multiplying length times width.
Garden:
$A = \ell \times w$
$A = 8 \times 7$
$A = 56$ sq ft

The area of the garden is 56 ft^2.

Find the area of each figure.

1.

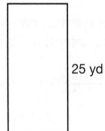

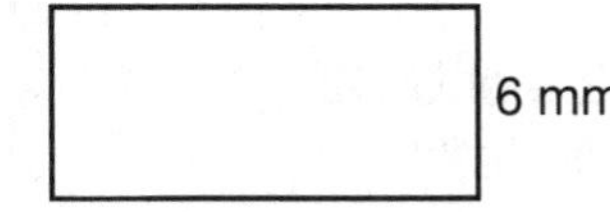

____

2.

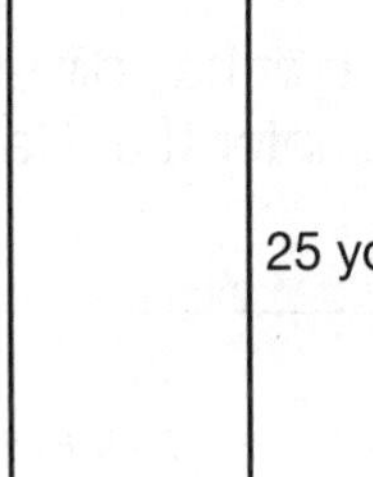

____

3.

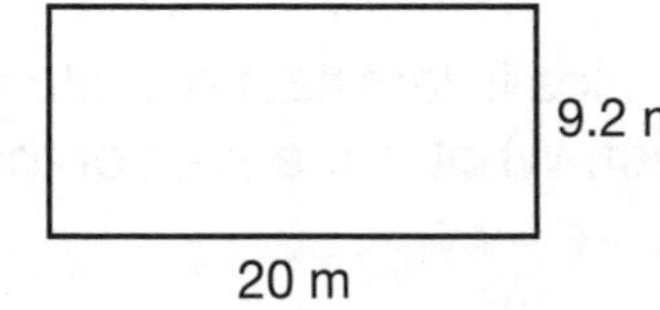

____

4. Suppose a rectangular garden measures $4\frac{1}{2}$ feet by 10 feet. What is the area of the garden? _______________

Name ______________________

Area of Rectangles

Find the area of each figure.

1.
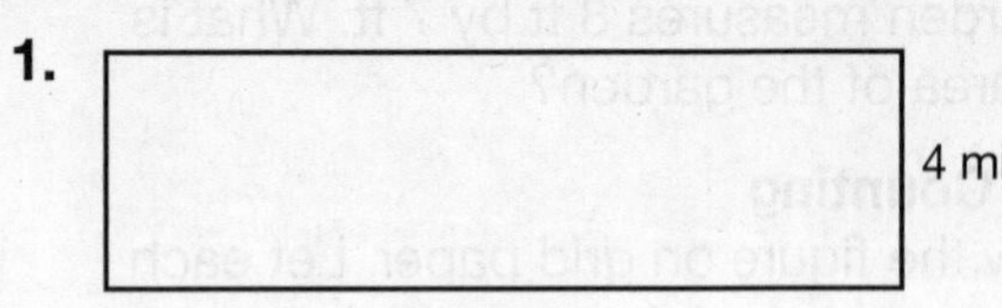

2.
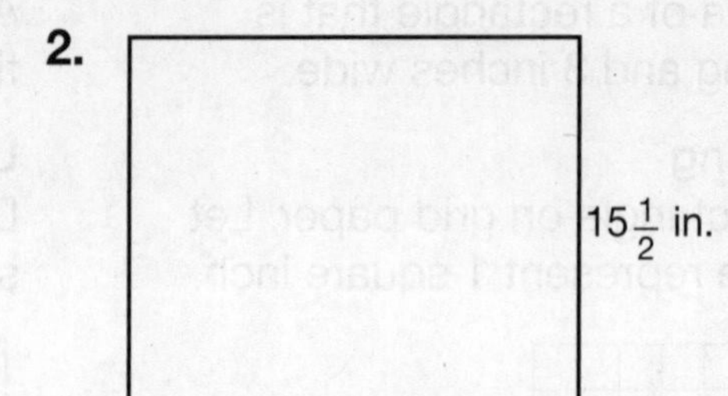

3.
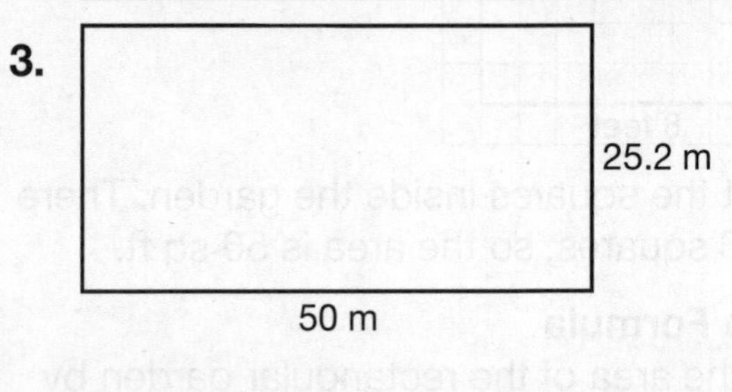

4.
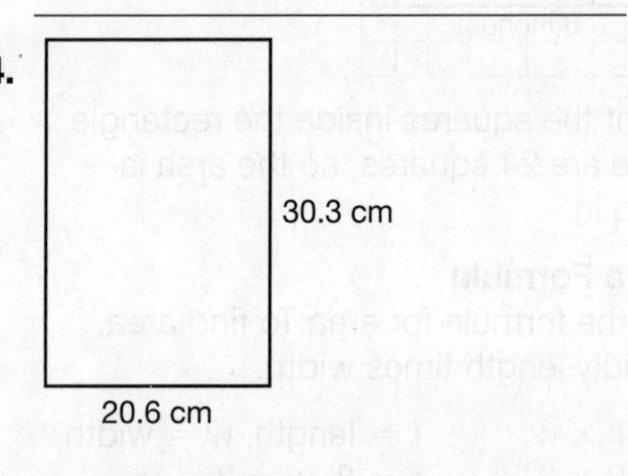

For **5** and **6**, draw and label the figures described using grid paper. Then calculate the area of each figure.

5. A rectangle that is 13 units by 9 units

6. Carlos is laminating a kitchen counter that has dimensions of 12 feet by 3 feet. What is the area of the kitchen counter that Carlos will laminate?

7. What is the area of a square that is 30 centimeters on one side?

A 60 cm^2 **B** 120 cm^2 **C** 300 cm^2 **D** 900 cm^2

8. **Writing to Explain** If you know the area of a rectangle, can you determine its length and width? Explain.

Name ____________________

Area of Parallelograms and Rhombuses

Find the area of this parallelogram.

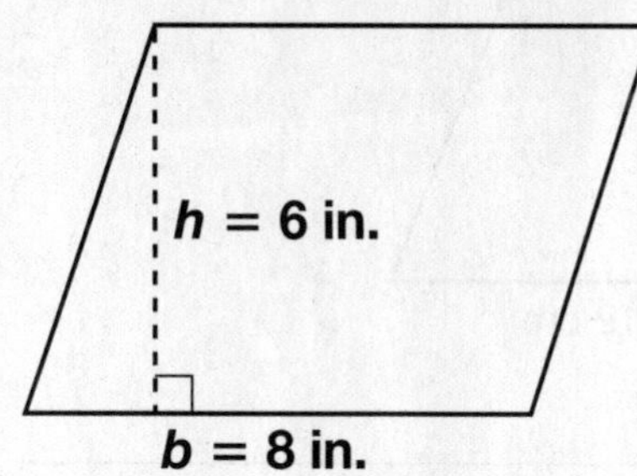

Use the formula $A = bh$.

$A = 8 \times 6$

$A = 48 \text{ in}^2$

The area of the parallelogram is 48 sq in.

Find the area of this rhombus.

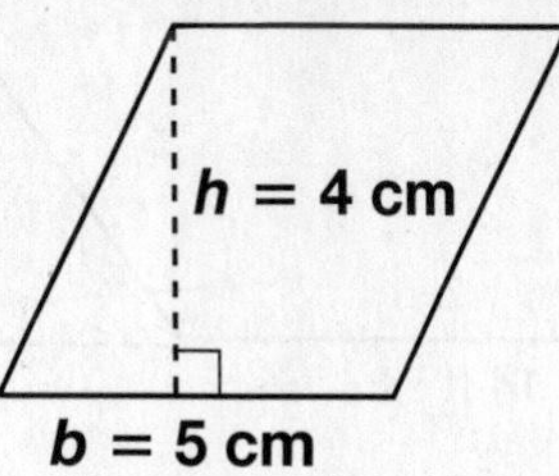

Use the formula $A = bh$.

$A = 5 \times 4$

$A = 20 \text{ cm}^2$

The area of the rhombus is 20 cm^2.

Find the area of each parallelogram or rhombus.

1.

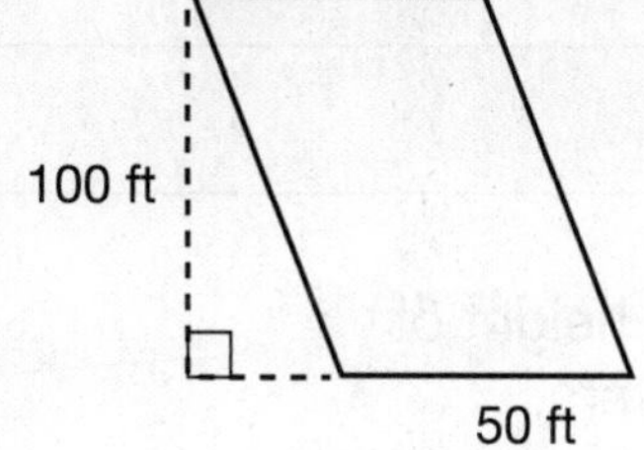

____

2.

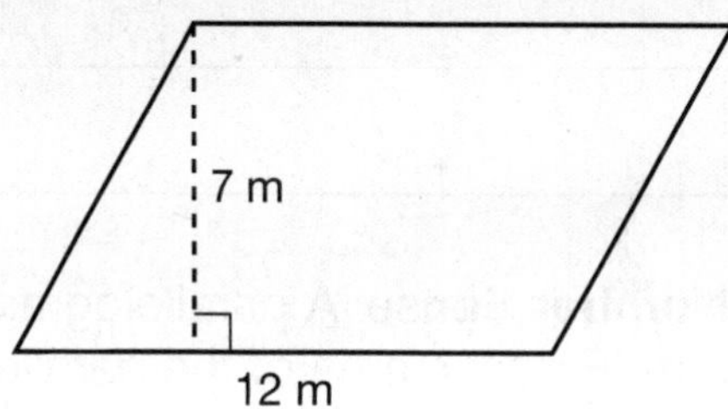

____

3. Rhombus: $b = 6$ ft, $h = 4$ ft ____________________

4. Parallelogram: $b = 18$ m, $h = 13.5$ m ____________________

5. Parallelogram: $b = 20$ in., $h = 9\frac{1}{2}$ in. ____________________

6. Writing to Explain Tony says he does not have enough information to find the area of this parallelogram. Is he correct? Explain.

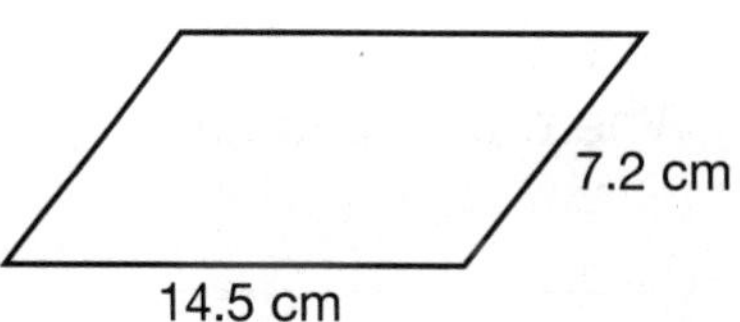

____

Name ______________________________

Area of Parallelograms and Rhombuses

Find the area of each parallelogram or rhombus.

1.

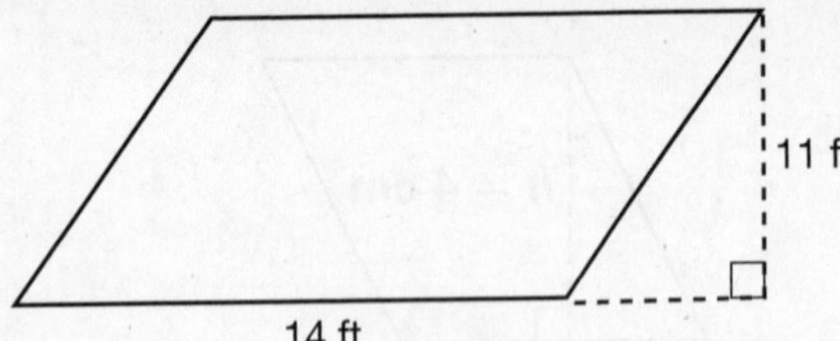

____

2.

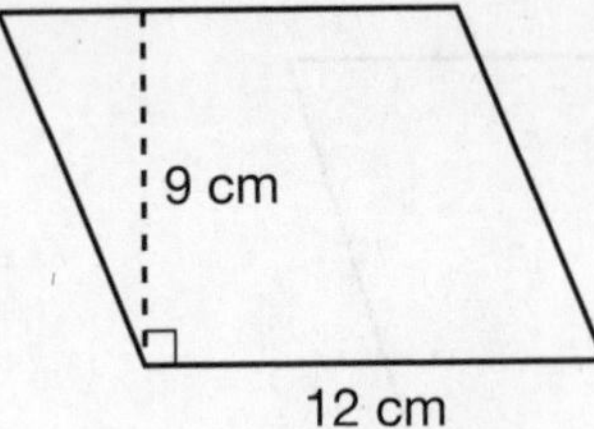

____

3. Rhombus
$b = 30$ m
$h = 15.5$ m

____

4. Parallelogram
$b = 18$ in.
$h = 2\frac{1}{2}$ in.

____

5. Parallelogram
$b = 20$ ft
$h = 3$ yd

____

6. Writing to Explain The area of a parallelogram is 42 square inches. The parallelogram's base is 6 inches. Find the height of the parallelogram. Explain how you do it.

____

____

7. Number Sense A parallelogram has a base of 4 m and a height of 3 m. Find the area of the parallelogram in square centimeters.

____

8. Estimation Which is the best estimate of the area of a parallelogram that has a base of 11.42 cm and a height of 8.33 cm?

A 200 cm^2 **B** 160 cm^2 **C** 100 cm^2 **D** 50 cm^2

9. Reasoning The area of a figure is 36 cm^2. Give 3 possible shapes of the figure. Where possible give 3 possible sets of dimensions for each possible shape.

____

____

____

____

Name ______________________

Area of Triangles

Find the area of this triangle.

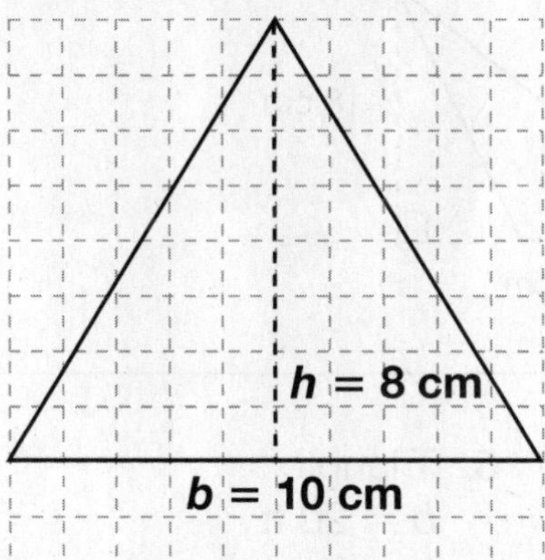

Use the formula $A = \frac{1}{2}bh$.

$A = \frac{1}{2} \times 10 \times 8$

$A = 5 \times 8$

$A = 40 \text{ cm}^2$

The area of the triangle is 40 cm^2.

Find the area of each triangle.

1.

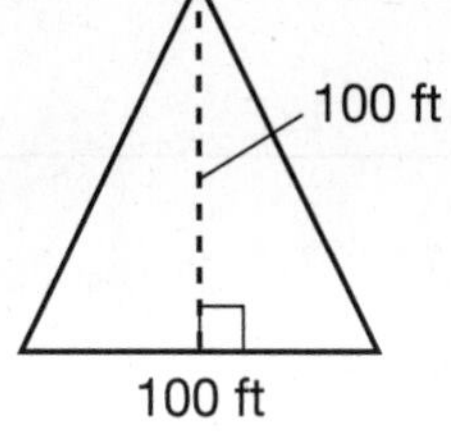

2.

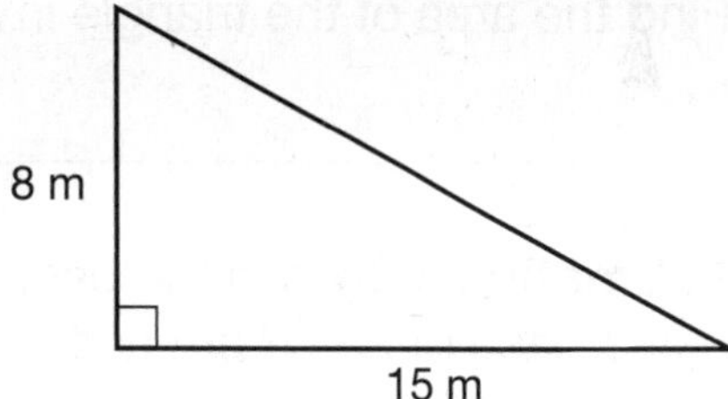

______________________ ______________________

3. Triangle: $b = 6$ ft, $h = 9$ ft ______________________

4. Triangle: $b = 18$ m, $h = 13$ m ______________________

5. Triangle: $b = 20$ in., $h = 9\frac{1}{2}$ in. ______________________

6. Writing to Explain Rebekah needs to find the area of a right triangle. She knows all the side lengths of the right triangle, but she says that she also needs to know the height. Is she correct? Explain.

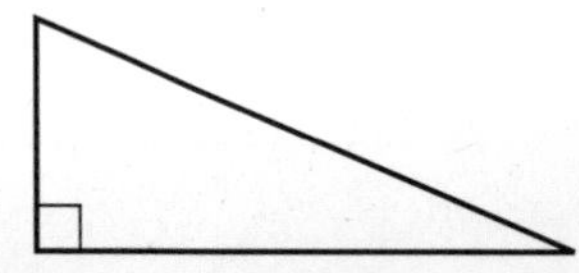

____

Name ______________________

Practice

12-3

Area of Triangles

Find the area of each triangle.

1.

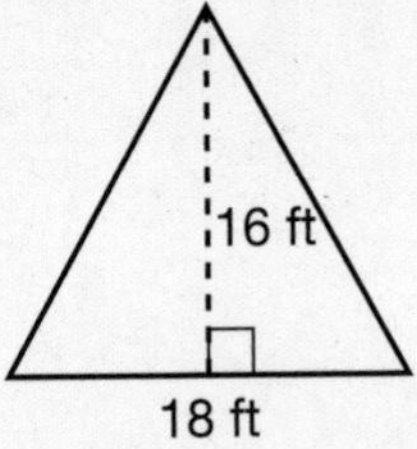

2.

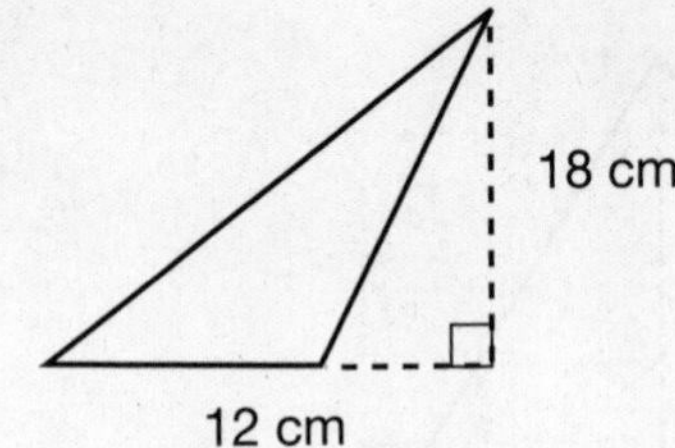

______________ ______________

3. Triangle
$b = 30$ m
$h = 15.6$ m

____

4. Triangle
$b = 18$ in.
$h = 6\frac{1}{2}$ in.

____

5. Triangle
$b = 20$ ft
$h = 3$ yd

____

6. Writing to Explain The area of a triangle is 42 square inches. The triangle's base is 6 inches. Find the height of the triangle. Explain how you do it.

____

____

7. Number Sense A triangle has a base of 2 m and a height of 4 m. Find the area of the triangle in square millimeters.

____

8. Estimation Which is the best estimate of the area of a triangle that has a base of 23.62 cm and a height of 8.33 cm?

A 200 cm^2 **B** 160 cm^2 **C** 100 cm^2 **D** 50 cm^2

9. Reasoning The area of a triangle is 36 cm^2. Give 3 possible sets of dimensions for the triangle and explain whether or not you can also give the triangles' side lengths.

____

____

____

____

____

Name ______________________________

Reteaching **12-4**

Area of Special Quadrilaterals

Find the area of this trapezoid.

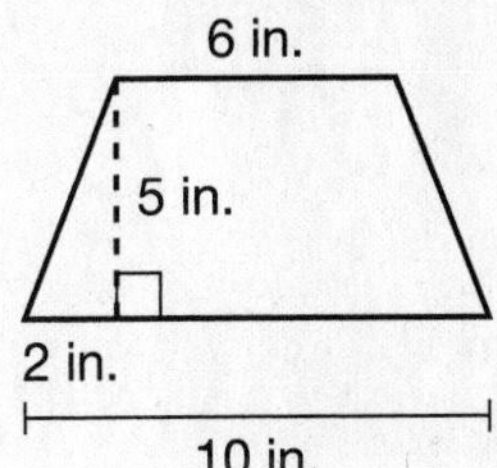

Find the area of each part.

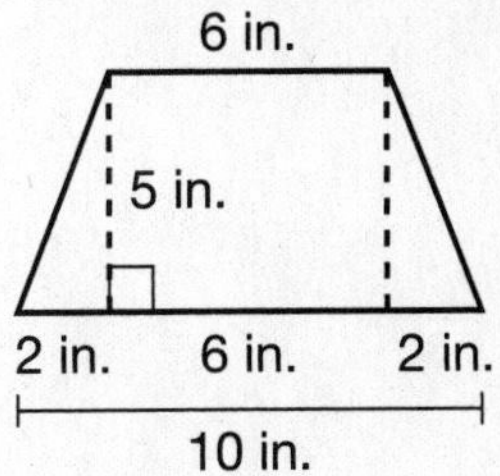

Each Triangle
$A = \frac{1}{2}bh = \frac{1}{2} \times 2 \times 5 = 5 \text{ in}^2$

Rectangle
$A = lw = 6 \times 5 = 30 \text{ in}^2$

Add the areas together.
$5 + 5 + 30 = 40 \text{ in}^2$

Find the area of this kite.

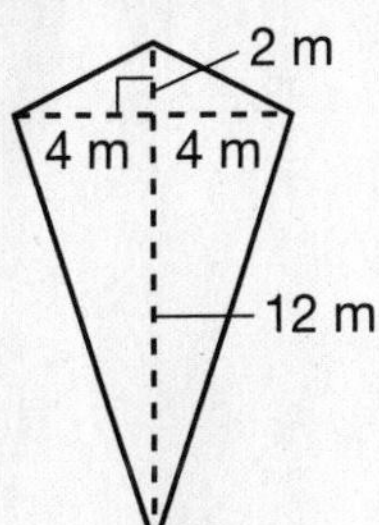

You can find the area of a kite by dividing it into two identical triangles and finding the area of each triangle.

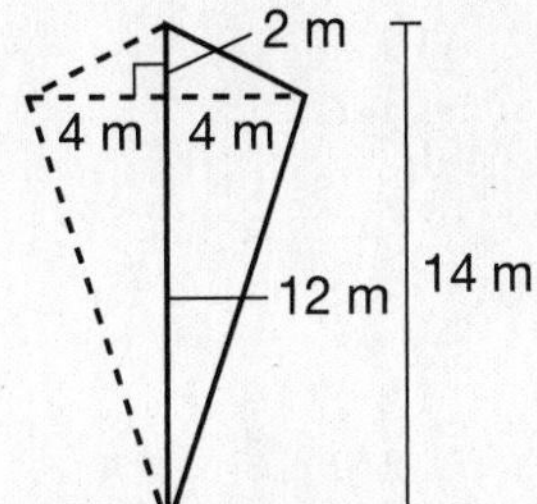

$A = \frac{1}{2}bh = \frac{1}{2} \times 14 \times 4 = 28$

The area of the kite is $2 \times 28 = 56 \text{ m}^2$.

Find the area of the trapezoid or kite.

1.

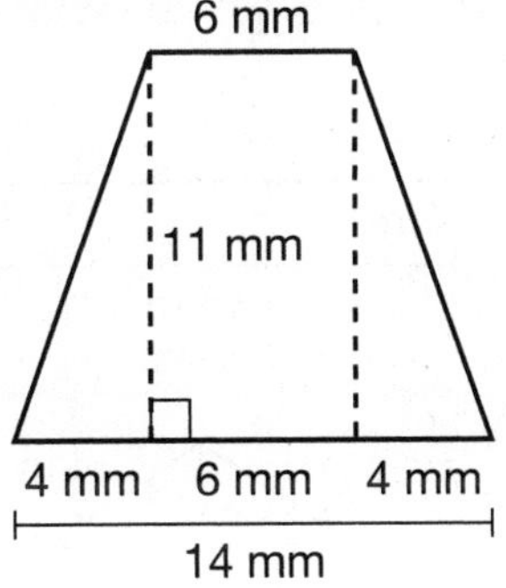

____

2.

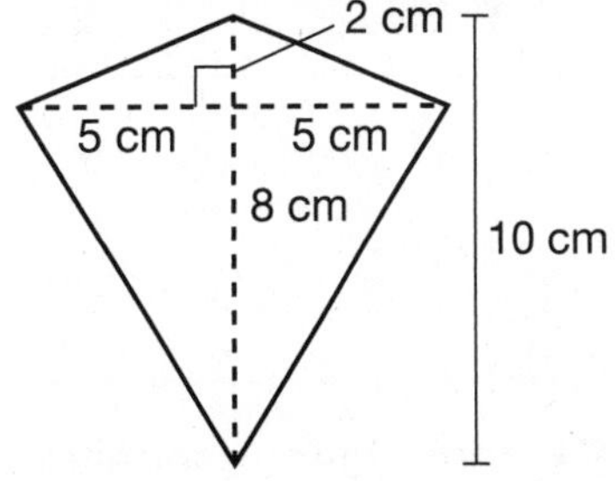

____

3. Which figure above has a greater area, the trapezoid or the kite? Explain your answer.

____

Name ___________________________

Practice
12-4

Area of Special Quadrilaterals

Find the area of each figure.

1. 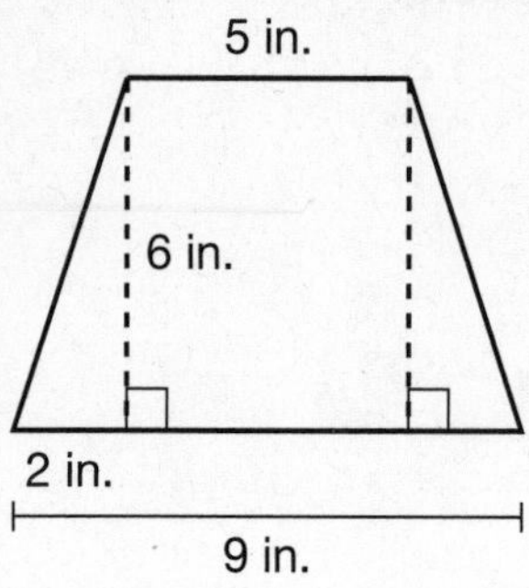

____

2. 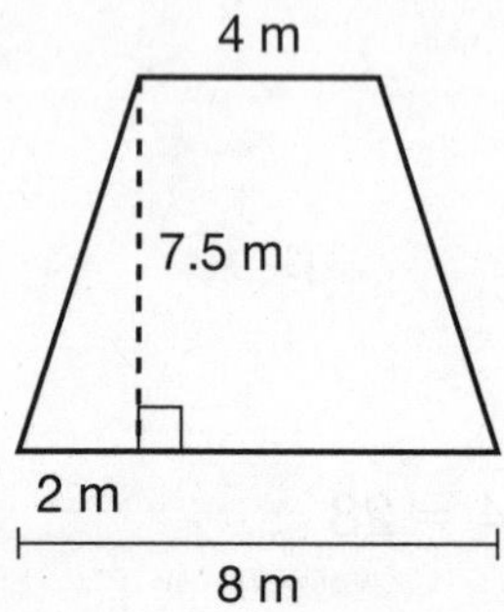

____

3. 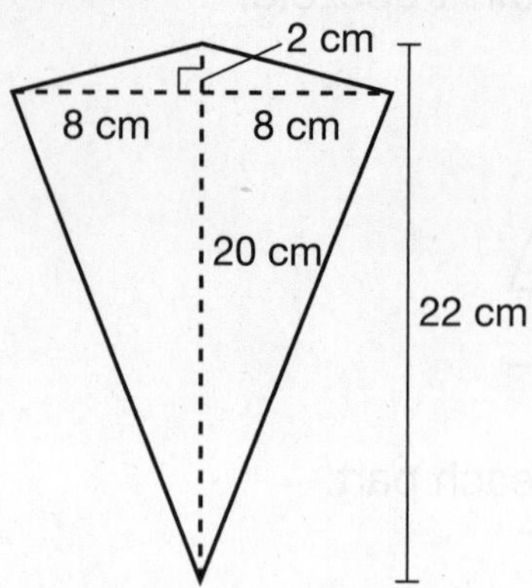

____

4. 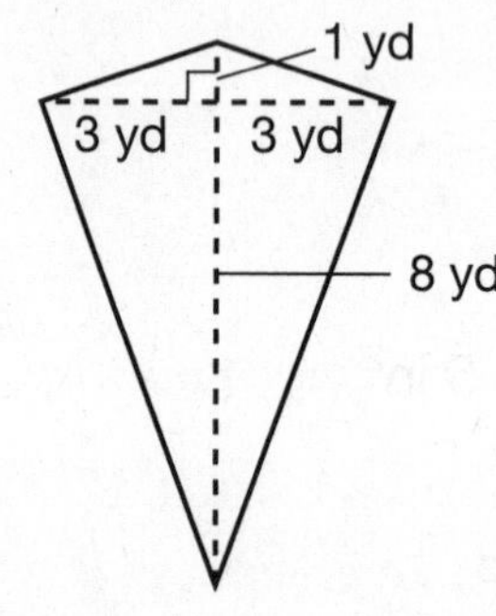

____

Solve each problem.

5. Rita wants to paint the area shown at the right. What is the area that she needs to cover?

____

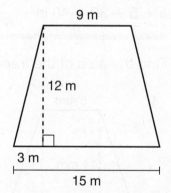

6. **Writing to Explain** Joshua received this kite as a gift. The dimensions were labeled as shown. Joshua says that he does not have enough information to find the area of the kite. Is he correct? Explain your answer.

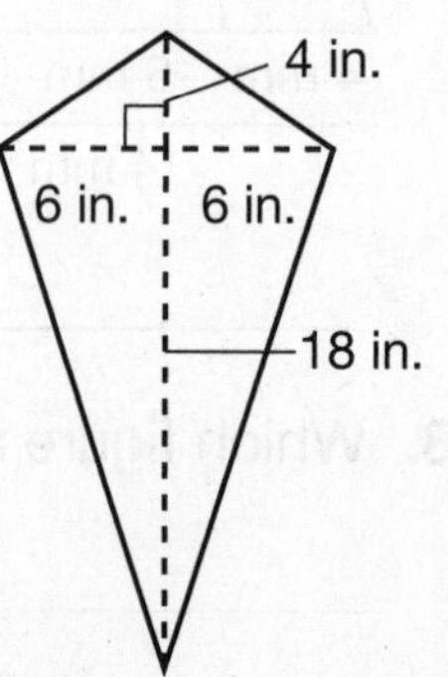

____

____

Name ______________________________

Reteaching
12-5

Finding Areas of Polygons

Find the area of this polygon.

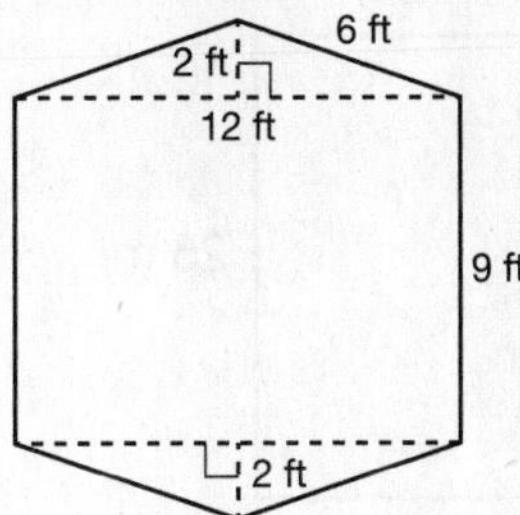

Find the area of each part.

Each Triangle:
$A = \frac{1}{2}bh = \frac{1}{2} \times 12 \times 2 = 12 \text{ ft}^2$

Rectangle:
$A = \ell w = 9 \times 12 = 108 \text{ ft}^2$

Add the areas together.
$12 + 12 + 108 = 132 \text{ ft}^2$

The area of the polygon is 132 ft^2.

A path around a garden measures 8 m by 7 m. The garden measures 4 m by 3 m. What is the area of the path?

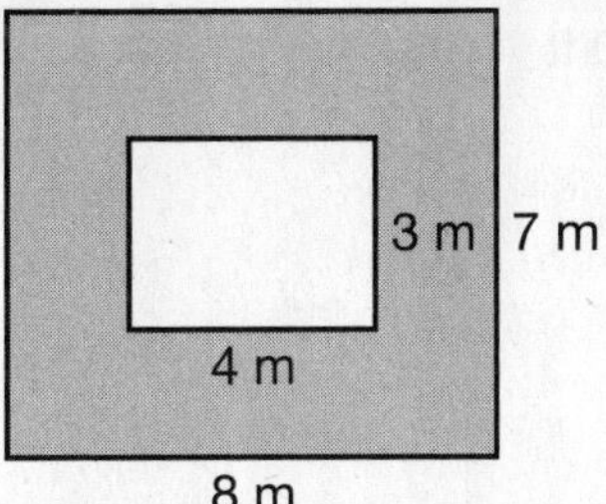

Find the area of the path and the garden together. Then subtract the area of the garden.

Path and garden together:
$A = \ell w$
$A = 8 \times 7$
$A = 56 \text{ m}^2$

Garden:
$A = \ell w$
$A = 4 \times 3$
$A = 12 \text{ m}^2$

$56 - 12 = 44$, so the area of the path is 44 m^2.

Find the area of each figure.

1.

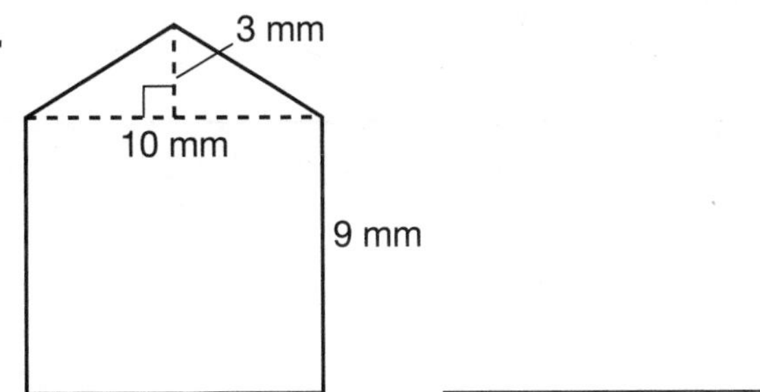

____

2.

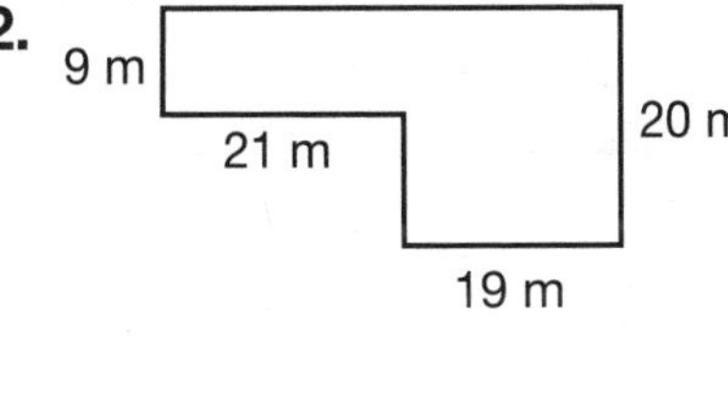

____

3. The outside of a rectangular path around a rectangular garden measures 4 meters by 7 meters. The garden measures 3 meters by 6 meters. What is the area of the path?

____

Name ____________________

Finding Areas of Polygons

Find the area of each figure.

1.

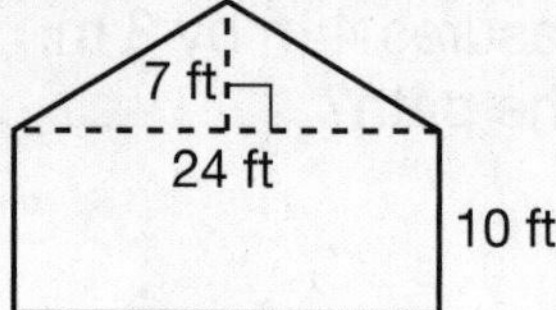

____

2.

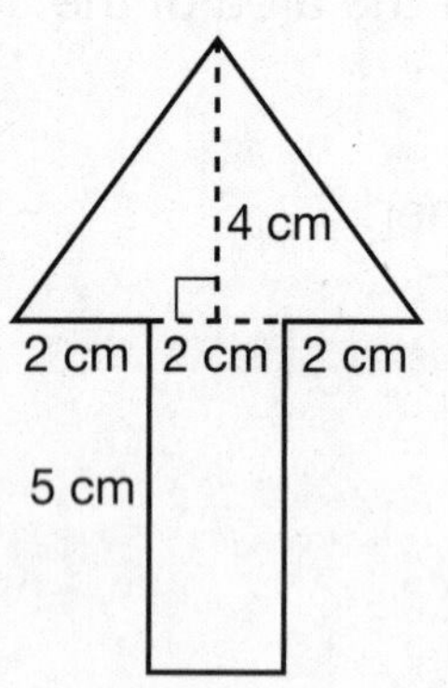

____

3.

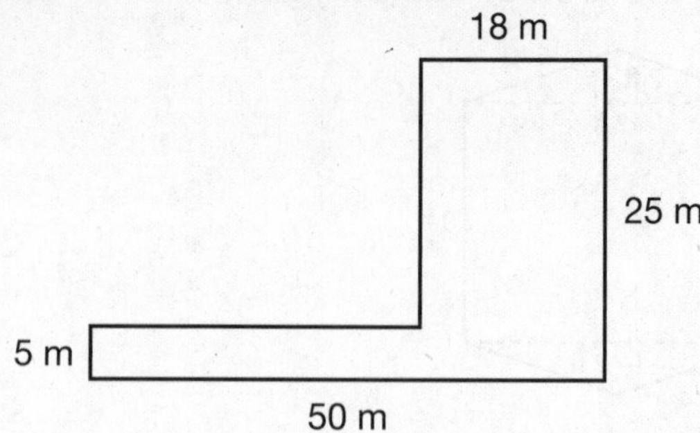

____

4.

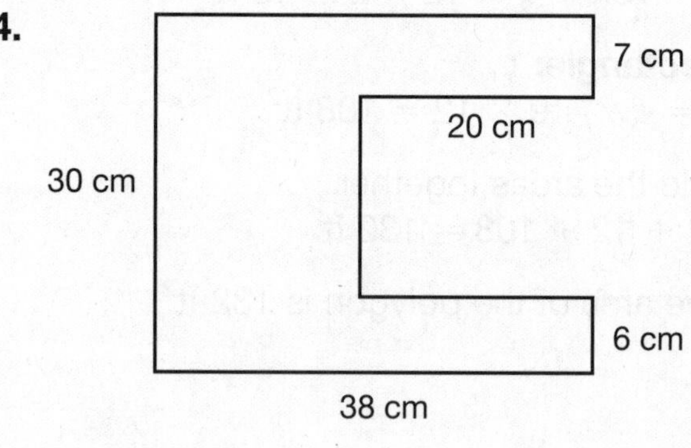

____

Read and solve each problem.

5. Carlos is tiling a kitchen counter that is 12 feet by 3 feet. The counter has a rectangular hole 3 feet by 2 feet cut in it for a sink. What is the area of the kitchen counter that Carlos will tile?

____

6. Writing to Explain Explain into which shapes you could break this polygon in order to find its area. Find the area.

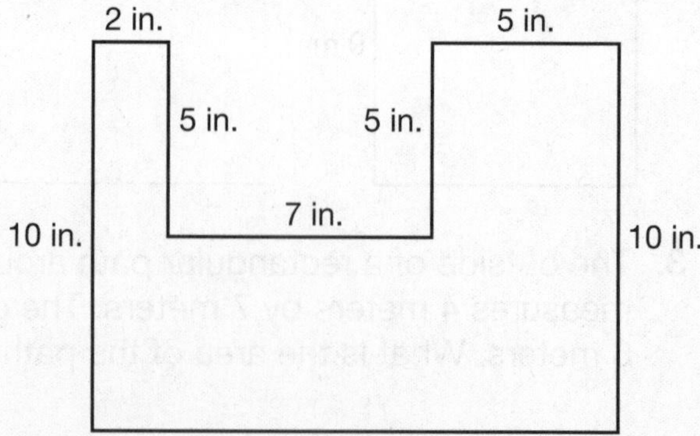

____

____

____

____

Name ____________________

Areas of Polygons on the Coordinate Plane

To find the area of the polygon on the coordinate grid below, divide the trapazoid into 2 triangles and 1 rectangle. Next, count the squares on the grid or use the absolute value to find the base and height of each triangle and the length and width of the rectangle. Then use these measurements to calculate the area of each part.

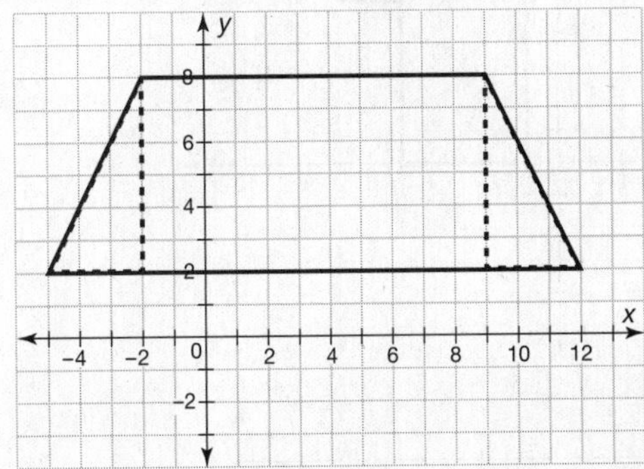

Area of each Triangle
$b = 3, h = 6$
$A = \frac{1}{2}bh = \frac{1}{2} \times 3 \times 6 = 9$ sq units

Area of the Rectangle
$\ell = 11, w = 6$
$A = \ell w = 11 \times 6 = 66$ sq units

Add the areas of the smaller shapes to find the total area of the polygon.

$9 + 9 + 66 = 84$ square units

Find the area of each polygon.

1. 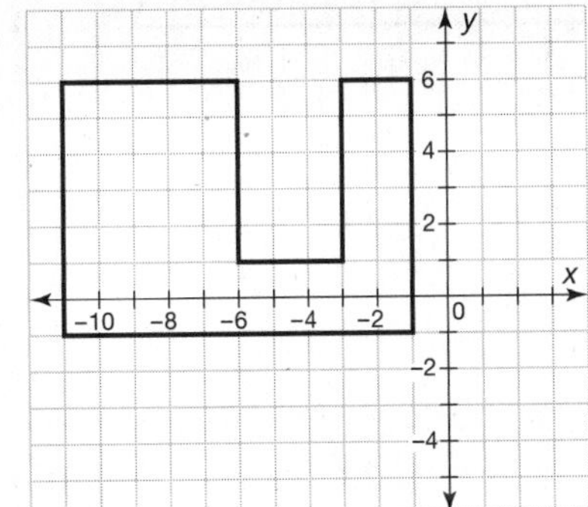

2. 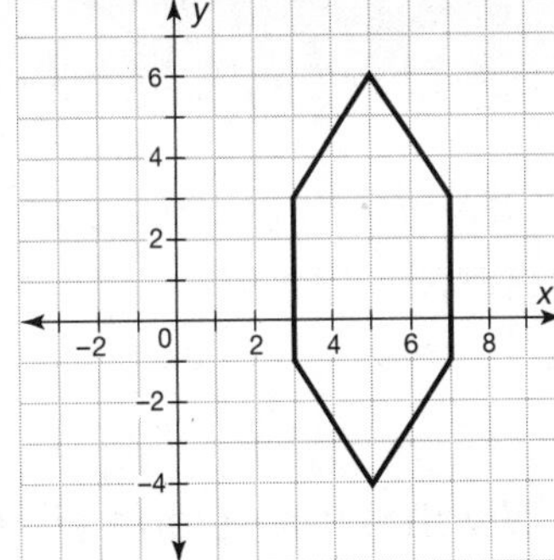

____________________ ____________________

3. Writing to Explain Jamal drew a sketch of the garden he is going to plant. Each grid represents 1 sq ft. Each different vegetable will need 3 sq ft, and he wants to plant 12 different vegetables. Does he have enough space in his garden? Explain you answer.

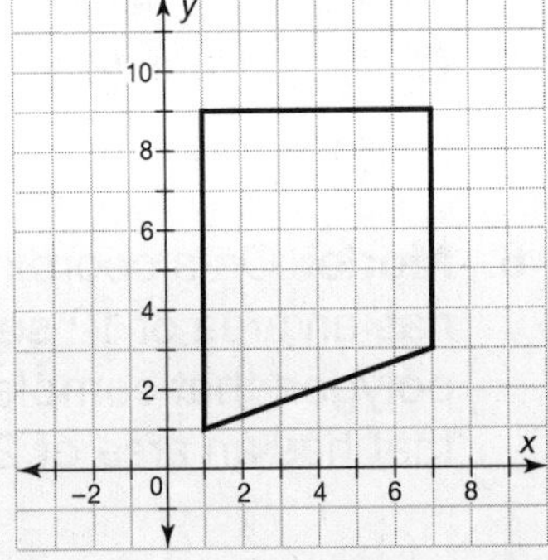

____

____

Name ___________________________

Practice
12-6

Areas of Polygons on the Coordinate Plane

Find the area of each figure.

1.

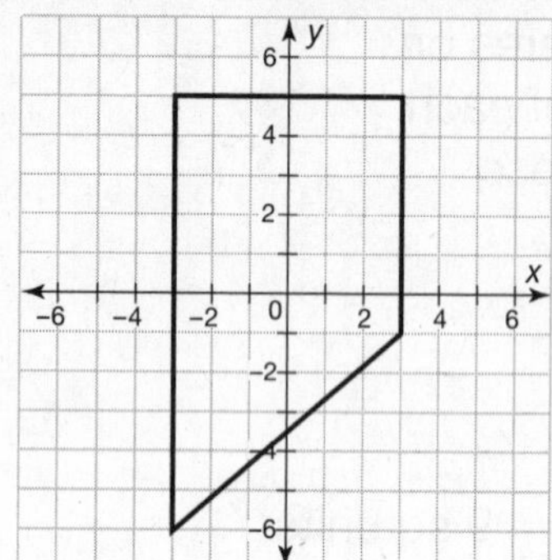

____

2.

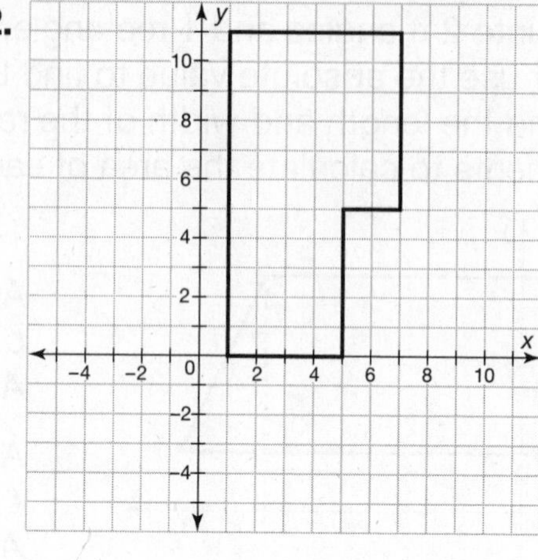

____

3.

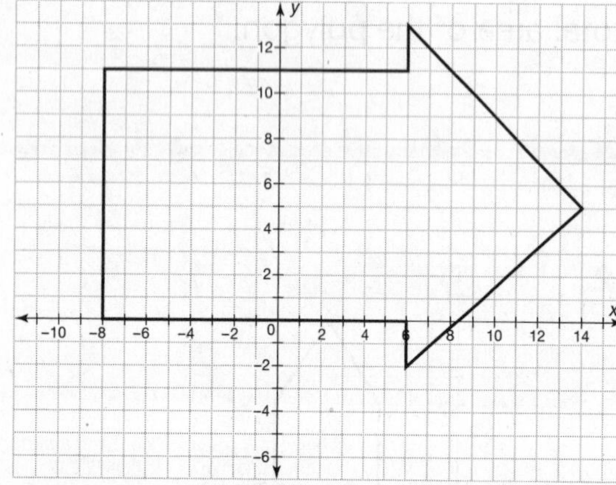

____

4.

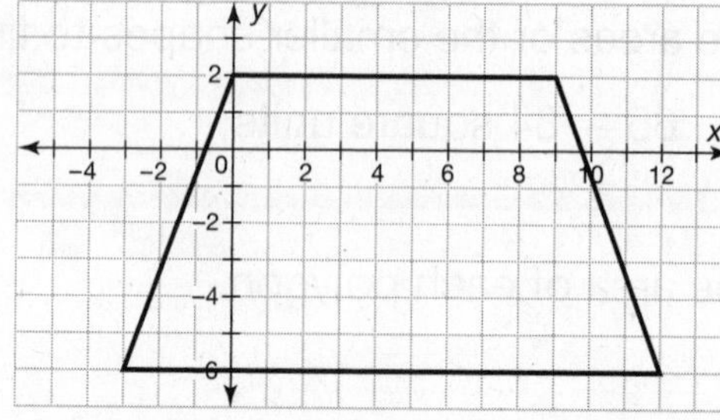

____

5. Reasoning Which expression can you use to find the area of this figure?

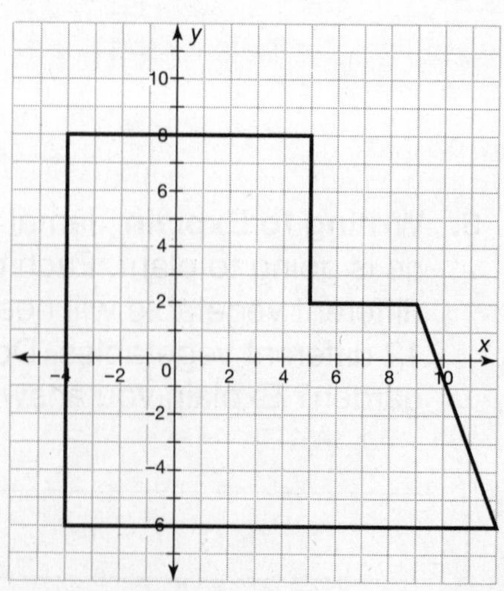

A $(9 \times 14) + (8 \times 4) + \frac{1}{2}(8 \times 3)$

B $(8 \times 14) + (9 \times 4) + \frac{1}{2}(9 \times 3)$

C $(9 \times 14) + (8 \times 4) + (8 \times 3)$

D $(9 \times 14) + (8 \times 4) + \frac{1}{4}(8 \times 3)$

6. Model On a coordinate grid, draw a polygon that has an area of 12 square units. Draw a second polygon that completely encloses the first polygon that has an area of 24 square units.

Name ______________________________

Problem Solving: Use Objects

Pentomino Construction Company There are 12 different pentominoes. Which two pentominoes can be used to make this shape?

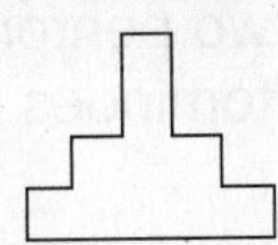

Read and Understand

What do you know? There are 12 different pentominoes. Two pentominoes are used to construct this shape.

What are you trying to find? The two pentominoes used to make the shape.

Plan and Solve

What strategy will you use? Use objects, in this case pentominoes.

Study the shape and compare the corners and angles to the group of pentominoes. Choose two pentominoes to make the figure.

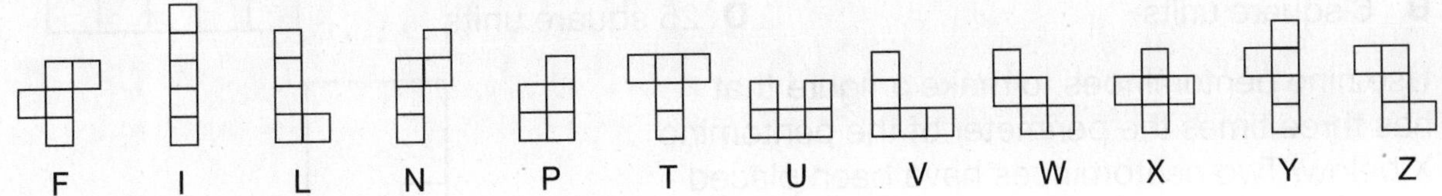

Since the base is 5 units, try the I and the T pentominoes. If your first choice does not work, try other pentominoes.

Look Back and Check

Is your answer reasonable? Yes. The two pentominoes make the same shape.

Fit two pentominoes together to create each shape. Draw the pentominoes used in each figure.

1. 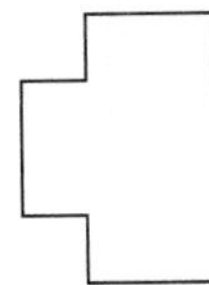

2. 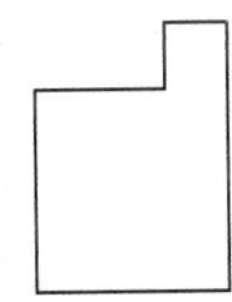

3. Writing to Explain A figure is made from three pentominoes. What is the area of the figure in square units? How did you find your answer?

____

Name ______________________________

Problem Solving: Use Objects

Fit two pentominoes together to create each shape. Draw the pentominoes used in each figure.

1. 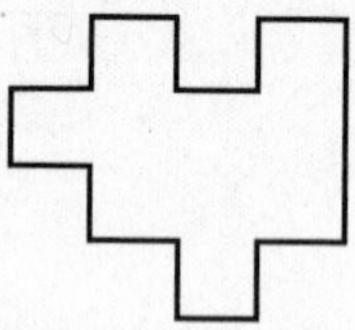

2. 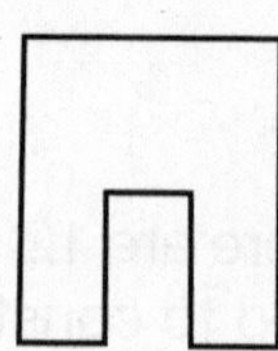

3. What is the area in square units of each figure you made in Problems 1 and 2?

____

4. Tessa used pentominoes to make this rectangle. The I pentomino is shown. What is the area of the rectangle in square units?

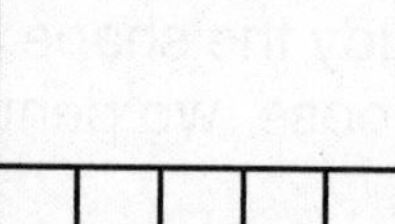

A 5 square units

B 6 square units

C 20 square units

D 25 square units

5. Use nine pentominoes to make a figure that has three times the perimeter of the pentomino X below. Two pentominoes have been placed to get you started.

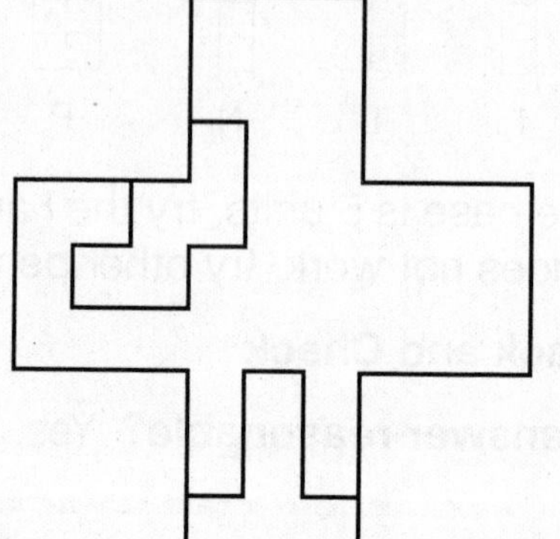

X

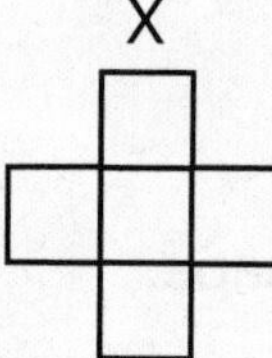

6. Writing to Explain Circle the pentominoes. Explain why any figures not circled are not pentominoes.

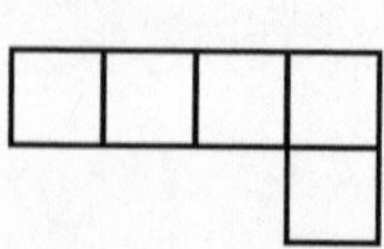

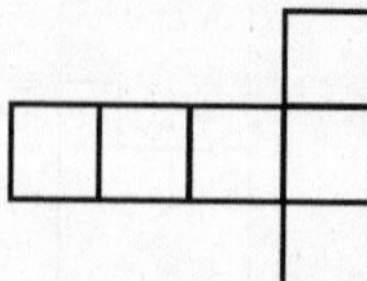

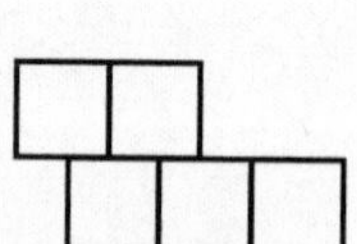

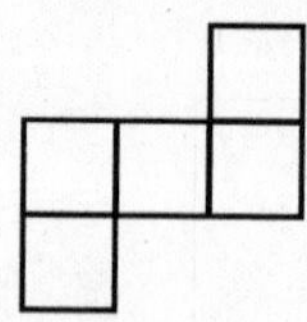

____

____

____

____

Name ____________________

Solid Figures and Nets

Polyhedrons

Prisms

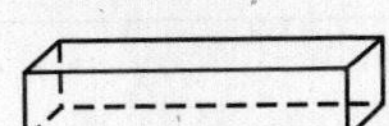
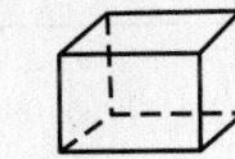
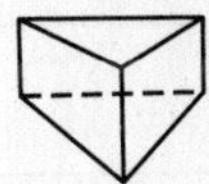

Pyramids

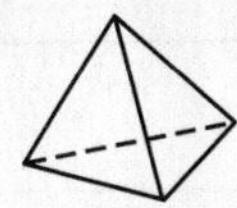
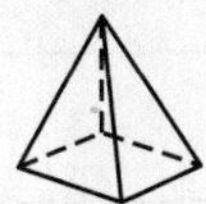
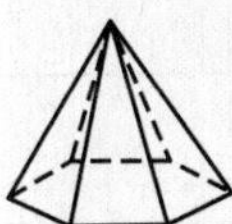

Not Polyhedrons

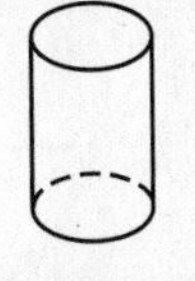
Cylinder

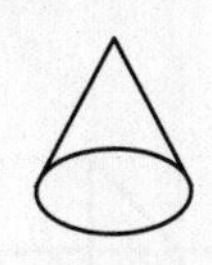
Cone

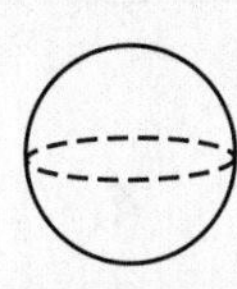
Sphere

Properties of polyhedrons include vertices, edges, and faces, and base(s).

Square Pyramid

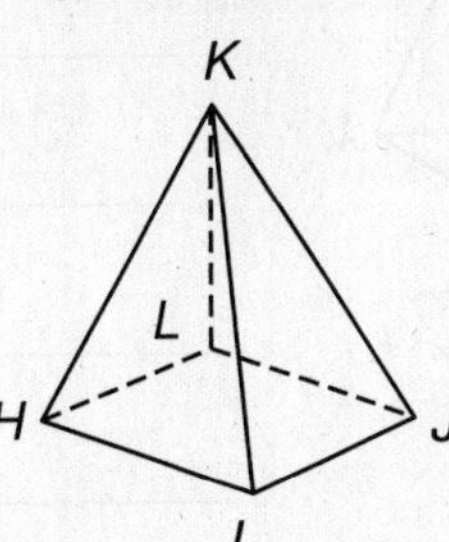

Vertices: *H, I, J, K, L*
Edges: $\overline{HI}$, $\overline{IJ}$, $\overline{JL}$, $\overline{LH}$, $\overline{HK}$, $\overline{IK}$, $\overline{JK}$, $\overline{LK}$
Faces: ΔHIK, ΔIJK, ΔJKL, and ΔHLK
Base: $\square HIJL$

Nets Identify solid figures from a net: a pattern that folds into the solid.

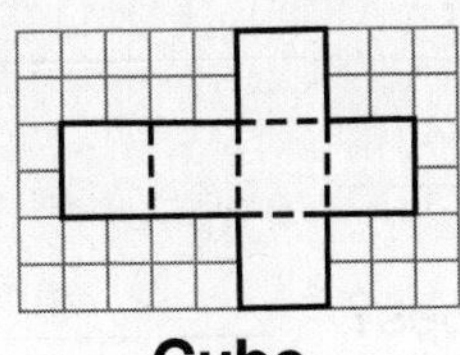
Cube

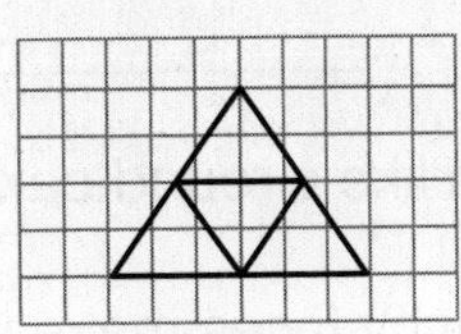
Pyramid

Classify the polyhedron. Name all vertices, edges, faces, and bases.

1.

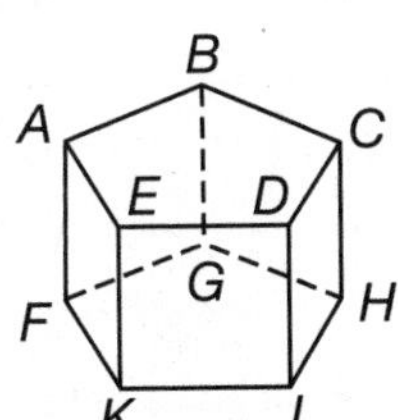

____

____

____

____

____

In **2** through **4,** classify each figure.

2.

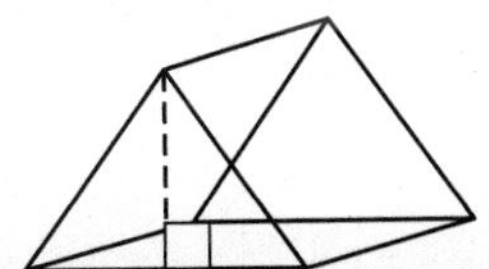

____

3.

____

4.

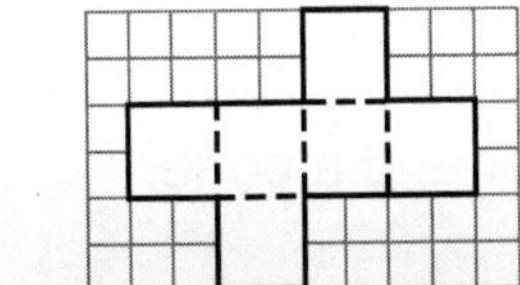

____

Name ______________________

Practice 13-1

Solid Figures and Nets

Classify the polyhedron. Name all vertices, edges, faces, and bases.

1. 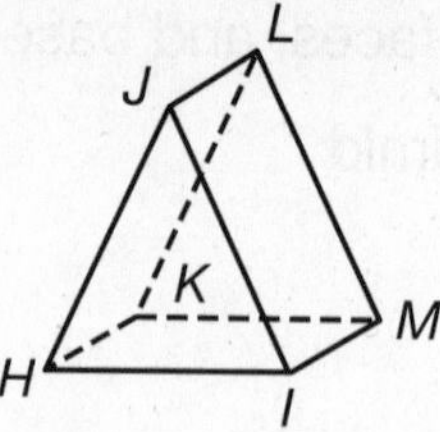

____

____

____

____

____

Classify each figure.

2. 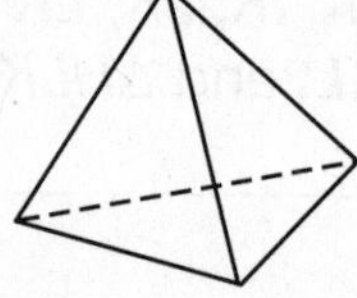

3. 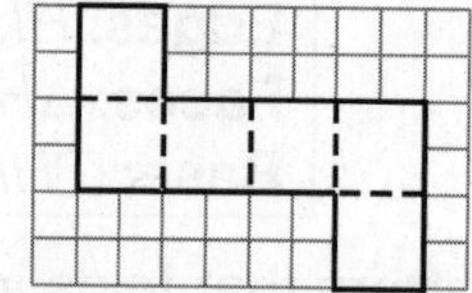

4. 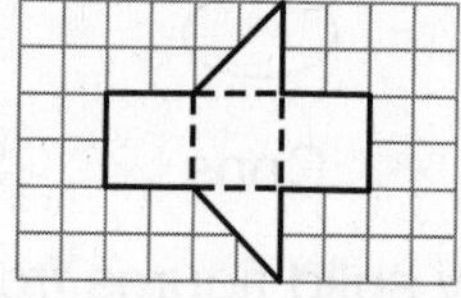

______________ ______________ ______________

5. Which solid figure looks like a round cake? ______________

6. **Number Sense** How many faces make up six number cubes? ______________

7. **Reasoning** A factory buys the boxes it needs in the form of flat nets. What advantages might the factory have in doing this?

____

____

8. What is the name of the polyhedron shown below?

A Rectangular prism

B Hexagonal prism

C Pentagonal prism

D Octagonal prism

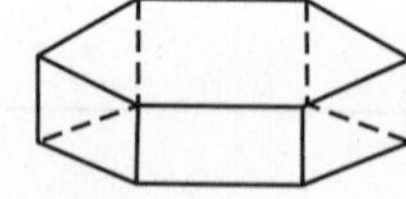

9. **Writing to Explain** Describe the similarities and differences of a cylinder and a cone.

____

____

____

Name ____________________

Surface Area of Prisms and Pyramids

You can use formulas to find the surface area of different solid figures. You can draw nets to help.

Rectangular Prism

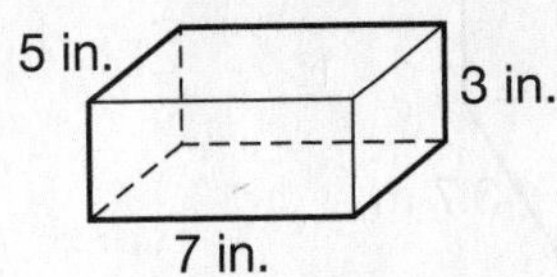

$SA = 2\ell w + 2\ell h + 2wh$

$= 2\ (5 \times 7) + 2\ (5 \times 3) + 2\ (7 \times 3)$

$= 70 + 30 + 42$

$= 142$

The surface area is 142 in^2.

Triangular Prism

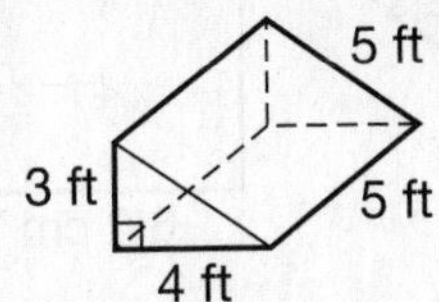

$SA = 2\ (\frac{1}{2} \times 4 \times 3) + (3 \times 5) + (4 \times 5) + (5 \times 5)$

$= 12 + 15 + 20 + 25$

$= 72$

The surface area is 72 ft^2.

Find the surface area of each figure.

1.

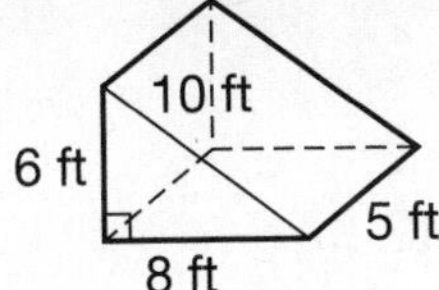

____

2.

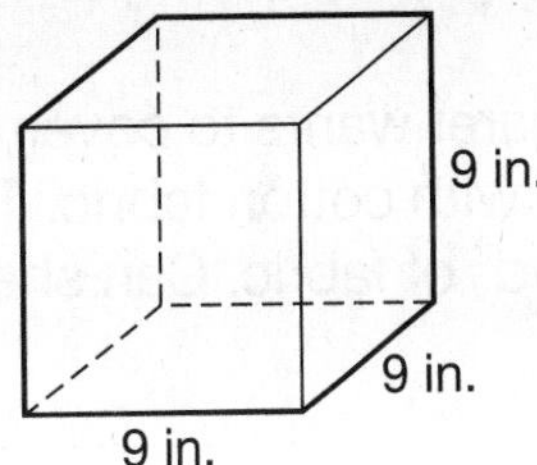

____

Find the surface area of each rectangular prism.

3. $\ell = 5.5$ cm, $w = 4.5$ cm, $h = 3.5$ cm ____________________

4. $\ell = 15$ in., $w = 9$ in., $h = 3.8$ in. ____________________

5. $\ell = 2$ yd, $w = 6$ yd, $h = 1.7$ yd ____________________

6. Reasoning Write the dimensions of two different rectangular prisms that have the same surface area.

____

____

____

Name ______________________

Practice
13-2

Surface Area of Prisms and Pyramids

Find the surface area of each figure. You can draw nets to help.

1.

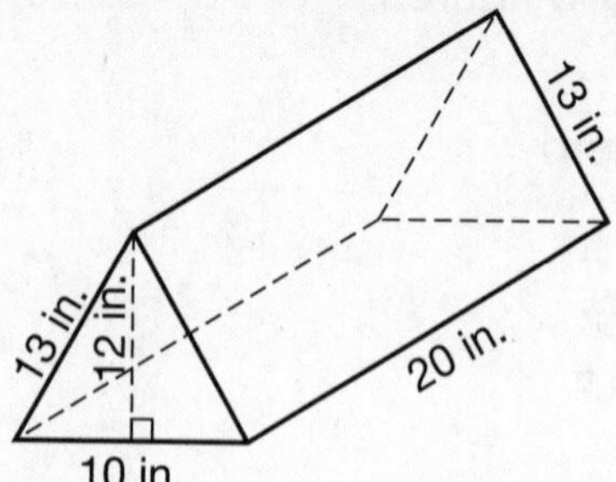

____

2.

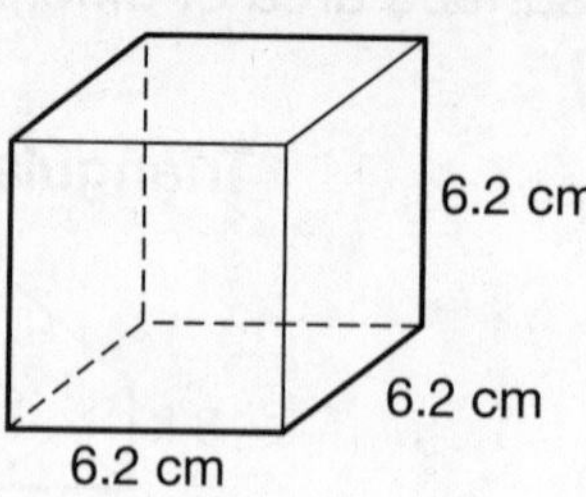

____

3.

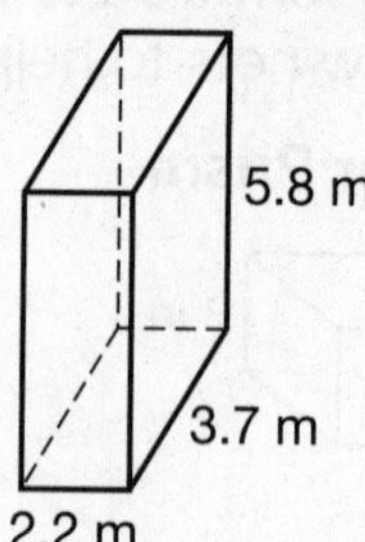

____

Find the surface area of each rectangular prism.

4. $\ell = 6.9$ mm, $w = 8.2$ mm, $h = 14$ mm ______________

5. $\ell = 3.4$ cm, $w = 12.7$ cm, $h = 16.5$ cm ______________

6. $\ell = 5.7$ yd, $w = 9$ yd, $h = 12.9$ yd ______________

7. Reasoning Margaret wants to cover a footrest in the shape of a rectangular prism with cotton fabric. The footrest is 18 in. $\times$ 12 in. $\times$ 10 in. She has 1 yd^2 of fabric. Can she completely cover the footrest?

____

____

____

8. Which is the surface area of a rectangular prism with a length of 2.3 in., a width of 1.1 in., and a height of 3 in.?

A 26.48 in^2 **B** 25.46 in^2 **C** 24.58 in^2 **D** 21.5 in^2

9. Writing to Explain A square pyramid has 2 m sides on the base. Each face is a triangle with a base of 2 m and a height of 1.5 m. Explain how to find the surface area.

____

____

____

Name ______________________________

Modeling Volume

Volume is the measure of space inside a solid figure. It is measured in cubic units. You can use a formula to find the volume of rectangular prisms: $V = B \times h$ where V stands for volume, B stands for the area of the base, and h stands for the height.

To find the volume of the rectangular prism at the right, first find the area of the base.

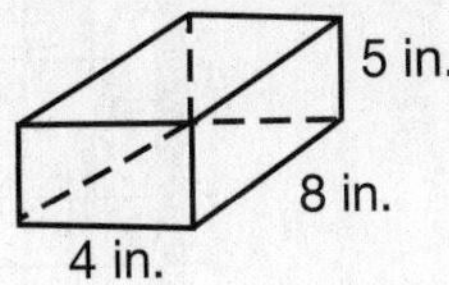

$B = \ell \times w$
$= 4 \times 8$
$= 32$ So the base is 32 sq in.

Then use the volume formula to find the volume.

$V = B \times h$
$= 32 \times 5$
$= 160$ So the volume is 160 sq in.

Find the volume of each rectangular prism. Don't forget to label the units.

1.

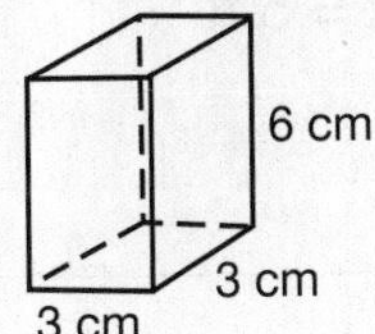

Area of Base ($B = \ell \times w$): __________

Volume ($V = B \times h$): __________

2.

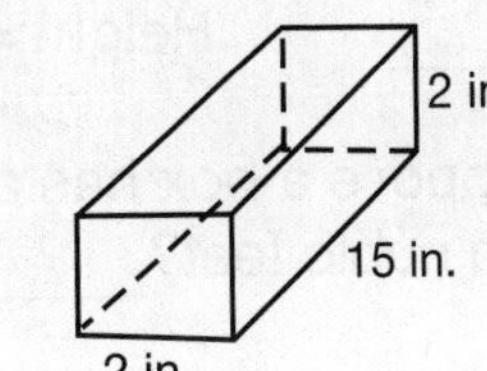

Area of Base ($B = \ell \times w$): __________

Volume ($V = B \times h$): __________

3.

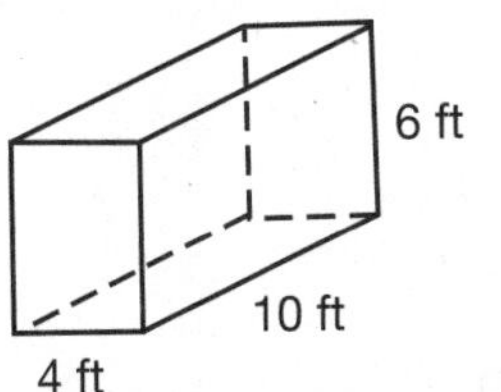

Area of Base ($B = \ell \times w$): __________

Volume ($V = B \times h$): __________

4.

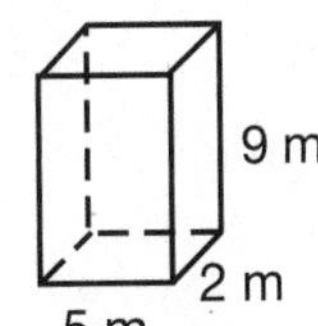

Area of Base ($B = \ell \times w$): __________

Volume ($V = B \times h$): __________

5. Find the volume of Rectangular Prism 1. How can you find the volume of Rectangular Prism 2 without using the volume formula?

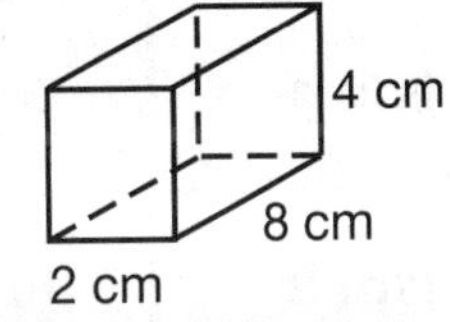

Rectangular Prism 1

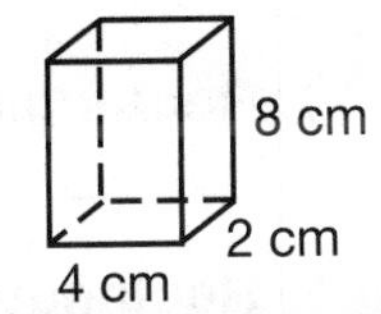

Rectangular Prism 2

____

____

____

Name ______________________

Modeling Volume

Find the volume of each rectangular prism.

1. 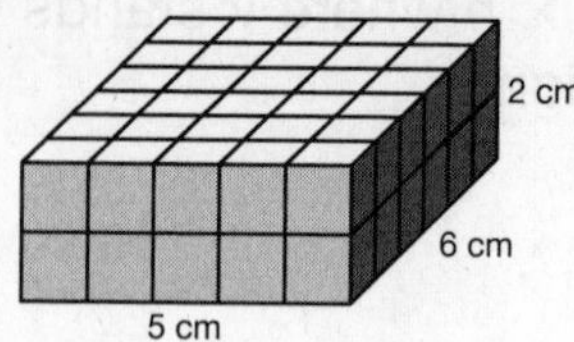

2. 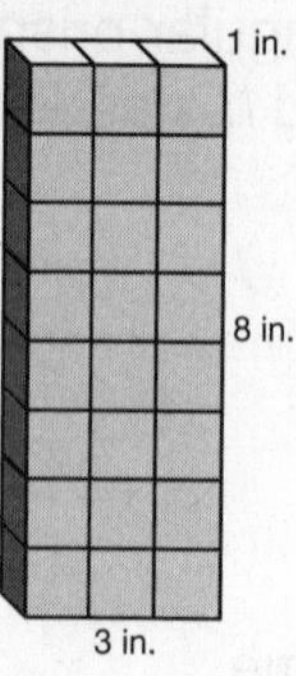

3. 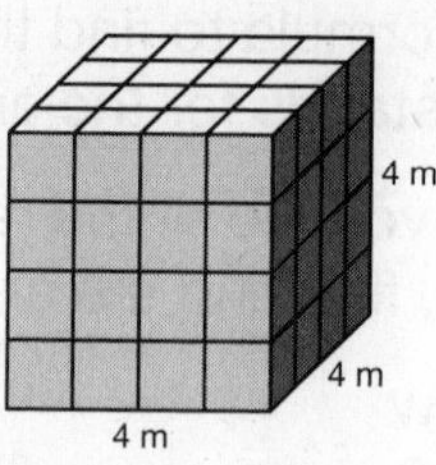

______ ______ ______

Find the missing value for each rectangular prism.

4. Volume = 6 cu in.
   Length = 3 in.
   Width = 2 in.
   Height = ______

5. Volume = 96 cu yd
   Length = ______
   Width = 6 yd
   Height = 8 yd

6. Volume = 125 cu ft
   Length = 5 ft
   Width = ______
   Height = 5 ft

7. **Number Sense** Suppose a box has a volume of 1 cu yd. What is its volume in cubic feet? ______

8. A rectangular prism has a base of 12 cm^2, a length of 3 cm, a width of 4 cm, and a height of 10 cm. Which is the volume of the prism?

   A 36 cm^3

   B 48 cm^3

   C 120 cm^3

   D 1,440 cm^3

9. **Writing to Explain** Find and compare the volumes of the two rectangular prisms below. How does doubling the measure of each dimension in a rectangular prism change the volume of the prism?

	Length	Width	Height	Volume
Rectangular Prism 1	5 ft	2 ft	10 ft	
Rectangular Prism 2	10 ft	4 ft	20 ft	

______

______

Name ______________________________

Volume with Fractional Edge Lengths

When finding the volume of a rectangular prism with fractional edge lengths, you have to find the number of cubes with fractional edge lengths that can fill the prism. What is the volume of the rectangular prism shown below at the right?

Consider a $\frac{1}{2}$-inch cube. 8 half-inch cubes can fill a 1-inch cube.

Next, figure out how many $\frac{1}{2}$-inch cubes will fill the prism. The prism can be filled with $5 \times 7 \times 3 = 105$ half-inch cubes.

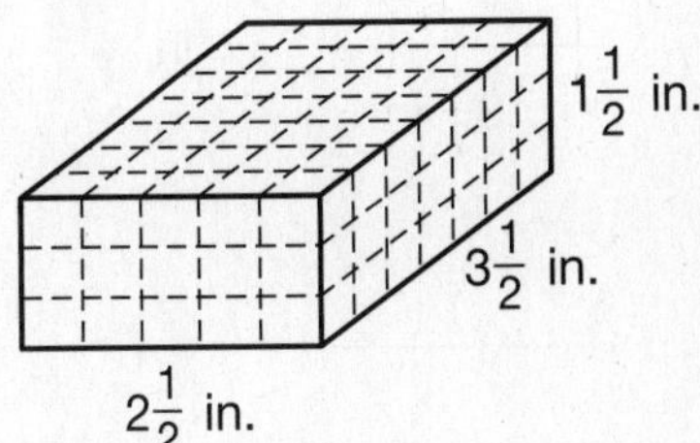

Divide 105 by 8 because 8 half-inch cubes make up a 1-inch cube. $105 \div 8 = 13\frac{1}{8}$

The volume of this rectangular prism is $13\frac{1}{8}$ in^3.

For **1** through **4**, find the volume of each rectangular prism.

1.

$1\frac{1}{2}$ in.

$3\frac{1}{2}$ in.

10 in.

Fraction cubes have _____ in. lengths.

V = ______________________________

2.

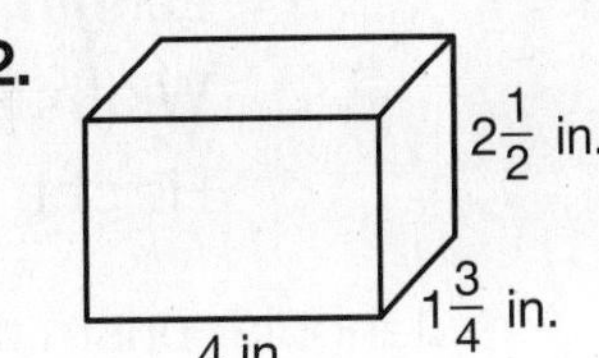

Fraction cubes have _____ in. lengths.

V = ______________________________

3.

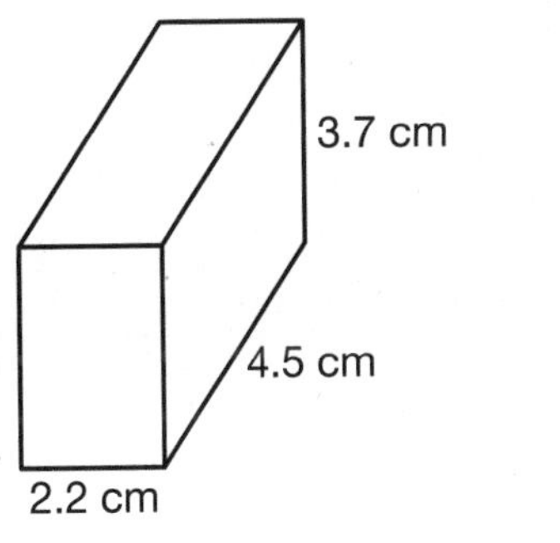

V = ______________________________

4.

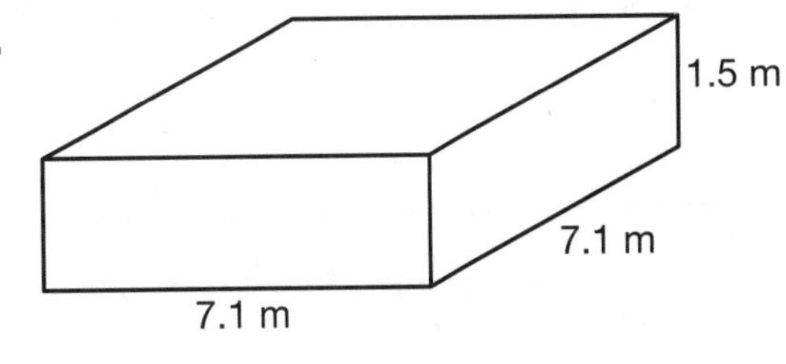

V = ______________________________

5. **Writing to Explain** How many $\frac{1}{2}$-inch cubes could fit inside the rectangular prism shown in Exercise 1? Explain how you know.

____

____

Name ______________________

Volume with Fractional Edge Lengths

Find the volume of each rectangular prism.

1. 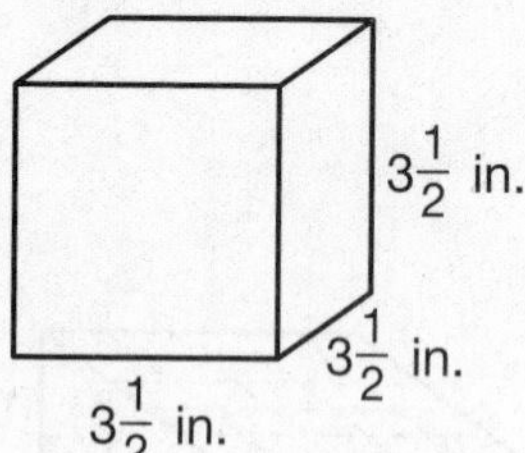

____

2. 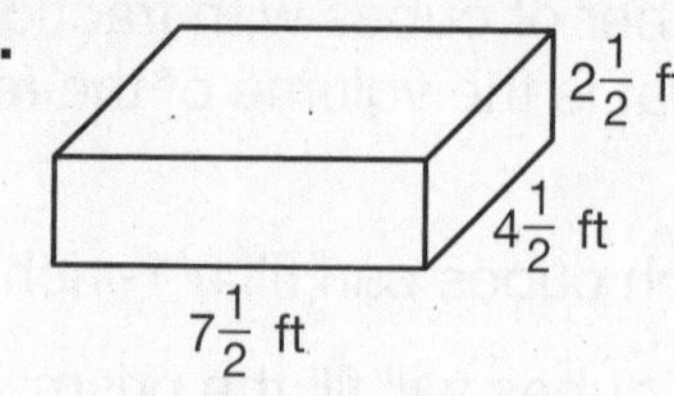

____

3. 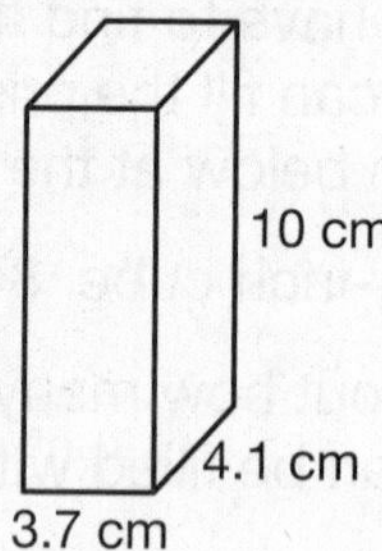

____

Find the missing value for each rectangular prism.

4. Volume: $111\frac{3}{8}$ in^3
Base: $20\frac{1}{4}$ in^2
Height: ________

5. Volume: $8\frac{2}{3}$ ft^3
Length: ________
Width: $4\frac{1}{3}$ ft
Height: $\frac{2}{3}$ ft

6. Volume: 758.16 mm^3
Length: 13 mm
Width: ________
Height: 7.2 mm

7. **Number Sense** A rectangular prism can be filled with 210 half-inch cubes. How many $\frac{1}{4}$-inch cubes would it take to fill the same prism?

____

8. A rectangular prism has a base with an area of 31.5 cm^2 and a height of 4.7 cm. What is the volume of the prism?

A 36.2 cm^3 **C** 148.05 cm^3

B 72.4 cm^3 **D** 296.1 cm^3

9. **Writing to Explain** Find and compare the volumes of the two rectangular prisms below. How does dividing each dimension of the larger prism by 2 affect the volume of the smaller prism?

Length	Width	Height	Volume
5 in.	$4\frac{1}{2}$ in.	6 in.	
$2\frac{1}{2}$ in.	$2\frac{1}{4}$ in.	3 in.	

____

____

Name ______________________________

Problem Solving: Use Objects and Reasoning

Each cube has a volume of 1 cm^3.

The area of one face of the cube is 1 cm^2.

The surface area of the cube is the sum of the area of each face of the cube.

To find the surface area of a figure of cubes, count only the faces that are exposed.

$V = 2(1 \times 1 \times 1) = 2 \text{ cm}^3$
$SA = 10(1 \text{ cm}^2) = 10 \text{ cm}^2$

The arrangement of cubes can affect the surface area, but the same number of cubes will always have the same volume.

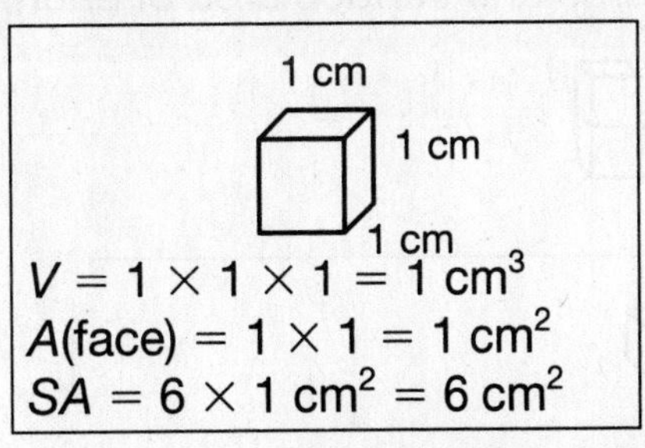

$V = 1 \times 1 \times 1 = 1 \text{ cm}^3$
$A(\text{face}) = 1 \times 1 = 1 \text{ cm}^2$
$SA = 6 \times 1 \text{ cm}^2 = 6 \text{ cm}^2$

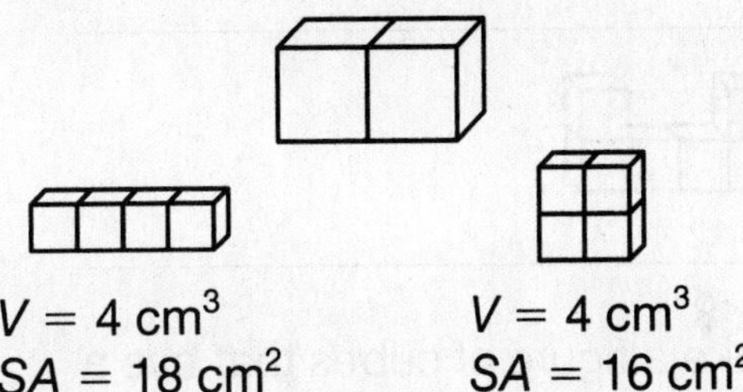

$V = 4 \text{ cm}^3$
$SA = 18 \text{ cm}^2$

$V = 4 \text{ cm}^3$
$SA = 16 \text{ cm}^2$

1. Find the volume and surface area of the figure.

____

2. Make a figure of cubes that has a volume of 7 cm^3 and a surface area of 26 cm^2. Draw your figure.

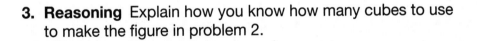

3. **Reasoning** Explain how you know how many cubes to use to make the figure in problem 2.

____

4. Find the volume and surface area of the figure.

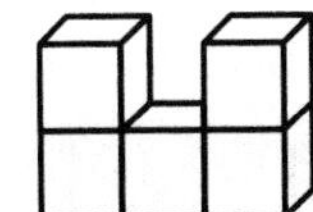

____

5. **Geometry** If the cubes in problem 4 were increased to 3 cm on a side, how would the volume and surface area be affected?

____

____

Name ______________________________

Practice
13-5

Problem Solving: Use Objects and Reasoning

Find the volume and surface area of each figure of centimeter cubes.

1. 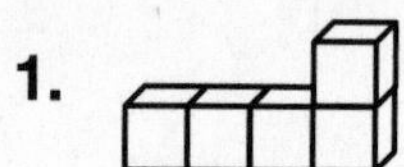

____

2. 

____

3. 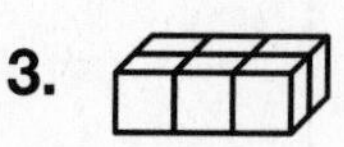

____

4. 

____

5. 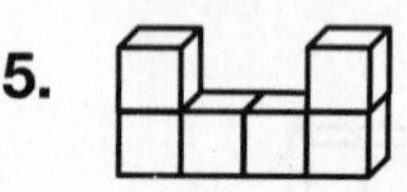

____

6. 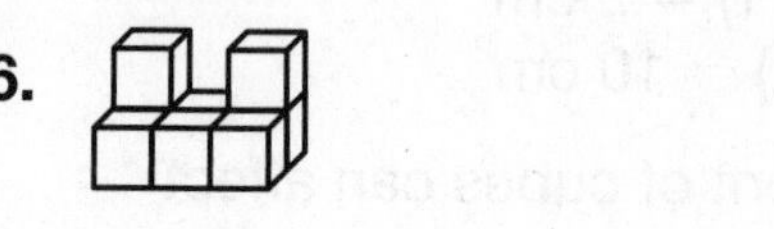

____

7. Make a figure of cubes that has a volume of 6 cm^3 and a surface area of 22 cm^2. Draw your figure.

8. Critical Thinking Without building a model, tell whether a long row of 8 cubes or a cube made from 8 cubes would have a greater surface area. Explain.

____

____

9. Make a figure that has the same volume as the diagram, but a greater surface area. Draw your figure.

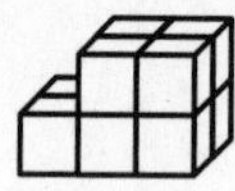

10. Writing to Explain Find the volume and surface area of these figures. Then describe the pattern(s) you see. Can you determine the volume of the next element in the pattern? The surface area? Explain.

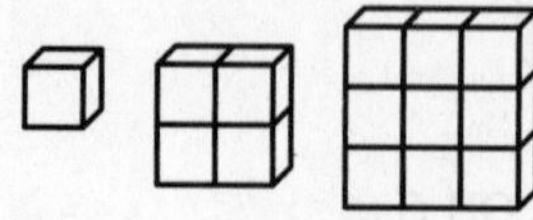

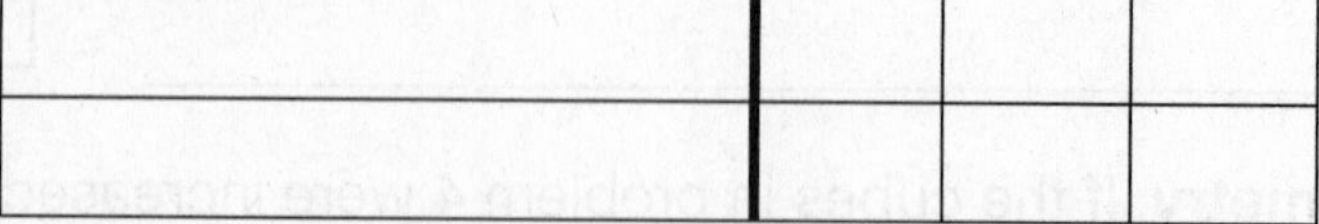

____

____

____

Name ______________________

Statistical Questions

To determine if a question you want to ask a group of people is statistical, ask yourself if it has several different answers.

How many nickels are in a dollar? **Not statistical**
How many nickels are in your bank? **Statistical**

A dot plot shows one way to display data collected from a statistical question.

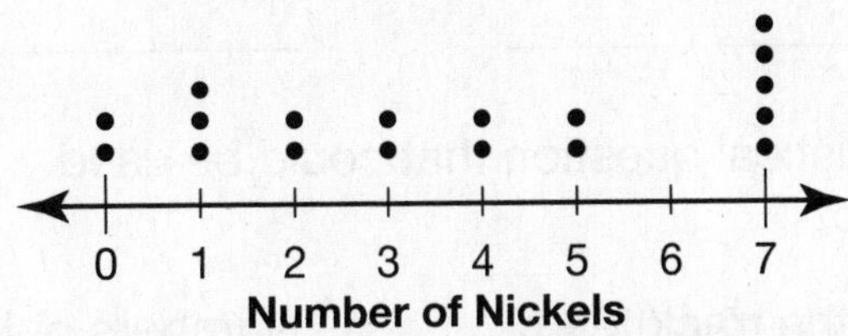

For **1** through **6**, tell whether or not each question is statistical.

1. How many of the cards are baseball cards?

____

2. When does summer break begin?

____

3. Who is the current President of the United States?

____

4. Who are the debate team members' favorite presidents?

____

5. How long does it take sixth-grade students to eat lunch?

____

6. Where are your classmates' favorite places to vacation?

____

7. Writing to Explain Explain why *How many days did it rain in September this year?* is not a statistical question.

____

8. Dean asked his class, *How many apples do you eat in a week?* He got the following responses: 7, 5, 5, 5, 7, 3, 2, 1, 0, 0, 4, 3, 2, 1, 0, 7, 5, 6, 7, 0, 2, 2, 1, 4. Make a dot plot to display the data.

Name ______________________________

Statistical Questions

For **1** through **4,** tell whether or not each question is statistical.

1. What was the low temperature each day last month?

____

2. What color shirt am I wearing?

____

3. What size shoes do the students in your class wear?

____

4. How long does it take students in a class to read a book?

____

For **5** through **8**, write a statistical question that could be used to gather data on each topic.

5. Distances members of the track team jogged last week

____

6. Numbers of letters in name of street you live on

____

7. Cost of a restaurant dinner

____

8. Numbers of cars of different colors in a parking lot

____

9. The data shown are the responses to the question, *How tall, in centimeters, is each bean plant?* Make a dot plot to display the data.

8	6	7	5	8	6	8	7	9	4
5	2	8	6	9	5	7	6	7	7

10. What statistical question might Brittany have asked to get this data?
18 min, 20 min, 30 min, 16 min, 45 min.

A How long did you spend on homework last night?

B How long do the directions say to cook the pie?

C At what time does school end?

D How many minutes does it take Eric to get to school?

11. Writing to Explain Wyatt says that statistical questions must involve numbers in the question. Do you agree with Wyatt? Explain.

____

____

Name ______________________

Looking at Data Sets

You can describe a data distribution, or how data values are arranged, by looking at its overall shape, its center, and its least and greatest values.

By looking at this dot plot, you can describe the data distribution as being spread out to the right and not symmetric. The data is grouped between 50 and 51, and there is a gap between 55 and 60.

Temperatures in September

50° 51° 52° 53° 54° 55° 56° 57° 58° 59° 60°

Temperature (°F)

The center of the data can be found by looking for the middle number in the largest group of data. A good estimate would be 50 or 51 because that is where most of the temperatures are plotted.

Use the dot plot to the right to answer the following questions.

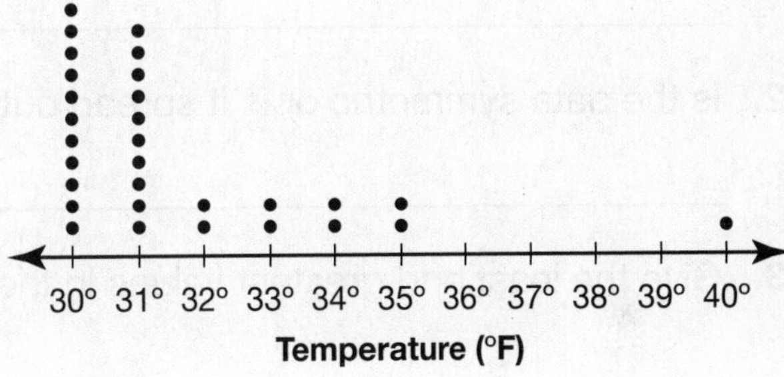

1. What is the least temperature? Greatest temperature?

   ____

2. Are there any gaps in the data? If so, where?

   ____

3. What temperature would be considered an outlier?

   ____

4. Is the data symmetric or spread out to one side?

   ____

5. **Writing to Explain** Where do you think the center of the data is in the dot plot? Explain how you found your answer.

   ____

   ____

   ____

Name ______________________

Looking at Data Sets

For **1** through **4**, use the dot plot.

Maria took a school survey to find out how many hours per week students watch television. Her results are in the dot plot below.

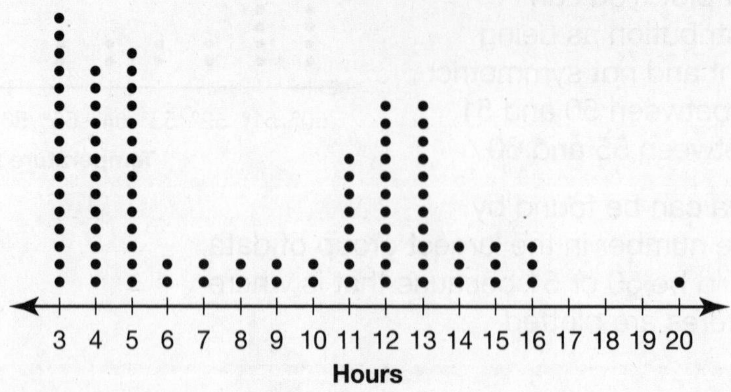

1. Where are there groupings of data?

____

2. Is the data symmetric or is it spread out to one side?

____

3. Give the least and greatest values in the data.

____

4. **Writing to Explain** Using the dot plot for the hours students spend watching TV, where do you think the center of the data is? Explain how you found your answer.

____

____

For **5** and **6**, use the line plot.

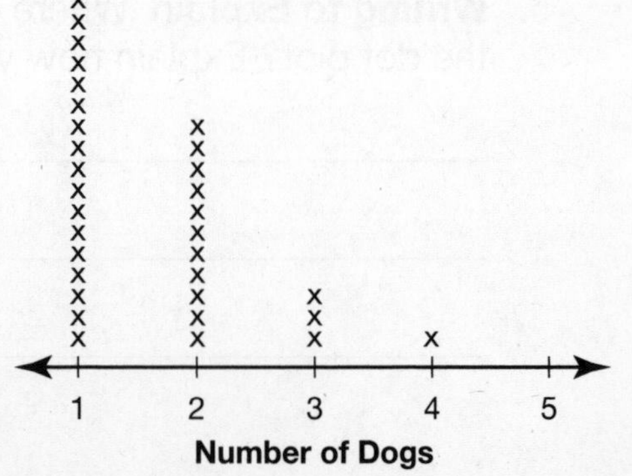

5. Which is the best representation of the center of this data set?

A 2 dogs **B** 3 dogs
C 4 dogs **D** 5 dogs

6. Which best describes this data set?

A Spread out to the left **B** No noticeable shape
C Spread out to the right **D** Symmetric

Name ______________________

Mean

The mean is the sum of all the values in a set divided by the number of items in the set. The mean is also called the average.

How to find the mean of a set of data:

Eduardo surveyed 7 of his friends to find out how many books they read during the month. The frequency table shows the data. What is the average number of books read by Eduardo's friends?

Book Reading	
Friend	**Number of books read**
Jean	2
Raul	3
Sally	8
Jonathan	5
Haley	6
Kristen	3
Owen	1

1. Add the number of books read by each friend. $2 + 3 + 8 + 5 + 6 + 3 + 1 = 28$

2. Divide the sum by the number of friends. $\frac{28}{7} = 4$

3. Use the average to answer the question. Eduardo's friends read an average of 4 books during the month.

1. Find the mean of this set of data: 241, 563, 829, 755. ______

2. This frequency table shows the number of silver medals won by American athletes in Summer Olympic Games between 1972 and 2000. What is the mean of this set of data?

______

US Silver Medals Summer Olympic Games	
Year	**Medals**
2000	24
1996	32
1992	34
1988	31
1984	61
1980	0
1976	35
1972	31

3. Estimation What is the approximate average of these three numbers: 9, 18, and 31? ______

4. Explain It Explain how you would find the mean of this set of data: 4, 3, 5.

______

______

Name ______________________

Practice
14-3

Mean

Find the mean of each set of data.

1. 2, 5, 9, 4 ______

2. 44, 73, 63 ______

3. 11, 38, 65, 4, 67 ______

4. 3, 6, 3, 7, 8 ______

5. 120, 450, 630 ______

6. 4.2, 5.3, 7.1, 4.0, 11.9 ______

Gene's scores were as follows: 8, 4, 10, 10, 9, 6, 9.

7. What was his average score? ______

8. If Gene gets two more scores of 10, what is his new average? ______

9. **Reasoning** Krishan wants his quiz average to be at least 90 so that he can get an A in the class. His current quiz scores are: 80, 100, 85. What does he have to get on his next quiz to have an average of 90?

A 85 **B** 90 **C** 92 **D** 95

10. **Explain It** Suppose Krishan's teacher says that he can drop one of his test scores. Using his test scores of 80, 100, and 85, which one should he drop, and why? What is his new average?

______

______

Name ___________________________

Median, Mode, and Range

The median, mode, and range are each numbers that describe a set of data.

Here is Eduardo's survey of how many books his friends read last month.

What are the median, mode, and range of Eduardo's survey?

Book Reading	
Friend	**Number of books read**
Jean	2
Raul	3
Sally	8
Jonathan	5
Haley	6
Kristen	3
Owen	1

Median: The median is the middle number in a set of data. To find it:

1. Arrange the data in order from least to greatest.
2. Locate the middle number. 1, 2, 3, 3, 5, 6, 8

↑ middle number = 3

The median number of books read is 3.

Mode: The mode is the data value that occurs most often. To find it:

1. List the data. 1, 2, 3, 3, 5, 6, 8
2. Find the number that occurs most. 3

The mode of the books read by Eduardo's friends is 3 books.

Range: The range is the difference between the greatest and least values. To find it:

1. Identify the greatest and least values. 8 and 1
2. Subtract the least from the greatest value. $8 - 1 = 7$

The range of the books read by Eduardo's friends is 7 books.

1. Find the median of this data set: 12, 18, 25, 32, 67. ________

2. Find the mode of this data set: 123, 345, 654, 123, 452, 185. ________

3. Find the range of this data set: 24, 32, 38, 31, 61, 35, 31. ________

Name ____________________

Practice
14-4

Median, Mode, and Range

1. Find the range of this data set: 225, 342, 288, 552, 263. ________
2. Find the median of this data set: 476, 234, 355, 765, 470. ________
3. Find the mode of this data set: 16, 7, 8, 5, 16, 7, 8, 4, 7, 8, 16, 7. ________
4. Find the range of this data set: 64, 76, 46, 88, 88, 43, 99, 50, 55. ________
5. **Reasoning** Would the mode change if a 76 were added to the data in Exercise 4?

____

____

The table below gives the math test scores for Mrs. Jung's fifth-grade class.

76	54	92	88	76	88
75	93	92	68	88	76
76	88	80	70	88	72

Test Scores

6. Find the mean of the data. ________
7. Find the mode of the data. ________
8. Find the median of the data. ________
9. What is the range of the data set? ________
10. Find the range of this data set: 247, 366, 785, 998.

A 998 **B** 781 **C** 751 **D** 538

11. **Explain It** Will a set of data always have a mode? Explain your answer.

____

Name ______________________________

Frequency Tables and Histograms

Maya recorded the number of bags of popcorn she sold each day at the carnival, and then represented the data in a frequency table and histogram.

Bags of popcorn: 62, 65, 58, 31, 64, 58, 66, 68, 56, 67, 68, 51

Make a Frequency Table

Choose a Range: The range should cover all of the data. Divide the range into equal intervals or groups.

Range in popcorn data: 68 − 31 = 37
You can make intervals of 10 by using a range of 30 to 69.

Tally Marks: Record a tally mark for each value in the range.

Frequency: Count the tally marks and record.

Bags	Tally	Frequency
30–39	I	1
40–49		0
50–59	IIII	4
60–69	~~IIII~~ II	7

Make a Histogram

Choose a Title: Bags of Popcorn Sold
Choose a Scale for the Vertical Axis: Use frequency of the data for the scale.
List Intervals on Horizontal Axis

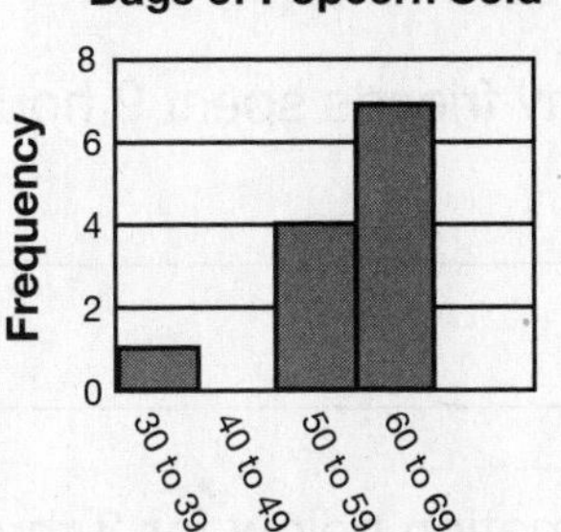

Use a Histogram

Look for clusters, gaps, and outliers.

Clusters: 50–69 for popcorn data
Gaps: 40–49; no bags sold in this interval
Outliers: 1 bag sold in 30–39 range

Use the information below for **1** through **3**.

Tickets Sold to Charity Ice-Skating Event							
72	81	88	51	90	89	85	74
87	100	80	99	87	96	99	84
84	86	94	88	91	85	78	90

1. Represent the data in the table in a histogram.
2. Where do most of the data in your histogram cluster?

____

3. **Reasoning** Describe any outliers or gaps in the data.

____

____

____

Name ____________________

Frequency Tables and Histograms

Conrad recorded the total number of hours 14 friends spent on the Internet in a week. He made a frequency table of the data. Use the table for **1** through **2**.

Hours on the Internet	
Hours	**Frequency**
0–4	2
5–9	3
10–14	7
15–19	0
20–24	0
25–29	2

1. What is the mode of the data? Explain.

2. How many friends spent 9 hours or less on the Internet that week? Explain.

Use the information below for **3** through **5**.

Ages of Players at Castle Miniature Golf				
14	7	6	24	15
9	19	25	10	17
51	8	21	48	12

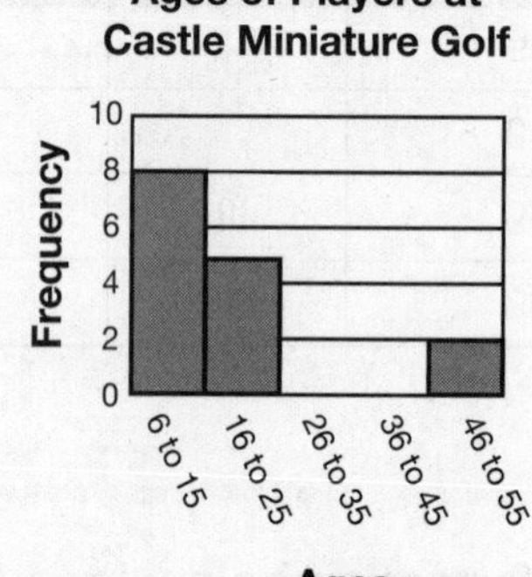

3. How many of the players are over 25? Explain.

4. Where do most of the data in the histogram cluster?

A 6–15
B 16–25
C 26–55
D Over 15

5. Writing to Explain Explain how you can tell whether a histogram has an outlier.

Name ________________________________

Box Plots

To create a box plot for a data set, follow these steps:

Step 1: Check to see if the numbers are in order from least to greatest. If they are not, place them in that order. Draw a number line using an appropriate scale to include the numbers.

Step 2: Find the least value and greatest value. The least is the *minimum*. The greatest is the *maximum*.

Step 3: Find the number that is midway between the minimum and maximum. This value is the *median*.

Step 4: Find the value that is halfway between the minimum and the median. This is the *first quartile*.

Step 5: Find the value that is halfway between the median and the maximum. This is the *third quartile*.

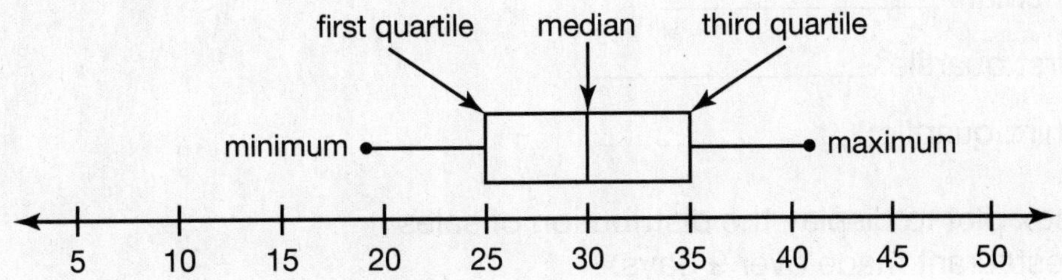

For **1** through **5**, use the five-step process for the following data:

8, 9, 3, 1, 2, 6, 5, 7, 4, 0, 10

1. Are the data in this set in order? If not, write them in order.

____

2. What is the median? How can you tell?

____

3. What is the minimum?
The maximum?

____

4. What is the first quartile?
The third quartile?

____

5. Draw a box plot for this data.

Name ______________________________

Practice
14-6

Box Plots

In **1** and **2** find the median, the first quartile, and third quartile.

1. In a bowling tournament, Sylvan got the following scores.

167, 178, 193, 196, 199, 199, 203, 209, 217, 220, 221

a. The median: ______________

b. The first quartile: ______________

c. The third quartile: ______________

2. Sarina raised flowers. In a competition with other flower growers, she earned the following scores.

7, 10, 10, 6, 7, 8, 8, 7, 9

a. The median: ______________

b. The first quartile: ______________

c. The third quartile: ______________

3. Make a box plot to display the distribution of sales Solon's restaurant made over 9 days:

$1,074, $1,209, $1,315, $1,360, $1,391, $1,442, $1,482, $1,569, $1,601

4. Which describes how to find the first quartile in a data set?

A Find the median of the data set.

B Find the median of the upper half of the data.

C Find the median of the lower half of the data.

D Count 3 spaces to the right from the minimum.

5. **Writing to Explain** David wants to make a box plot showing his team's points for the year. The median score was 7, first quartile was 4, and third quartile was 10. The minimum was 2 and the maximum was 20. Explain how David can draw the box plot.

____

____

____

Name ______________________________

Measures of Variability

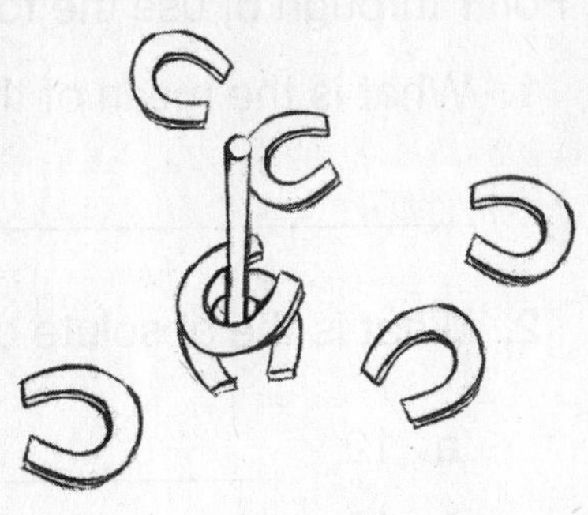

Variability describes how clustered or spread out data is. You might think of variability in terms of a game of horseshoes. The goal of the game is to get as many horseshoes as you can to “ring,” or hook around, a post. Once a player has taken a turn, the horseshoes—or data—look something like this picture.

One way of measuring variability of data is by finding the *mean absolute deviation*.

Step 1. Find the mean of the data. To do this, you add the data values and divide by the number of values in the set. Suppose you have 20, 40, 60, 80, 100 as the data. The sum of these numbers $20 + 40 + 60 + 80 + 100 = 300$. Since there are 5 items in the set, $300 \div 5 = 60$.

Step 2. Find the absolute deviation for each value in the data set. To do this, find each absolute value of the difference between the mean and each number in the set. So, for the numbers in the set, you get:

$|60 - 20| = \mathbf{40}$

$|60 - 40| = \mathbf{20}$

$|60 - 60| = \mathbf{0}$

$|80 - 60| = \mathbf{20}$

$|100 - 60| = \mathbf{40}$

Step 3. Find the mean of the absolute deviations. You find the mean of the absolute deviations by adding $40 + 20 + 0 + 20 + 40 = 120$. Then divide by the number of values, 5, which gives you 24. So the mean absolute deviation for 20, 40, 60, 80, 100 is 24.

Use the 3-step process to find the mean absolute deviation for each set of data. Give the mean of the original set, the sum of the absolute deviations, and the mean absolute deviation.

1. 10, 15, 20, 30, 50

____

____

2. 500; 1,000; 1,500; 2,000

____

____

Name ______________________________

Practice 14-7

Measures of Variability

For **1** through **6**, use the following data set: 12, 20, 16, 10, 17, 9, 23, 13

1. What is the mean of this set?

____

2. What is the absolute deviation from the mean for the following values:

a. 12 ____________

b. 16 ____________

c. 20 ____________

3. Which value in the original set has the greatest absolute deviation from the mean? Which has the least absolute deviation?

____

4. What is the mean absolute deviation for the set?

____

5. What is first quartile for the set? The third quartile?

____

6. What is the IQR for the set?

____

For **7** and **8**, use the following data set: 3, 7, 11, 15, 20, 31, 39, 42

7. Writing to Explain The data set shows the approximate hourly tides in feet recorded at a beach during an 8-hour period. What is the mean absolute deviation for the data set? Explain how you found it.

____

____

____

____

8. Which is the IQR for the set?

A 26 **B** 28 **C** 35 **D** 36

Name ______________________________

Appropriate Use of Statistical Measures

Paige tracked the number of points scored so far this season by each member of her basketball team: 28, 30, 28, 30, 40, 30, 34, 32. Which measure of center and measure of variability best describe the typical number of points scored?

Make a dot plot to organize the data and identify any outliers.

The median and mode are 30. The mean is 31.5. There is a gap between 34 and 40, and 40 is an outlier.

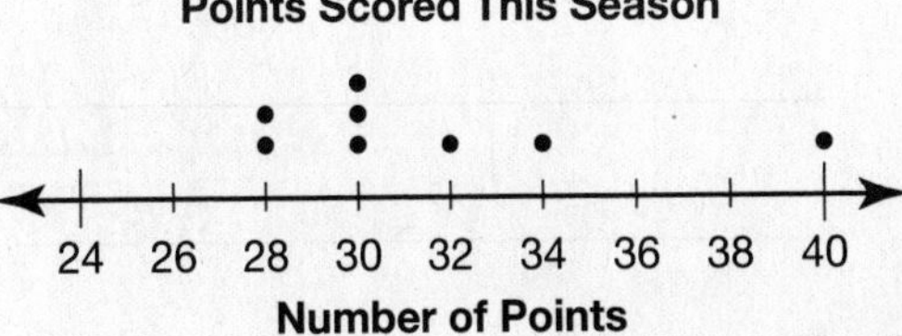

Since the outlier, 40, affects the mean, the median is the best measure of center for the data. For measures of variability, use the mean absolute deviation when the mean is the appropriate measure of center. Use the interquartile range when the median is more appropriate. Since the median is the best measure of center, you would use the IQR to measure variability of this data.

1. Make a dot plot using this set of data:
38, 68, 78, 88, 98

2. Which measure of center and measure of variability best describes this data set? Why?

____

____

____

3. Make a dot plot using this set of data:
35, 38, 40, 35, 37, 38, 36, 40, 43

4. Find the mean, median, and mode of the data set.

____

5. Which measure of center best describes this data set? Why?

____

____

Name ______________________

Practice
14-8

Appropriate Use of Statistical Measures

1. Find the mean, median, and mode of this data set:
76, 74, 78, 72, 73, 80, 49, 72, 83

2. Which measure of center best describes the data set? Why?

3. Find the IQR and mean absolute deviation of the data set below. Round the mean absolute deviation to the nearest hundredth.
13, 19, 17, 15, 11, 19, 18

4. Which measure of variability best describes the data set in Exercise 3? Why?

5. Find the mean, median, and mode of this data set:
150, 138, 130, 127, 140, 108, 138

6. **Critical Thinking** What number could be added to the data set in Exercise 5 so that the mean, median, and mode are all the same?

7. **Writing to Explain** Ava found the mean, median, and mode of a data set. Then she discovered that she had not included a very high outlier in her calculations. How will the mean, median, and mode be affected by the inclusion of this outlier? Explain.

Name ______________________

Reteaching **14-9**

Summarizing Data Distributions

The box plot to the right displays data for the number of days the temperature was over 80°F for the month of July. Data in displays can be summarized.

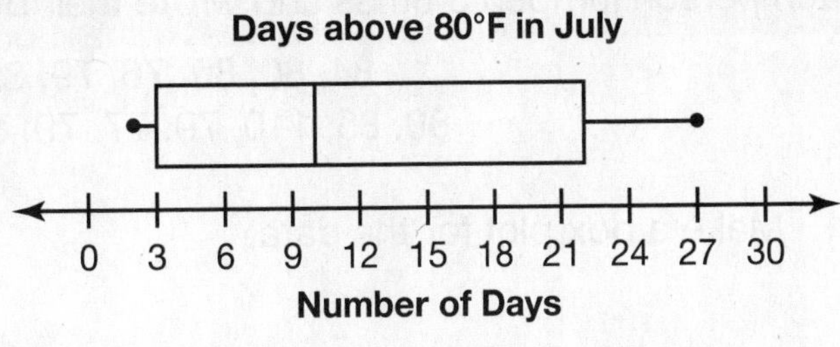

You can summarize this data set by choosing some ways to describe it. The data are spread out to the right. The median is 10, and it describes the center of the data. The first quartile is 3 and the third quartile is 22. The interquartile range, or IQR, describes the variability and it can be found by subtracting the first quartile (3) from the third quartile (22) to get 19.

Use the box plot to answer Questions **1** through **4**.

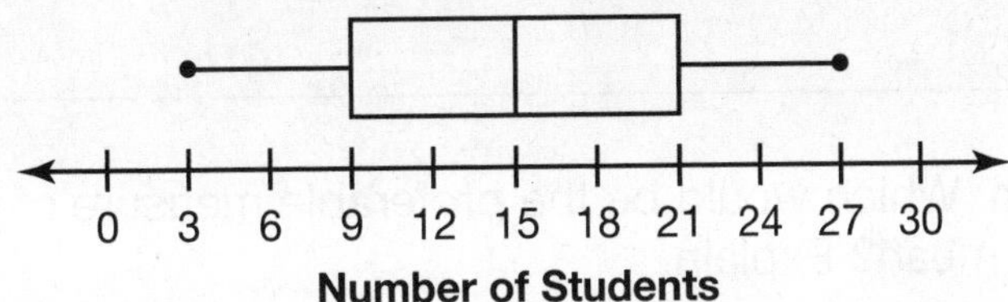

1. What is the greatest number of students in a classroom who have a dog? The least? ______________

2. a. What is the median? ______________

b. What are the first and third quartiles? ______________

c. What is the interquartile range? ______________

3. Describe the shape of the data distribution.

____

4. **Writing to Explain** If a dot plot was used to display the same data, make a prediction about how the data would look.

____

____

Name ____________________

Practice **14-9**

Summarizing Data Distributions

For **1** through **5** use the data set below.

Mr. Hansen's physical education class did a long jump competition. Each person jumped 3 times and wrote their best long jump (in inches).

84, 80, 80, 76, 79, 82, 89, 72, 76, 78,
80, 85, 110, 79, 77, 79, 81, 79, 80, 81, 72, 83

1. Make a box plot for the data.

2. a What is the mean? The median? ____________________

b What are the first and third quartiles? ____________________

c What is the interquartile range? ____________________

3. Describe the shape of the data distribution.

____

4. Writing to Explain Which would be the preferable measure of center, the median or the mean? Explain.

____

____

5. Would the median or the mean be more affected if a long jump of 140 inches was added to the data? Explain how you know.

____

____

6. Which is the best representation of the center of this data set?

A 2 fish　　**C** 4 fish

B 3 fish　　**D** 5 fish

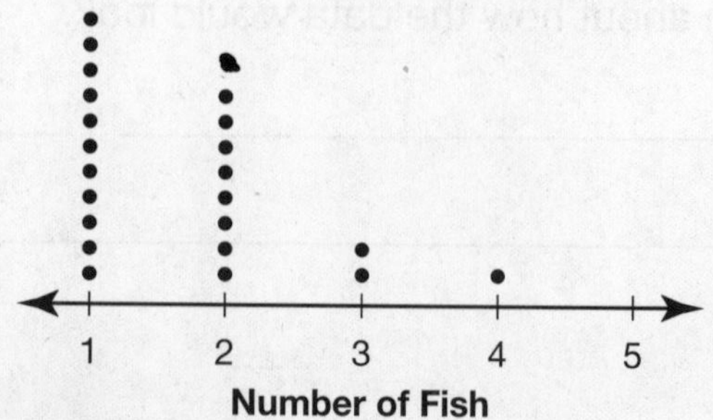

Name ______________________________

Problem Solving: Try, Check, and Revise

Audrey bowled 3 games. Her mean score was 148. Each score was different. Name three possible scores. Remember that the highest possible score in bowling is 300.

Use the problem solving plan.

Read and Understand:

What do you know?
Audrey bowled 3 games.
Her mean score was 148.

What are you trying to find?
Three scores that have a mean of 148.

Plan and Solve:

What strategy will you use?
Try, check, and revise.

Try 156, 140, 160. The mean is
$(156 + 140 + 160) \div 3 = 456 \div 3 = 152$.

The mean is too high by 4 points:
$152 - 148 = 4$.
Try subtracting 4 points from each score.
$156 - 4 = 152$, $140 - 4 = 136$,
$160 - 4 = 156$.

Check:
Check to see if the mean is 148.

$(152 + 136 + 156) \div 3 = 444 \div 3 = 148$

1. The median time 5 people waited to ride on the "Whirl and Twirl" was 38 minutes. List 5 possible times they may have waited.

____

2. Ben checked the price of the camera he wants at 4 stores. Each price was different. The mean price was $238. What are 4 possible prices for the camera?

____

3. Five hamsters weigh between 12 and 20 ounces. The mode weight of the 5 hamsters is 18 ounces. List the possible weights of the hamsters.

____

4. The mean, median, and mode of a set of 4 numbers is 100. Name 4 numbers that could make up the set.

____

5. The mean and median of a set of 6 numbers is 140. Name 6 numbers that could make up the set.

____

Name ______________________________

Practice
14-10

Problem Solving: Try, Check, and Revise

1. The mean number of passengers on a daily flight from Los Angeles to San Francisco is 82. The plane holds a maximum of 102 passengers. List the possible number of passengers on the flight over the past 5 days.

____

2. Four adult pandas weigh between 200 and 275 pounds. Their median weight is 240 pounds. List four possible weights for the pandas.

____

3. Over the past 7 years the median rainfall in West Berry has been 74 inches. The greatest rainfall was 102 inches. The least was 52 inches. List possible rainfall amounts for the 7 years.

____

4. The mean number of miles Mr. Austin drove in six days was 96. The mode was 82. The median was 97. What are possible distances Mr. Austin drove in the 6 days?

____

5. **Writing to Explain** The mode of the heights of 5 sunflowers is 70 inches. The median is 68 inches. What are some possible heights of the 5 sunflowers? Tell how you decide.

____

____

____

6. **Number Sense** Three consecutive odd integers have a sum of 195. What are the integers?

____

7. **Geometry** The area of a rectangle is 180 square inches. The length and width share no common factors other than one. What are the dimensions of the rectangle?

A 30 in. by 6 in. **C** 14 in. by 16 in.

B 20 in. by 9 in. **D** 12 in. by 15 in.

Name ____________________________________

Adding Integers

You can use a number line or rules to add integers. On a number line, start at 0. Move right to add a positive number. Move left to add a negative number.

Add two integers with different signs.

Find $3 + (-4)$.

Start at 0. Move 3 units to the right. Then move 4 units to the left.

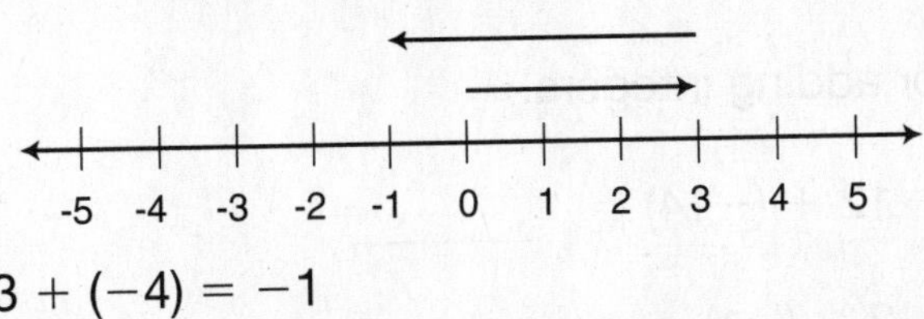

$3 + (-4) = -1$

Find the absolute value for each addend.
$|-4| = 4$ and $|3| = 3$

Subtract the smaller absolute value from the greater: $4 - 3 = 1$

Give the difference the same sign as the addend with the greater absolute value. Because +4 has the greater absolute value ($4 > 3$), this difference receives a negative sign.

$3 + (-4) = -1$

Add two integers with the same sign.

Find $-1 + (-2)$.

Start at 0. Move 1 unit to the left. Then move 2 more units to the left.

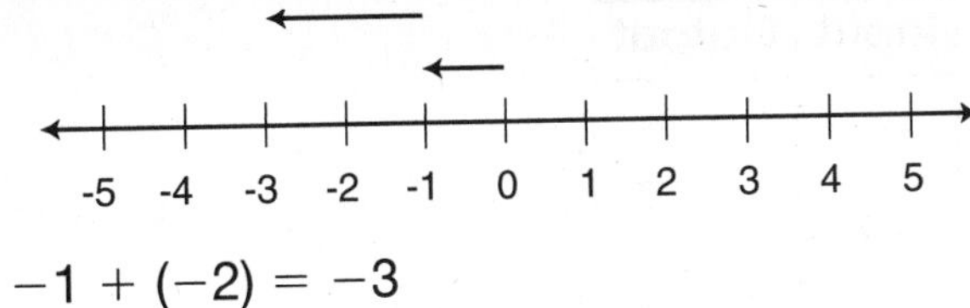

$-1 + (-2) = -3$

Find the absolute value for each addend.
$|-1| = 1$ and $|-2| = 2$

Add the absolute values. $1 + 2 = 3$

Give the sum the same sign as the addends.

$-1 + (-2) = -3$

Find each sum. Use the number line or rules.

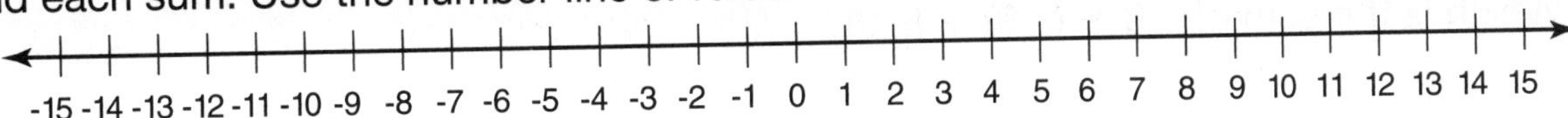

1. Find $-5 + 7$.
Move *left* _____ spaces. Move *right* _____ spaces. So, $-5 + 7 =$ _____

2. $8 + 4 =$ _____ **3.** $3 + (-5) =$ _____ **4.** $-7 + (-8) =$ _____

5. $-4 + (-4) =$ _____ **6.** $-5 + 3 =$ _____ **7.** $7 + (-3) =$ _____

8. $10 + (-1) =$ _____ **9.** $-8 + 6 =$ _____ **10.** $2 + (-3) =$ _____

11. $11 + 3 =$ _____ **12.** $-9 + 6 =$ _____ **13.** $-2 + 12 =$ _____

14. Algebra The rule is Add –5. The input is 10. What is the output? _____

Name ____________________

Step-Up 1
Practice

Adding Integers

1. Draw a number line to find 3 + (−4).

Find each sum. Use a number line or the rules for adding integers.

2. 4 + (−12) = ______

3. −12 + (−14) = ______

4. 10 + (−1) = ______

5. −2 + (−1) = ______

6. −50 + (−1) = ______

7. 8 + (−4) = ______

8. −9 + 7 = ______

9. −3 + (−6) = ______

Algebra Use the rule to complete each table.

10. **Rule: Add -6**

Input	Output
5	
3	
−1	

11. **Rule: Add 2**

Input	Output
−7	
−4	
0	

12. Which is the sum of −6 + (−9) + (−9)?

A −24

B −12

C −6

D 24

13. **Writing to Explain** Explain how you would solve −4 + 4 + 5.

____

____

Name ____________________

Subtracting Integers

Step-Up 2
Reteaching

You can use this rule to subtract integers.

Rule: To subtract an integer, add its opposite.

Examples:

Find: 8 − (−3)
The opposite of −3 is 3.
Add: 8 + 3 = 11
So, 8 − (−3) = 11

Find: −6 −7
The opposite of 7 is −7.
Add: −6 + (−7) = −13
So, −6 − 7 = −13

Find: −3 − (−9)
The opposite of −9 is 9.
Add: −3 + 9 = 6
So, −3 − (−9) = 6

Find each difference.

1. 5 − (−1)
The opposite of −1 is 1

Add: 5 + ____ = ____

2. −10 − 3
The opposite of 3 is ____

Add: −10 + ____ = ____

3. −7 − (−2)

____

4. − 9 − 4

____

5. 6 − (−10)

____

6. −1 − (−3)

____

7. Writing to Explain Without computing, how do you know that the answer to 7 − (−15) is positive?

____

____

____

8. Draw a Picture In one football game the Wildcats gained 5 yards on one play, lost 8 yards on the next play, and gained 6 yards the next play. In all, how many yards did they gain or lose?

____

Name ______________________________

Step-Up 2

Practice

Subtracting Integers

For **1** through **3** use the number line below to find each difference.

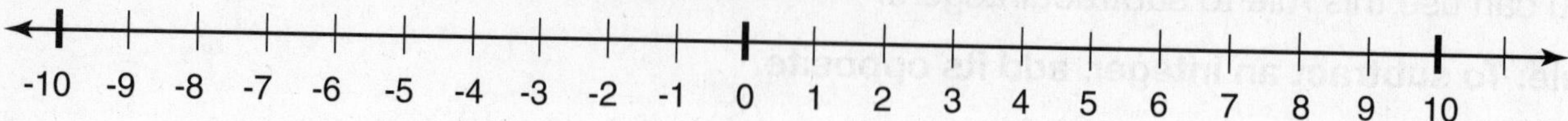

1. $5 - 10$ ________

2. $-4 - 4$ ________

3. $6 - (-3)$ ________

For **4** through **9**, use a number line or the rules for adding integers to find each difference.

4. $-6 - (-1)$ ________

5. $-12 - 10$ ________

6. $25 - (-5)$ ________

7. $14 - 22$ ________

8. $7 - |-6|$ ________

9. $|-2| - |2|$ ________

For **10** through **12**, evaluate each expression for $m = -5$.

10. $52 - m$ ________

11. $m - (-15)$ ________

12. $18 - |-3| - m$ ________

13. Writing to Explain Explain when you use the word "minus" and when you use the word "negative." Give an example.

____

____

14. Number Sense Ben's first score on a video game was 12. His second score was −15. Which expression can he use to find how many more points he got in the first game?

A $-12 + 15$

B $12 - 15$

C $12 + -15$

D $12 - (-15)$

Name ______________________

Multiplying Integers

To multiply integers, remember these rules:

• The product of two positive integers is positive.	$4 \times 5 = 20$
• The product of two negative integers is positive.	$-4 \times -5 = 20$
• The product of one positive integer and one negative integer is negative.	$-4 \times 5 = -20$ $4 \times -5 = -20$

A simple multiplication sentence will have two negative terms or no negative terms. If you see one negative term, look to find the other negative term.

Multiply.

1. $6 \times 3 =$ ________ **2.** $5 \times (-6) =$ ________

3. $-4 \times 0 =$ ________ **4.** $12 \times (-5) =$ ________

5. $-4 \times (+9) =$ ________ **6.** $22 \times 4 =$ ________

7. $(-1)(-37) =$ ________ **8.** $(-7)(-7) =$ ________

9. $(2)(4)(-3) =$ ________ **10.** $(-8)(-7) =$ ________

11. $(-3)(-5)(-3) =$ ________ **12.** $(5)(-3)(2) =$ ________

Evaluate each expression for $d = -3$.

13. $-4d =$ ________ **14.** $d \times (-6) =$ ________

15. $-10d - 3 =$ ________ **16.** $9 + (-2d) =$ ________

17. $5d + 38 =$ ________ **18.** $(2d)(-4)(-2) =$ ________

19. Number Sense Is the product of four negative integers positive or negative? Explain.

____

____

Name ____________________

Step-Up 3
Practice

Multiplying Integers

Find each product.

1. $(-8)(-2) =$ ________

2. $7 \times (-10) =$ ________

3. $5 \times 3 =$ ________

4. $(-9)(-6) =$ ________

5. $(-6)(-3) =$ ________

6. $3 \times (-18) =$ ________

7. $-9 \times -41 =$ ________

8. $(-6)(-21) =$ ________

Number Sense Use order of operations to evaluate each expression.

9. $(-3) + 5 + 4 - 9 \times 3 =$ ________

10. $(-6) - 4 \times 8 + 11 \times 2 =$ ________

Algebra Evaluate each expression when $r = 8$.

11. $-12r - 120 =$ ________

12. $7r + -5 =$ ________

13. $(-4r)(-30) - (-8) =$ ________

14. $(-2r)(8) + (-25) =$ ________

15. From 1950 to 1970, some glaciers thinned by an average of 1.7 ft per year. What was the change in glacier thickness during this period?

____

16. From 1995 to 2000, the glaciers thinned by 6 ft per year. What was the change in glacier thickness during this period?

____

17. Which is the product of $(-4)(-12)$?

A -48

B -36

C 36

D 48

18. **Writing to Explain** Explain how to evaluate $5p + (-6)$ when $p = -4$.

____

____

____

____

Name ______________________________

Step-Up 4
Reteaching

Dividing Integers

Rules for dividing integers:

- The quotient of two integers with the same sign is positive.
- The quotient of two integers with different signs is negative.

$54 \div (-6)$

$54 \div 6 = 9$

Because the signs of the two integers in the original problem are different, the sign of the quotient is negative.

So, $54 \div (-6) = -9$.

$-36 \div (-3)$

$36 \div 3 = 12$

Because the signs of the two integers in the original problem are the same, the sign of the quotient is positive.

So, $-36 \div (-3) = 12$.

Find each quotient.

1. $-18 \div (-3)$ __________ **2.** $-28 \div 4$ __________ **3.** $-50 \div (-5)$ __________

4. $-24 \div 6$ __________ **5.** $30 \div 6$ __________ **6.** $48 \div (-8)$ __________

Use order of operations to evaluate each expression for $n = -4$.

7. $-40 \div n$ __________ **8.** $n \div 4$ __________ **9.** $76 \div n$ __________

10. $8n \div 2$ __________ **11.** $14 + (n \div 2)$ __________ **12.** $-3n \div (-3)$ __________

13. Nathan and Haley went scuba diving. It took 3 minutes to dive 18 meters. What was the average descent rate of their dive? Find $-18 \div 3$.

____

14. Reasoning Without computing the answer, how do you know if the quotient $-232 \div 11$ is negative or positive?

____

15. Algebra Write the next two integers in the pattern −48, −24, −12, ____, ____

____

Name ______________________

Step-Up 4
Practice

Dividing Integers

Find each quotient.

1. $80 \div (-8)$ ______

2. $-75 \div (-5)$ ______

3. $-49 \div 7$ ______

4. $-45 \div (-9)$ ______

5. $0 \div (-14)$ ______

6. $-81 \div (-3)$ ______

Use order of operations to evaluate each expression for $c = -8$.

7. $-96 \div c$ ______

8. $c \div 4$ ______

9. $-144 \div c$ ______

10. $13 - (c \div 2)$ ______

11. $(3c + 4) \div 5$ ______

12. $c \div (-4) + 6$ ______

13. **Reasoning** Is $120 \div -6 \times -3$ positive or negative? Explain.

____

____

____

14. **Algebra** A roller coaster dropped 224 feet in 2 seconds. What was the rate of change in height per second? Find $-224 \div 2$.

____

15. What is the quotient of $-162 \div (-9)$?

A -18

B -16

C 16

D 18

16. **Writing to Explain** Jill says that the rules for multiplying and dividing integers are alike. Do you agree? Explain.

____

____

____

Name ______________________

Equations with More Than One Operation

Some equations require more than one operation to solve. When you solve an equation with more than one step, undo the operations in this order:

- First undo addition or subtraction.
- Then undo multiplication or division.

Solve $5x - 10 = 95$.	
Step 1: Undo subtraction. Add 10 to both sides.	$5x - 10 = 95$ $5x - 10 + 10 = 95 + 10$ $5x = 105$
Step 2: Undo multiplication. Divide both sides by 5.	$\frac{5x}{5} = \frac{105}{5}$ $x = 21$
Step 3: Check by substitution.	$5x - 10 = 95$ $5(21) - 10 = 95$ $105 - 10 = 95$ $95 = 95$ ✔
Solve $10 = \frac{n}{5} + 6$	
Step 1: Undo addition. Subtract 6 from both sides.	$10 = \frac{n}{5} + 6$ $10 - 6 = \frac{n}{5} + 6 - 6$
Step 2: Undo division. Multiply both sides by 5.	$4 = \frac{n}{5}$ $4 \times 5 = \frac{5 \times n}{5}$ $20 = n$
Step 3: Check by substitution.	$10 = \frac{n}{5} + 6$ $10 = \frac{20}{5} + 6$ $10 = 4 + 6$ $10 = 10$ ✔

Solve each equation and check your solution.

1. $8b + 16 = 64$ ____________

2. $2y - 4 = 24$ ____________

3. $\frac{q}{10} + 5 = 10$ ____________

4. $\frac{m}{3} + 2 = 17$ ____________

5. $\frac{p}{4} + 13 = 21$ ____________

6. $5b - 8 = 17$ ____________

7. $\frac{a}{3} - 17 = 14$ ____________

8. $3d + 17 = 24.5$ ____________

9. **Number Sense** Would you expect the solution of $4x + 12 = 36$ to be greater than or less than 36? Explain.

____

Name ____________________

Step-Up 5
Practice

Equations with More Than One Operation

1. $12a + 24 = 48$ ______

2. $4z - 8 = 32$ ______

3. $\frac{x}{5} - 10 = 2$ ______

4. $\frac{p}{3} + 6 = 42$ ______

5. $5b + 15 = 30$ ______

6. $7n + 14 = 21$ ______

7. $\frac{c}{4} + 3 = 5$ ______

8. $\frac{q}{2} - 4 = 18$ ______

9. $17 + 3y = 38$ ______

10. $\frac{m}{4} - 17 = 4$ ______

11. $\frac{c}{12} + 12 = 21$ ______

12. $8z - 13 = 7$ ______

For **13** and **14**, write and solve an equation.

13. Yoshi's age is twice Bart's age plus 3. Yoshi is 13 years old. How old is Bart?

______

14. Caleb and Winona both travel by car to their friend's home. The distance Winona traveled was 124 miles less than twice the distance Caleb traveled. If Winona traveled 628 miles, how far did Caleb travel?

______

15. Critical Thinking Explain the mistake in this solution and find the correct solution.

$6x + 15 = 69$
$6x = 84$
$x = 14$

______

______

16. Number Sense Which is the value of n when $4n + 16 = 64$?

A $n = 4$ **B** $n = 8$ **C** $n = 12$ **D** $n = 16$

17. Writing to Explain Explain how to solve the equation $6x - 3 = 39$.

______

______

Name ______________________________

Circles

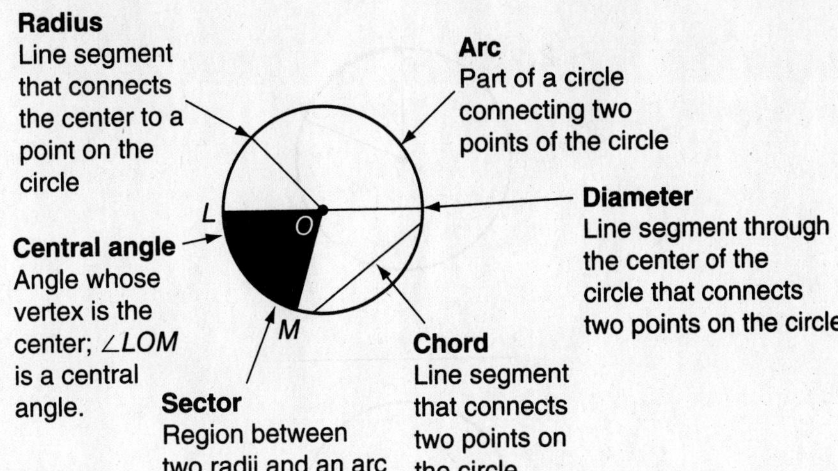
Radius
Line segment that connects the center to a point on the circle
Arc
Part of a circle connecting two points of the circle
L
O
M
Diameter
Line segment through the center of the circle that connects two points on the circle
Central angle
Angle whose vertex is the center; ∠LOM is a central angle.
Chord
Line segment that connects two points on the circle
Sector
Region between two radii and an arc

Identify the figure or portion of the figure that is drawn in each circle.

1.

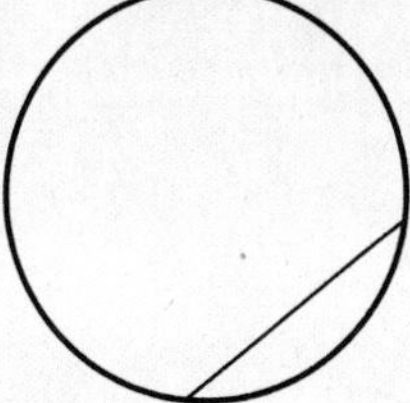

____

2.

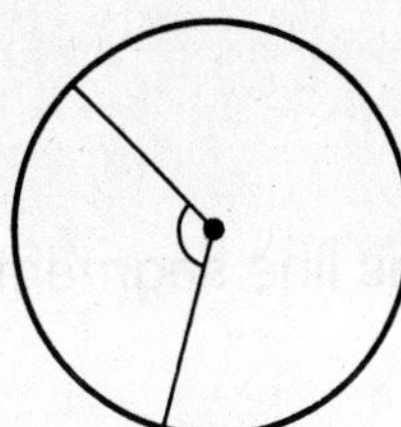

____

3.

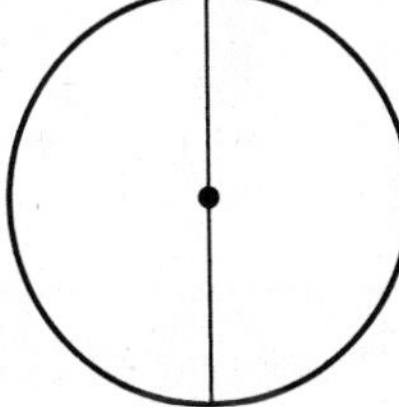

____

4.

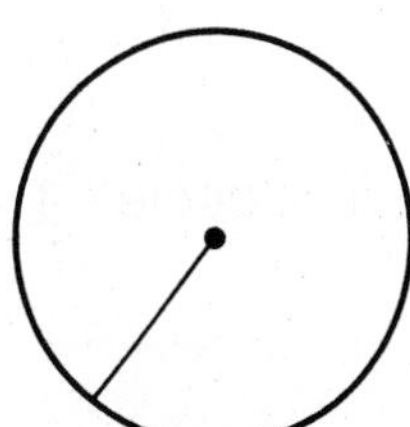

____

5.

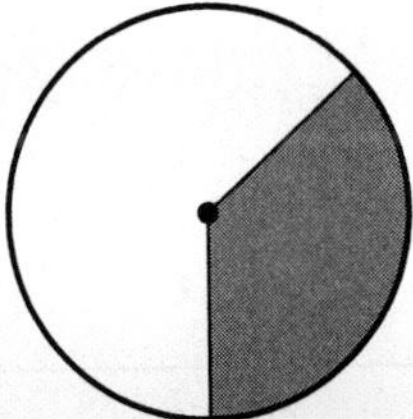

____

6.

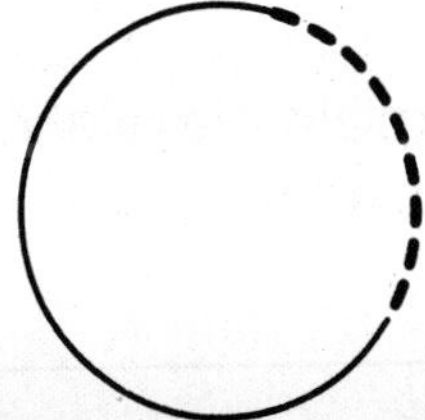

____

Name ______________________________

Circles

Identify the figure shown in bold.

1.
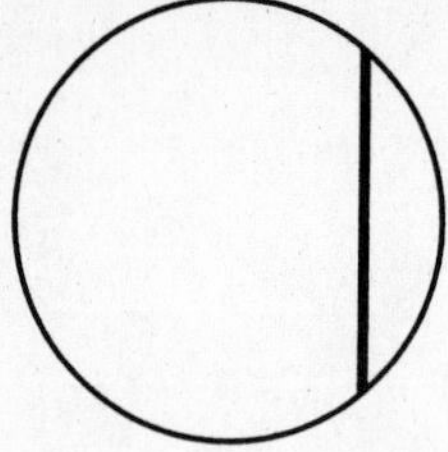

____

2.
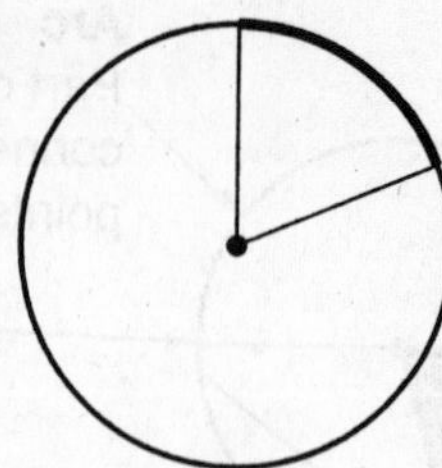

____

3.
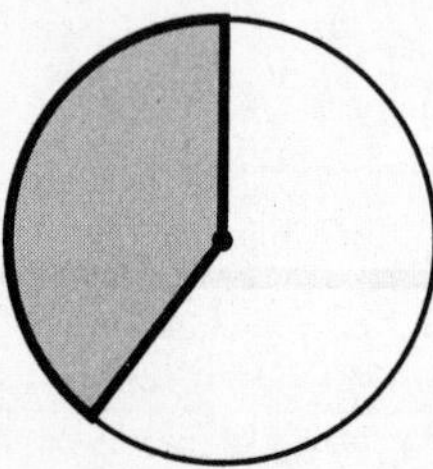

____

4.
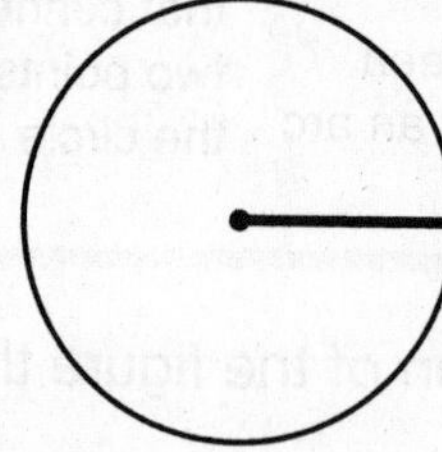

____

5. What part of the circle is line segment *FG*?

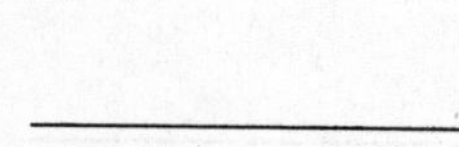

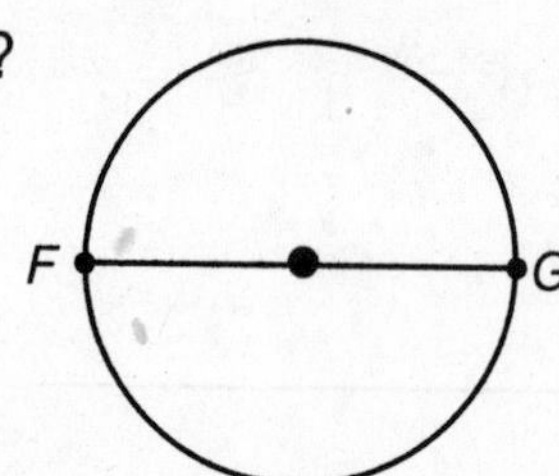

____

6. How many degrees are in a circle?

A 90°

B 120°

C 180°

D 360°

7. **Writing to Explain** Explain the relationship between the radius and the diameter of a circle.

____

____

Name ___________________________

Step-Up 7
Reteaching

Circumference

Find the circumference. Use 3.14 or $\frac{22}{7}$ for π.

Use the formula $C = 2\pi r$.

$C = 2\pi r$
$C = 2 \times 3.14 \times 8$
$C = 6.28 \times 8$
$C = 50.24$ m

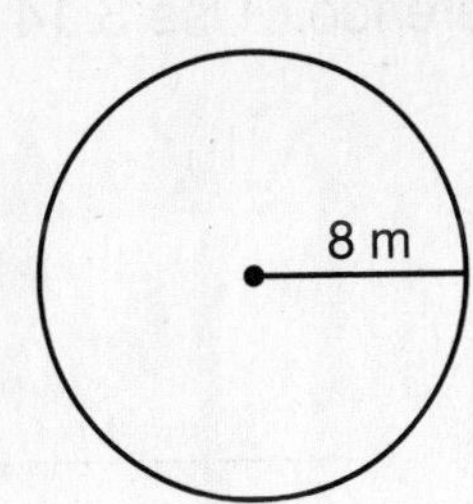

Find the diameter and the radius of a circle with a circumference of 65.94 in.

Divide by π to find the diameter.

$65.94 \div \pi = d$
$65.94 \div 3.14 = 21$
$d = 21$ in.

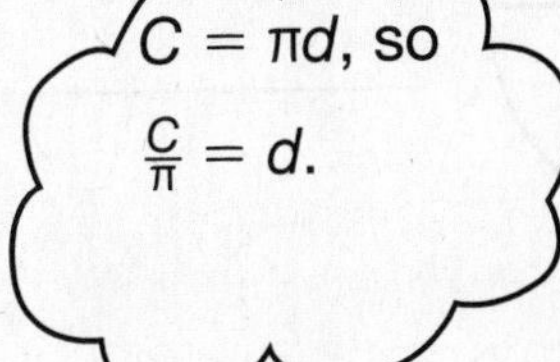

To find the radius, divide the diameter by 2.

$21 \div 2 = 10.5$
$r = 10.5$ in.

Find each circumference. Use $\frac{22}{7}$ or 3.14 for π.

1. 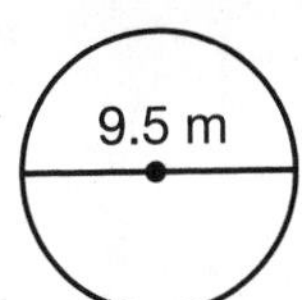

____

2. 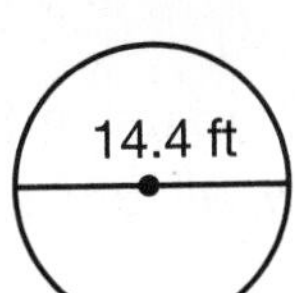

____

3. 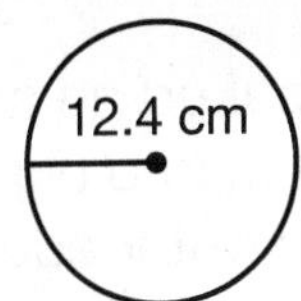

____

Find the missing measurements for each circle. Round to the nearest hundredth.

4. $C = 39.25$ ft.

$d =$ ___________

5. $C = 63.3024$ m

$r =$ ___________

6. $r = 5.95$ yd

$C =$ ___________

7. Number Sense Which circle has the greater circumference: a circle with a diameter of 13.2 in., or a circle with a radius of 6.9 in.? Explain.

____

____

____

Name ________________________

Circumference

Step-Up 7
Practice

Find each circumference. Use 3.14 or $\frac{22}{7}$ for π.

1. 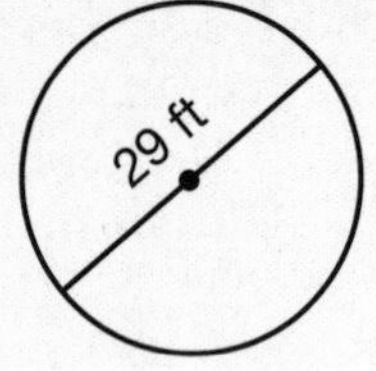

____

2. 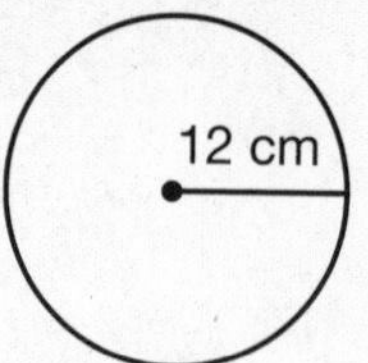

____

3. 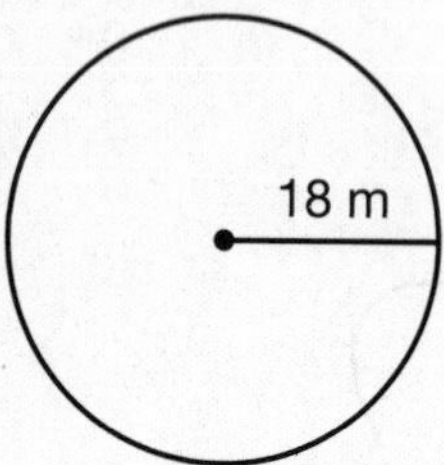

____

4. 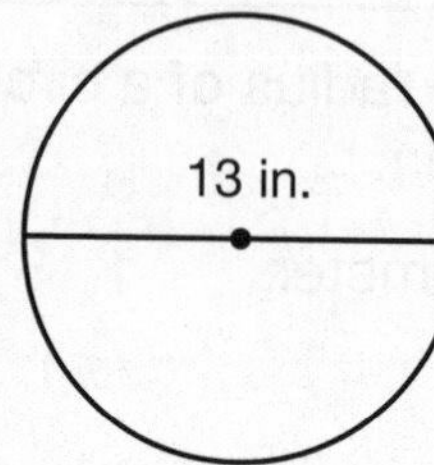

____

Find the missing measurement for each circle. Round to the nearest hundredth.

5. $C = 60.288$ cm, $d =$ ________

6. $C = 11.304$ m, $r =$ ________

7. **Estimation** CD's have a diameter of about 5 in. Estimate the circumference of a CD.

____

8. Angela baked an apple pie that had a radius of 6 in. She wants to cut the pie into eight equal slices. How wide will each piece of pie be at the outer edge?

A 5.2 in. **B** 4.7 in. **C** 4.4 in. **D** 4.2 in.

9. **Writing to Explain** Based on the diagram, is it correct to say that the smaller circle has one half the circumference of the larger. Why?

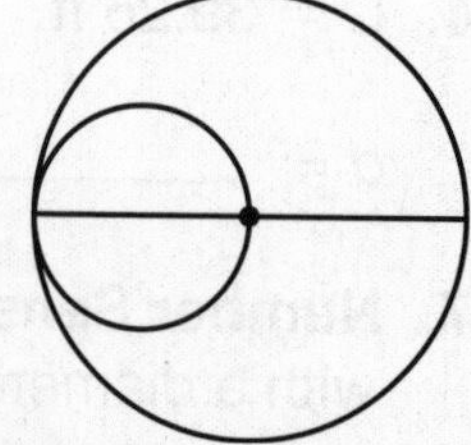

____

____

____

____

Name ______________________________

Area of a Circle

A circular bucket has a radius of 6 in. Find the area of the bottom of the bucket. The formula for finding the area of a circle is $A = \pi r^2$.

One Way

Use 3.14 for π.

$A = \pi r^2$
$= 3.14 \times 6^2$
$= 3.14 \times 36$
$= 113.04 \text{ in}^2$

Another Way

Use $\frac{22}{7}$ for π.

$A = \pi r^2$
$= \frac{22}{7} \times 6^2$
$= \frac{22}{7} \times 36$
$= \frac{22}{7} \times \frac{36}{1}$
$= \frac{792}{7}$
$= 113.14 \text{ in}^2$

With a Calculator

Press:   6  =

Display: 113.09734

The bucket's area is about 113 in^2.

Find the area of each circle to the nearest whole number. Use 3.14 or $\frac{22}{7}$ for π.

1.

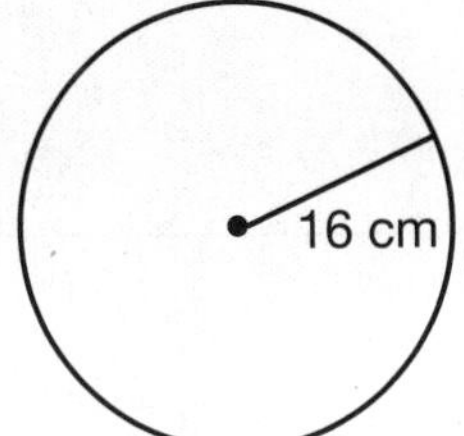

____

2.

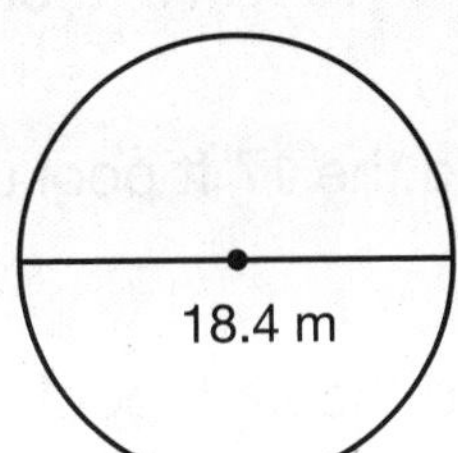

____

3.

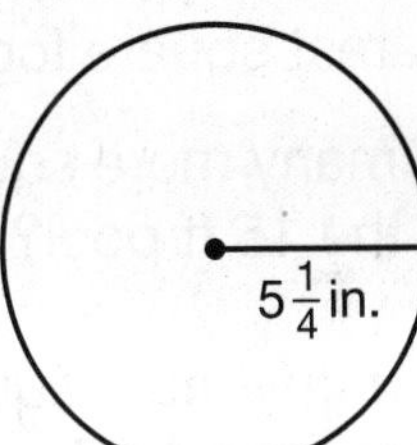

____

4. $r = 9$ yd ______________

5. $d = 20$ m ______________

6. $r = 14$ cm ______________

7. $d = 2.4$ ft ______________

8. $r = 22$ cm ______________

9. $d = 8.8$ m ______________

10. $d = 32$ cm ______________

11. $r = 5.3$ m ______________

12. Reasoning If the circumference of a circle is 18π, what is the area of the circle? ______________

Name ____________________

Area of a Circle

Find the area of each circle to the nearest whole number. Use 3.14 or $\frac{22}{7}$ for π.

1.

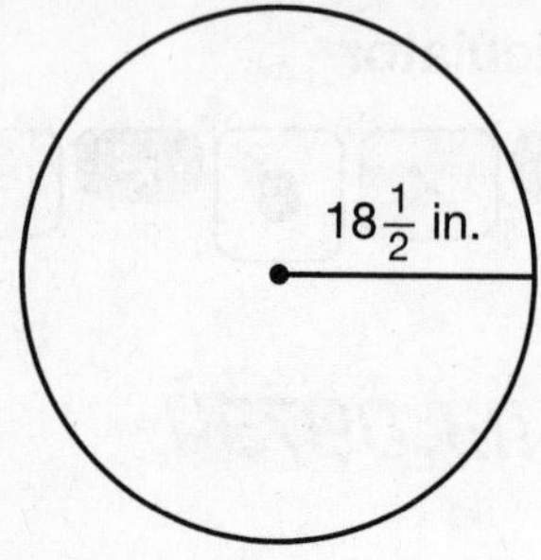

2.

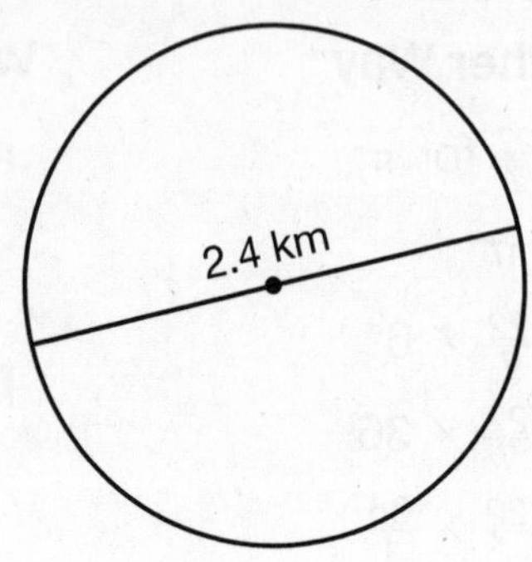

3.

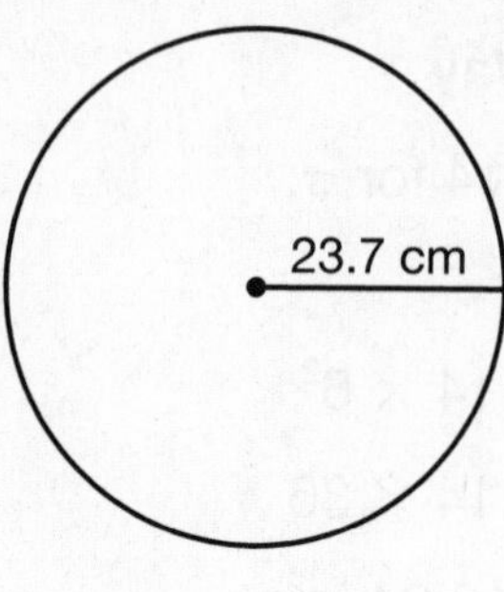

____________________ ____________________ ____________________

4. $d = 14$ in. ____________________

5. $r = 11.25$ cm ____________________

6. $d = 2$ mi ____________________

Brian's dad wants to put a circular pool in their backyard. He can choose between pools with diameters of 15 ft, 17 ft, or 22 ft. Round to the nearest square foot.

7. How many more square feet would the 17 ft pool use than the 15 ft pool? ____________________

8. How many more square feet would the 22 ft pool use than the 17 ft pool? ____________________

9. On a water ride at the amusement park, a rotating valve sprays water for 15 ft in all directions. What is the area of the circular wet patch it creates?

A 30 ft^2

B 31.4 ft^2

C 94.2 ft^2

D 706.5 ft^2

10. Writing to Explain Explain how to find the radius of a circle with an area of 50.24 mi.

____

____

____